Edward Garbett

God's Word written

The Doctrine of the Inspiration of Holy Scripture explained and enforced

Edward Garbett

God's Word written
The Doctrine of the Inspiration of Holy Scripture explained and enforced

ISBN/EAN: 9783337183431

Printed in Europe, USA, Canada, Australia, Japan

Cover: Foto ©ninafisch / pixelio.de

More available books at **www.hansebooks.com**

GOD'S WORD WRITTEN:

THE DOCTRINE

OF THE

INSPIRATION OF HOLY SCRIPTURE

EXPLAINED AND ENFORCED.

BY THE

REV. EDWARD GARBETT, M. A.,

AUTHOR OF "RELIGION IN DAILY LIFE;"

INCUMBENT OF CHRIST CHURCH, SURBITON; BOYLE LECTURER FOR 1861, 1862, AND
1863; SELECT PREACHER TO THE UNIVERSITY OF OXFORD IN 1862 AND 1863.

"Holy men of God spake as they were moved by the Holy Ghost." 2 PET. 1:21.

PUBLISHED BY THE
AMERICAN TRACT SOCIETY,
150 NASSAU-STREET, NEW YORK.

PREFACE.

The object of the following pages is to explain, and in explaining to enforce, the doctrine of the plenary inspiration of Holy Scripture. On the general subject I believe an entire concurrence of opinion to exist between myself and the Society under whose auspices the work has been prepared. But for the method of the argument, and the detailed views maintained in the course of it, I am solely responsible.

The method adopted will probably appear to some minds to include matters not strictly related to the subject of which I profess to treat. I earnestly crave the indulgence of my readers on this point, and ask for their patient forbearance during the earlier stages of the argument. In support of this plea I am anxious briefly to explain for what reasons this particular line has been selected. It will appear, I believe, that no topic has been introduced devoid of an immediate and important bearing on the specific question of inspiration, and not requisite for the elucidation of some vital principle.

The most embarrassing difficulty in the settlement of this great question has long appeared to me to consist in the ambiguous use of terms. So long as the same words or phrases convey different meanings to the various parties to the controversy, there cannot be the slightest chance of even an approximation to unity of opinion. There is not a distinctive phrase employed in the discussion which has wholly escaped this ambiguity of usage. The term "inspiration" is itself no exception. All parties PERFECTLY UNDERSTAND the nature of the thing denoted, and the bearings of the question at issue; but they differ very considerably in the definition they are prepared to accept. The familiar terms "mechanical" and "dynamical" afford another example. We are told, for instance, that verbal inspiration must necessarily be mechanical; and the writer who makes the assertion, consistently enough with his own theory, considers himself to have proved that the inspiration of the Scriptures was not verbal, when he has proved that it was not mechanical. In other quarters the significance and relative bearing of the words "inspiration" and "revelation" have been eagerly discussed. The expressions "Divine element" and "human element" have been the centre of a circle of ambiguities of their own. An able writer of late date maintains that verbal inspiration is logically inconsistent with the admission of a human element in Scripture; while a learned professor in one of our ancient universities has publicly employed the words "human element" as avowed equivalent to the asserted fact of human mistakes in the sacred writings.

These complicated misapprehensions render the employment of the utmost caution necessary in all who desire to maintain a positive doctrine of inspiration. They embarrass a believer in proportion as they supply valuable weapons to the skeptic. To commence a work of this kind with a string of definitions, before some common truths have been reached and common principles accepted, would be to plunge headlong into the very perplexities which it is a matter of the highest moment to remove. I have, therefore, been anxious to avoid all definitions during the earlier steps of the argument, and to reserve such formal propositions as might be necessary for its latest stages. The inductive method offered the only means of securing this object. I have, therefore, endeavored to base my arguments on facts, and from facts to ascend to principles.

Two advantages are secured by this plan. The course of the inquiry is simplified. At each step of it the reader has but to ask, Are these things so? And if the answer be in the affirmative, to consider for himself the conclusions founded on them. I have also been enabled to avoid, in a great measure, the ambiguous terms already alluded to. With the exception of the word "inspiration" itself, and the phrases "Divine element" and "human element," which I have found it impossible to avoid without prolixity, none of them will be found in these pages.

It would be presumptuous to expect that their contents will carry conviction to all classes of readers. To some I venture to hope that the argument will carry the same conclusiveness which it has to my own mind. Where it does not convince, it may yet assist in some measure towards laying down a broader and more satisfactory platform for the discussion of this great and vital question. It is too great to be hedged up into some special corner of theology; for it pervades all theology from end to end. I commend these pages to the blessing of God, with a profounder conviction than ever of the supreme authority and absolute truth of God's Word written.

EDWARD GARBETT.

Surbiton, Surrey.

CONTENTS.

GOD'S WORD WRITTEN.

CHAPTER I.

WHAT IS CHRISTIANITY?

Relation of Christianity to the Christian Scriptures—Christianity a Definite Historical System—Origin and Meaning of the Word—Christianity as a Faith. and the Christian Church as a Society—Influence of Christianity upon the World—Elements of its Power — Its Supernatural Element — Its Doctrinal Form — Church Creeds—Their Circumstantial Diversities and Substantial Identity.

"God's Word written," is the title applied by the church of England to the Scriptures of the Old and New Testaments ; and the phrase expresses the concurrent belief of the church catholic throughout all lands and ages. The title either expresses one of the grandest facts it is possible for us to conceive, or one of the fondest delusions ever palmed by religious enthusiasm upon the credulity of mankind. A revelation from God, as truly his as if his voice of thunder uttered it audibly from the skies, would be among the grandest of known facts. The application of so great a title as "God's word written" to a fragmentary collection of human traditions and human theories, would be among the fondest of existing delusions. It is certain that the early fathers, and also the great divines of the church of England, from the Reformation period down to recent times, accepted the Scriptures as the infallible word of God, conclusive on all questions of religious belief, and binding on faith and conscience. Modern rationalism loudly affirms this belief to be a mistake, and irreconcilable with the results of modern criticism. To examine the grounds of this allegation, and gather, from a careful induction of all the facts of the case, what are the true character and authority of the Scriptures, is the object of the present work.

Foremost among these facts is the relation held by the canonical Scriptures towards Christianity itself. It is sometimes asserted that they are wholly independent of each other. It is necessary, therefore, to carry the inquiry a step backward, and ask, What is it we mean by Christianity?

St. Luke records, in the Acts of the Apostles, 11 : 26, that the disciples were called Christians first at Antioch. The epithet is an evident enlargement of the honored name of Christ, the official title of the Saviour of the world, and suggests the intimate dependence of the religion professed upon the person of its divine Founder. The recognition of places and persons as a bond of union between sections of mankind, and the consequent derivation from them of distinctive names, had long been familiar before the times of our Lord. All the great kingdoms of antiquity supply instances of generic names. This was probably the beginning of the habit. It soon acquired more particular application. The schools of ancient philosophy followed each other in rapid succession; and each of them, as it took definite form and gathered disciples, gave rise to a corresponding name. Stoics and Academics derived their name from the localities where the respective systems were taught; Pythagoreans, Epicureans, and Platonists, from the person of the teacher. It was natural, therefore, that the verbal analogy should be followed in the case of the disciples of our Master; and that the lively inhabitants of Antioch, famous for wit and satire, should be the first to suggest it. The disciples were called Christians from Christ, as others were called Pythagoreans from Pythagoras, Epicureans from Epicurus, Platonists from Plato. Another natural step in advance formed the name of the system from the name of the men who followed it. As Stoicism expressed the bond of union common to all Stoics; Platonism the bond common to all Platonists; so Christianity expresses the bond of union common to all Christians.

The analogy illustrates not only the origin of the name, but likewise the ideas involved in it, and the necessary limits of its use. The ideas involved are two: the idea of a society more or less intimate, more or less organized according to the nature of the case; and the idea of a defined system of thought out of which it has grown. The claim of membership in the society would include discipleship to the system. No man, for instance, could fairly appropriate the name of Platonist who did not share the opinions of Plato. To originate a new system, either by the omission of some essential principles from the old, or by the addition of new particulars, and yet to call it by the old name, would not be consistent with either truth or honesty. It would not be consistent with truth, because the title and the thing signified by it would no longer correspond; it would not be consistent with honesty, because such an ambiguous use of words would only deceive. This rule would become more absolute in proportion to the length of time during which the name has been thus appropriated, and the number and publicity of the events associated with it. Established usage and historical association would combine to invest the title both with definiteness and with authority. The principle has been admitted and acted upon in past times. After the establishment of Christianity, a great effort was made, both within and without the limits of the church, to combine the principles of Plato with the teaching of the Christian Scriptures; but the advocates of the system did not venture to call it by the old name, Platonism; recognizing its distinctness alike of internal character and of historical descent, they modified the name accordingly, and called it Neo-Platonism.

The same principles of usage should, in all candor, be applied to Christianity. To form an ideal person, different from the historical personage born at Bethlehem and crucified upon Calvary—to surround him with attributes and characteristics different from what are imputed to him in the authoritative records of the faith—to connect him with a system of teaching varying from the doctrines inaugurated under his authority, and then to call this new production Christianity, is to do in regard to things religious what no man has ventured or would venture to do in regard to things secular. The morality of religious controversy would be lowered, by assent to such an act, below the standard of all other controversy. Mutual misapprehension and dangerous mistakes could be its only result. The name of Christianity is already appropriated to one defined form of religion, by virtue alike of the society called into existence and of the belief on which it is founded, and cannot be transferred to any other. The two have ever existed together from the beginning of the Christian era to our own day. Down the whole line of these nineteen hundred years, the outward society has existed alike by unbroken descent and by continuity of belief. The creed taught by the church of England, from the times of the Reformation to the present day, can be shown by undoubted proofs to be the same as was taught in the primitive and apostolic times. The reformers laid great stress upon this fact. The Romish church admits it equally. Her documents claim the right to add additional truth to the body of doctrine held by the reformed churches; but they never deny that this body of doctrine is both primitive and apostolical. The whole of Christendom may, therefore, be called as witness to the existence of an identical faith in the church of Christ from the day of Pentecost till now. This faith has, moreover, been maintained and handed down by a society comprising many branches, and subject to many modifications, but identified, nevertheless, throughout them all, by points of external habit and organization, such as public worship, the sacraments, and the ministry. This defined and continuous society is the church of Christ; and the system constituting its bond of union, alike in its inward life and its outward doctrines, is Christianity.

By Christianity, therefore, we do not mean any imaginary belief about any imaginary Christ, but we mean the definite religion preached, in its completed form, in the first century of our era, centred around the personal Christ described by the four evangelists, incorporated in the society specified in the Acts of the Apostle, expanded in the doctrines of the apostolic epistles, and prophetically depicted in the great outlines of its outward fortunes in the book of the Apocalypse.

This identification of the word " Christianity " with a known historical system is confirmed when, having specified what we intend by it, we go on to examine more closely into its nature. Let us suppose the attention of a thoughtful and educated man to be seriously drawn for the first time to the claims and promises of this Christianity. Up to this time he has received the ordinary education given in a Christian household; but the subject has never previously interested his feelings or actively

occupied his understanding. Perhaps his studies
in other directions have brought him into contact
with the question. Perhaps the prominence of
modern controversy has called his attention to it.
Perhaps the influence of some Christian example
has reacted upon him, and he is tempted to inquire
into the sources of its spiritual power. Perhaps
the great questions of life and death have been
brought home to him, and the moral wants of his
own soul have begun to make themselves felt. Perhaps, in the spirit of a former Lord Lyttleton and
of Mr. West, he wishes to examine in order to refute;
and, like them, has the honesty to inquire and the
candor to be convinced. Whatever may be the
cause, he sits himself down to search into the question, and examine for himself the foundations of
Christianity.

His inquiry necessarily starts from the standpoint of his own times and his own position towards
them. It would not be just, nor is it possible for
him to leave them out of view. His object is to
investigate an actual, not an imaginary Christianity; and he must deal with the case, therefore, not
as it might conceivably have been, but as it actually is. The beginning of Christianity cannot be
the beginning of his inquiry about it. The first in
order of time is the last in order of investigation.
He begins from his own stand-point, and commences
with the facts of the case as presented in his own
times and related to his own position.

He finds Christianity to be the dominant religion of the world. This fact is the more striking

because it is not the religion of the greatest number of mankind. There are wide tracts of the earth's surface peopled by teeming millions either ignorant of its existence or contemptuously incredulous of its claims. The votaries of Buddha outnumber the disciples of Jesus of Nazareth beyond all comparison. But these wide regions are the sterile plains of the moral and intellectual world. A stereotyped civilization that has outgrown its own vitality, and is like a dead leaf retaining the form of its former self, but performing none of its functions; or a quiescent and self-satisfied stagnation of all life and activity brood over them, depressing energy and crushing effort. Every nation prominent in the transactions of the world is, without exception, professedly Christian. Within Christendom are included all the springs of enterprise and wealth; all the active influences of art, science, and civilization; all the wheels of the world's political action, and the secret causes of its movements. The portion of the globe occupied by Christianity constitutes a small portion of its surface, but reigns the acknowledged mistress of all the rest.

Within these limits Christianity exercises a moral influence without a parallel elsewhere. Unequally exercised, and exhibiting a restraining and ameliorating power even where its highest effects are absent, it stands without an equal, almost without a rival, in the education of mankind. No other power but itself claims to regenerate human nature after so lofty a model. The facts are too evident for denial, that it succeeds in making the drunkard sober, the profligate chaste, the liar truthful, the cheat honest, the idle industrious, the cruel gentle, the churl generous, the disorderly peaceful and obedient. It is accepted as an instrument of government where it is rejected as a means of personal happiness. It has covered the world with schools and hospitals and institutions—a costly and elaborate apparatus of benevolence, to which nothing remotely corresponding ever existed before. It has evoked a self-denying zeal and an amount of labor for the good of other men so enormous as to make adequate calculation impossible. No want appears to be too minute to escape the anxiety of Christian benevolence, no enterprise too gigantic to exhaust its energy. The voluntary efforts of individuals accomplish what no compulsory organization could attempt. In the course of these ceaseless and prodigious labors all over the world, it has wrought so great a change in human habits, opinions, and principles, as to amount to a revolution. Whether Christianity be true or false, it is confessedly the most amazing moral force ever exhibited in the history of mankind.

The adoption of this conclusion suggests a further inquiry relative to the sources of this power and the nature of the religion which exercises it. What is Christianity, and what the elements of its influence? The reply is given by putting into the hands of the inquirer some authorized confession of faith. Let us suppose it to be the Articles of the Church of England. A comparison of them with other church confessions serves easily to eliminate the distinctive peculiarities belonging to any particular branch of the universal society, and to leave behind the common principles of the Christian faith. These principles constitute a formal and complete body of doctrine, united by a close dependency of one part upon another. The truths themselves are of the grandest and most elevating description, including divine action as well as human, and extending to the prospects, wants, and hopes of universal human kind. Certain broad characteristics distinguish them sharply from all known systems of human thought. They are not speculations, a fabric woven out of the operations of the human mind, but definite statements made with the tone of conscious authority and truthfulness. They profess to be based throughout on a substructure of actual facts, events either completely transacted, or begun and still in process of transaction. These facts are partly supernatural, accomplished by God himself in the sphere of the unseen world; such as the session of Christ in glory, his mediation at the right hand of the Father, his government over the world, and the act of a sinner's justification before God. Others are historical events, matters lying within the sphere of things visible and known, actions accomplished upon the earth, cognizable by the senses, and admitting of being measured and tested by the ordinary methods of all historical investigation. Such are the facts relative to the birth, life, ministry, death, and resurrection of our Lord. Of all this portion of Christian faith, it may be asserted that it is by its very nature beyond the possibility of change. The only point of discussion is the truth of the facts. If the events have been transacted, or are in process of transaction, it is impossible that they can be undone. Any form of words expressive of the possibility destroys itself, and becomes a sound without a sense.

These facts constitute, however, but one portion of the Christian faith. The other portion consists of doctrinal truths, stated in the form of general principles, requiring belief in the first place, moral acceptance in the second, practical adoption in the third. Such, for instance, are the doctrines relative to justification, good works, Christ without sin, predestination, and similar articles of faith. It is observable, in regard to the whole of them, that more or less immediately they are dependent upon the historical facts ; and this so closely, that if the facts were disproved, the doctrines would be destroyed at the same time. The case is not, that the facts form one independent portion of the Christian faith, and the doctrines another; but that the two portions constitute one common and indivisible whole. The faith is a fabric so made up of both, that the act of taking away, not alone the facts in general, but any one part of the facts, loosens the coherence and destroys the nature of the fabric itself. If without irreverence such great matters may be illustrated by very familiar things, the faith may be compared in this respect to some production of the modern loom, manufactured of two materials, and deriving its name and qualities from the union of the two. Take either of them away, and the fabric ceases to be itself, and becomes something else.

This body of truth does not, however, make up the whole of Christianity. We need to add to it a living and superhuman power, working in and through the faith, and constituting the really efficient agent of its wonderful triumphs. This is the grace of God the Holy Ghost, and this is his special function in the plan of human redemption. It is not possible to sever these operations of the Spirit from the truths whereby he operates. The experienced result must be referred back to the corresponding doctrine in the Scriptures. It is exactly the result that might be expected to follow, if the doctrine be true, and it presents in its own nature exactly the characteristics the doctrine leads us to expect. If there be a Holy Ghost, and if his office in the scheme of salvation be to infuse a new life, and renew the soul after the image of Christ Jesus, then the facts of Christian experience could not be otherwise than they are; and being what they are, they confirm and verify the doctrine.

Hence, in asking what Christianity is, the truths of the Christian faith can alone supply the answer. There is an unseen and supernatural element about it. But this element, in its very nature, does not admit of intellectual inquiry and examination. As it presents itself for investigation, Christianity can only be resolved into the truths constituting the substance of the Christian faith.

Hence has arisen the use of church standards. The form of creed was at first exceedingly short and simple. As the church acquired a more perfect organization, and felt the necessity of guarding herself against false teaching within, as well as violence without, the formula of faith became more definite and exact. The three ancient creeds—the Apostles', the Nicene, and the Athanasian—exactly illustrate the process. The Apostles' Creed is the most ancient and the most simple. Although not composed by the apostles, its composition must be referred back to a period closely touching the apostolic days, and it undeniably embodies the doctrines of primitive Christianity. But they are stated in a very condensed form, and follow so strictly the baptismal formula given by our Lord himself, as to be only an amplification of it: "Go ye, teach all nations, baptizing them in the 'name of the Father, and of the Son, and of the Holy Ghost." The Nicene Creed was adopted by the Council of Nicea after the establishment of Christianity by Constantine, and when the Arian heresy already threatened to rend the unity of the faith. It is accordingly longer and fuller, and more controversial, and fills up in definite detail the apostolic outlines. The creed attributed to Athanasius was later in date by more than two centuries, and evidences in every part of it the adoption of an exact theological language. It deals primarily with two great doctrines only—the trinity of persons in the Godhead, and the unity of the divine and human natures in the one person of Christ, because these were the prominent subjects of debate in the sixth century.

The creeds of different branches of the church

of Christ have carried this expansion still farther. They have in all cases been colored by the circumstances of the times and the variations of controversy.   But although they vary in form and in the relative prominence given to truths, they are identical in substance, both with themselves and with the more ancient creeds.   The body of truth is one and identical.   I use the word *body* to express, not simply a collection of separate doctrines, but a connected and organized system of belief.   That the parts of this teaching are not isolated and fragmentary truths, but harmonious portions of one intelligent scheme, may be illustrated by such a work as Calvin's "Institutes," by the Westminster Confession, or by the Thirty-nine Articles of the Church of England.   The members of a body are not more closely united to each other than are the doctrines of the Christian faith.   The existence of such a body of truth is repeatedly asserted in Scripture under the expression "the faith," where the context defines the application of the phrase beyond the possibility of doubt; as, for instance, in the words of St. Jude, "The faith which was once delivered unto the saints."

Many lines of evidence thus concur in limiting even the name of Christianity to one recognized system of truth.   Its distinct origin, its definite history, its supernatural characteristics, its organized body of doctrine, its embodiment in visible churches, its distinctive principles, its world-wide effects, its series of creeds and formularies, its sacraments and institutions, its unbroken descent and perpetuity of life and power, belong to itself alone. Christianity in its outward form, and as presented for inquiry, is identified with a body of systematic truth, centring round the person and work of Christ, and has the church of the past and the present as its visible witness and embodiment.

CHAPTER II.

CHRISTIANITY IS IDENTIFIED WITH THE CHRISTIAN SCRIPTURES.

The Case regarded as a Matter of Fact—No other Source of Information within the Pale of the Christian Church—Origin of the Scriptures and their Recognized Authority—No Source of Information on Christian Doctrine Outside the Church—Profane History: what it supplies and does not supply—Human Philosophy: its Struggles and its Failure.

WE have seen that Christianity, in its outward aspects, consists of a series of definite and positive statements, constituting together a complete and harmonious body of doctrine. In this sense the word will be invariably used in the course of the present inquiry. I affirm nothing more about it at present. I neither pronounce upon its truth nor upon its obligation; I only define what it is. It may be right to reject it altogether, or it may be necessary to make a selection of its doctrines, and, separating what we conceive to be true from what we conceive to be false, blend them into another system. I only affirm that such a system would not be Christianity—that Christianity which points to its history in the past, exercises its influence in the present, and claims the promises of the future.

This being Christianity, the question is, Upon what authority are these doctrines taught, whence are they gathered, and what are their claims upon the acceptance and obedience of mankind? The success of Christianity, if it stood alone, would not of itself suffice to prove its Divine authority, however strong a presumption to that effect it might justify. It would remain open to dispute whether these alleged effects are attributable to Christianity or to some other cause; or, granting that they are its product, they might still be referred by an objector to the effect of one or two great truths embodied in Christianity, rather than to the whole body of its teaching. To ascertain whence these doctrines are derived is, therefore, the next essential step in the inquiry. The Bible, placed in the hands of the investigator, supplies the answer. Christianity is identified with the Christian Scriptures.

This is the answer of no one section of Christendom, but of Christendom at large. Wherever Christianity is found to flourish in its greatest activity and closest alliance with human liberty and civilization, the Bible is enthroned as the absolute rule of faith. That is the weapon of its warfare, this the instrument of its progress. The history of its missions is the history of the Book. To the heathen, on whose darkness is poured the light of the Christian day, its missionaries are the men of the Book. The Protestant divine, in constructing his scheme of theological belief, acknowledges no other authority; the private Christian derives from it his daily strength and comfort, and listens to its teaching as to the voice of God. It has become the centre of a prodigious and ever-enlarging literature. Even science, in all its branches, is deeply indebted to it :

and history, so far as it has any fixed and certain chronology, derives it from this source. Such a thing as a Christianity without the Bible is unknown. Its facts and its doctrines, its triumphs in the past, and its hopes for the future, its power, its character, its existence, its very self, are all derived from this fountain—this issuing forth of the divine mind in the written revelation.

The Bible is the source, and the only source, of information on Christian truth. Take away every thing derived from its authority, and Christianity would be gone. We should know nothing about it. Had not the Bible existed, there would have been no creeds to be believed, no promises to be remembered. It is exceedingly difficult even to conceive its absence, so inextricably has its influence become mixed up with the whole order and fortunes of the world. Our state without it would be simple heathenism, if not something worse; for it is very doubtful whether paganism, as it actually existed, could have ever grown into its life, such as it was, without the influence of the Hebrew revelation. The world without the Bible would be like a globe without light—a firmament without a sun.

I. There is no other source of information within the circle of Christianity itself. The church has no independent source of teaching. Neither a solitary fact nor a solitary truth has ever been added to the sum of Christian doctrine from any other quarter. It has been said that the church was before the Bible, and must, therefore, be independent of it; and in one very limited sense the assertion may be admitted. Undoubtedly the facts of our Lord's life, and the offer of salvation through his atoning death were preached before they were written in the New Testament Scriptures. Undoubtedly it is possible to conceive of Christianity apart from its inspired records; but it is useless to argue about what might might have been. It is in vain to tax the brain with ingenious suppositions relative to the life of Christianity, if the Scriptures never had been written, and the preservation of its doctrines had been intrusted to oral teaching alone. Such theories are valuable to the opponent of Christianity, because they enable him to lose sight of the case as it is, in a cloud of ingenious theories; but they should be rigidly watched, and most carefully avoided by the advocate of Christianity. What God might have done is a question for himself What he has done is the only question for us. Looking from the stand-point of our own times and our own circumstances, our sole and only knowledge of Christian facts and Christian doctrines is dependent on the Christian Scriptures.

The facts are few and simple. For a short period after the day of Pentecost the gospel was extended by oral preaching. But even during this period it was a preaching constantly referred back, as we see in the Acts of the Apostles and in the Epistles, to the prior authority of the Scriptures. The design of God in perpetuating the revelation of his will through the permanent form of written documents instead of by word of mouth, had undoubted reference to considerations as powerful, in the times after Christ, as in the times before. We find, accordingly, the same method to have been adopted by the apostles under the New Testament dispensation as by the prophets under the Old. The gospel of St. Matthew, the earliest of the New Testament books, has been ascribed to dates varying from one year to fifteen years after the ascension. The Revelation of St. John, the latest of the New Testament Scriptures, is by some referred to a date as early as A. D. 60, and by no critics to a later date than A. D. 96. Within the lifetime, therefore, of the last survivor of the apostles, the canon of the New Testament was finally completed. The oral teaching of living men passed away, and was succeeded by the teaching of authoritative Scriptures.

How completely these Scriptures stand alone as the sole fountains of revealed truth will be seen from a brief statement of the facts. The caution must be continually borne in mind, that we can only deal with the case as it is, not as we can conceive that it might have been. The number of believers was very large at the close of the apostolic period, and conceivably many writers, besides the inspired authors of the New Testament, might have written on the events and doctrines of Christianity. But as a matter of fact, we have no such sources of information. Christian books of the same antiquity as the canonical Scriptures lie within a very narrow limit. All that we possess are an epistle of doubtful genuineness, ascribed to Barnabas, the companion of St. Paul; part of a letter supposed to have been written by Clement, bishop of Rome; the

"Shepherd of Hermas," a work, like the letter of Barnabas, of disputed authority; the Seven Epistles attributed to Ignatius, A. D. 70; and a letter of Polycarp, bishop of Smyrna, A. D. 108. These are the sole extant remains of the Christian literature of the apostolic period. A broad gulf of time, as well as of character and position, separates all the other Christian fathers from the inspired writers of the New Testament.

These apostolic fathers, as the name signifies, lived during the first century, when the memory of Christ himself must have been fresh, and his divine voice, as it were, still thrilled upon the ears of men; when, consequently, a large amount of oral information, relative to him, must still have survived. They were acquainted with the apostles, and are said to have conversed with them. Yet, standing in this immediate contact with the sacred writers, they never professed to be themselves independent teachers; but both by direct statement, and still more by free reference and quotation, refer back to the authority of the Scriptures as their rule of faith. With exceptions equally slight and uncertain, not the word spoken, but the word written, was their professed guide and authority. Their writings, consequently, are only reflected copies of the Scriptures, and derive their teaching from the Scriptures they reflect.

The later Christian writers followed in their footsteps. As they lived and died they were but links in one successive chain—the first link of which rested on the written Word. If those who lived nearest the times when the New Testament canon was closed claimed to have, and had, no authority beyond what they derived from Scripture, still less had those farther off from them. It was but a remoter succession from one and the same beginning. Could it be conceived, therefore, that the original Scriptures had been allowed to perish, and that their contents had been perpetuated only in the writings of the uninspired successors of the apostles; even then these writings would have had no authority of their own, but would have possessed just that claim for credence which they derived from the original Scriptures and no more. If the Scriptures had not existed, neither would their writings have existed. The absence of the one would have included equally the absence of the other; and in the void thus produced we should possess no source of information whatever upon the subjects included within the range of Christian faith.

The claims of church authority, and of a tradition of divine truth, advanced by the church of Rome, constitute no exception to this principle. These claims are not only without evidence, but they are contradicted by the facts of history and experience. As a mere question of fact, no consentaneous and universal tradition of truth does exist, or has ever existed. But, putting this out of the question, the claim does not invalidate the fact that the Christian Scriptures furnish our exclusive source of information on the subject of Christianity; for the church of Rome rests it on the authority of Scripture, however falsely our Lord's words may be alleged for this purpose. If the Christian writers could not have existed without the Christian Scriptures, neither could Romish perversions have existed, since in the absence of the written Word there would have been nothing to pervert. I take the facts simply as they stand. As the case is, the absence of the written Word would have involved equally the absence of the false gloss, as well as of the truthful interpretation. There is, therefore, no other source of information on divine things within the circle of Christianity itself than the Christian Scriptures.

II. There is no other source of information outside the circle of Christianity. Let it be supposed that the Lord Jesus Christ lived, suffered, taught, and died; and that the apostles carried on the preaching of the gospel after his death; that all the facts of the New Testament history up to the day of Pentecost took place as they are recorded, but that no written Scriptures, and consequently, no patristic writings, founded on those Scriptures, survived. Let us suppose that this being the case, some of ourselves, nineteen hundred years afterwards, wished to inquire into the facts of Christ's life, just as we may inquire into the life of Julius Cæsar, or any other hero of antiquity, what authentic sources of information would be open for such an inquiry? The answer is, "Literally none." Were we confined to a knowledge of such facts relative to the person and work of our Lord, as profane history is able to supply, his nationality and his death would be nearly the whole of our information.

We cannot even say that the history of the church of Christ would, nevertheless, have continued to witness to his person and his doctrine, because this involves the assumption that the church would have flourished and triumphed all the same, if no authoritative records of his life and doctrine had been given. So far as can be judged, experience would directly disprove such an assumption. As a matter of fact, Christianity and the Christian Scriptures lived and triumphed together, and so far as we know, were never separated. Secular history might possibly have recorded the result of the apostolic labors, as it has recorded other temporary outbursts of human enterprise and enthusiasm; just as Tacitus has left on record the historical peculiarity of the Jews as they appeared to a heathen historian, and just as the letter of Pliny to Trojan has left on record the picture of Christianity and Christians as they appeared to a heathen philosopher; but this would have been all. A few distorted lineaments would have represented all the world could have known of the glorious Jesus of Nazareth, and of the sublime doctrines that he preached.

One other supposition only remains to be considered. Let it be supposed that neither Christ nor Christianity had existed, is there any other source whence mankind could have derived a knowledge of the lofty and animating doctrines relative to God and man contained in the Christian Bible, and constituting the substance of the Christian revelation? Should we know any thing of a personal God, his attributes of wisdom, love, and justice, or his moral government over the world; any thing of the past history of human nature, the immortality of the soul and the resurrection of the body; any thing of a man's justification before God; of the eternal distinctions of right and wrong; or of the relative and social duties between man and man? To take away these truths would be the same calamity to our moral life as it would be to our physical being were the sun extinguished in the midst of the heavens. Yet the history of pagan philosophy proves that we are entirely indebted for them to Christianity and the Christian Scriptures. This philosophy was already in its decline at the beginning of the Christian era, and profane history contains nothing more pathetic than its plaintive confession of its own absolute vanity.

The highest attainments of heathenism never exceeded a system of guesses. It was fertile in doubts; barren of fixed conclusions. Common principles, it had none; ascertained truth universally accepted, it had none; acknowledged creed, it had none. It was a thing many-shaped and many-colored, fickle and inconstant as the clouds across the summer sky. What one thinker suggested another thinker denied. It sometimes guessed what might be; it could never say what was. In its best and highest form, attained under Socrates and Plato, it caught some dim outlines of great truths; but could never give them definite form, frame them into intelligible truths, nor invest them with power over the intellect, or authority over the conscience.

2*

These guesses amounted, moreover, to very little solution of the great and pressing problems of human life and death. Was there a God at all? If so, was he a personal Being, or a universal all-pervading substance? Did he take notice of human affairs as the moral governor of the world; or did he repose idly in the abstract contemplation of his own glory? Was it an intellectual will or a blind fate whereby human affairs were ordered? Is there any other law for man than the instincts of his own nature? Has he a soul? and what will become of it at death? Is there another life? and what will be its character? Is there such a thing as truth? and if so, is every thing truth, or nothing truth? These are questions pressing so closely on the conscience, and brought so intimately into contact with the heart that some definite answer to them is necessary for happiness. Without some clear knowledge of them there can be neither security for life nor peace for death. Yet these vital questions heathenism left unsolved, and was as incompetent to solve them as the human hand is to bind the winds and change the ordinances of the sky.

We do not adequately appreciate what we owe to the Christian Scriptures, or what we should lose by their absence. Take them away, or destroy their authority, and we are absolutely ignorant on all these subjects. We should neither know what we ourselves are, nor what God is; neither understand the meaning of life, nor the significance of death. The moral and spiritual darkness of mankind would be as thick and absolute nineteen centuries after Christ as it was seven hundred years before Christ, when "darkness covered the earth, and gross darkness the people."   Isaiah 60:2.

Hence the inquiry on which we suppose ourselves to have entered has issued in one definite conclusion, one firm and solid link in the chain of truth—the Christianity of the historical past is identified with the Christian Scriptures.   As a matter of fact, it has been identified with them throughout.   As a matter of theory we are unable to conceive what would have been the present condition of the world had the two been separated.   For our present purposes the separation may therefore be considered as inconceivable.   Dealing with the case as it is, all our knowledge of the faith is derived from this source, and from this source only.   Christianity and the Christian Scriptures have ever stood together in the past, and for all that we can see, they must together stand or together fall in the future.

CHAPTER III.

THE AUTHORITY OF THE CHRISTIAN SCRIPTURES.

The Authority of the Scriptures as a Revelation from God—Its Threefold Grounds: I. The Inspired Character of their Authors, and the Scriptural Teaching on the Nature and Limits of their Commission—No other Writings of Inspired Men extant—II. The Structural Unity of the Whole Collection of Sacred Books and its Producing Cause—III. The Sublimity and Superhuman Character of its Contents.

In prosecuting an inquiry into the character of God's word written, every conclusion gained must be accepted as a settled principle, and as the basis of fresh conclusions. To go back and undo what has been done would make all definite result impossible. All our processes of thinking depend upon a number of conclusions, each one of which depends upon the one preceding it, like consecutive links of a chain. We must not disturb the foundations on account of any difficulty in the superstructure. Each link in the series cannot be too carefully tested, or too clearly understood. But once accepted, it must not be called into further question, but must be adopted as affording a firm hold for further progress.

The considerations presented in the preceding chapter prove the authority of Christianity to be identical with the authority of the Christian Scriptures, inasmuch as these records constitute our only source of information. Had they not existed, or existing, were their credibility now destroyed, we should find ourselves in almost absolute ignorance on all points relative to Christ and to his teaching.

This conclusion rests on a consideration of the facts of the case as they are, and not as they might conceivably have been. This caution cannot be too frequently reiterated, or too rigidly maintained. The facts of Christianity are clearly distinct from its records. The events themselves are different from our knowledge of the events. The work of Christ might have been completed in his life, death, and resurrection; his gospel might have been preached by the apostles, and been accepted by the world although no authoritative records had been given. An ingenious fancy might occupy itself with an imaginary history of Christianity under such circumstances. But a mental exercise of this kind can have no weight in a practical inquiry after truth, because this inquiry must deal with things as they are; and under the actual facts of the case the progress of Christianity has never been distinct from its authoritative records, but has been bound up with them in such a way that if the records had been absent all our knowledge of Christianity would have been absent likewise.

It is, for instance, conceivable in the nature of things that the knowledge of Christ and of his doctrine, as it existed during the lifetime of the companions and witnesses of his ministry, might have been perpetuated in a series of uninspired compositions linked in point of time to the New Testament writings, but independent of them for their authority. These conceivable writings might have derived their information on points of fact and doctrine from the oral tradition of the living church, and not from the inspired writings of the apostles. This is conceivable; but in point of fact it is not the case. No such writings exist. The earliest compositions of the primitive church are not independent witnesses, but witnesses dependent on the inspired writings, and consistently referring back to them. It is useless therefore to argue upon a theory devoid of correspondence with the actual facts of the case.

Or again, it is conceivable that the great Head of the church might have provided a succession of inspired men to perpetuate the oral teaching of the church, and have authenticated their inspiration by extraordinary signs and miracles. But this is not the case. Inspired men, attested by their possession of the powers of the world to come, have ceased to exist; and it is not only useless, but mischievous, to distract attention from the facts as they are, in order to fix it on the facts as they might have been, but are not.

Or again, it is conceivable that God might have laid up the gift of infallibility in his church, and constituted the succession of her ministry into an authoritative instructor in all truth, qualified to pronounce what is and what is not true. But God has not done this. For centuries after Christ, no whisper of any such claim was heard. When the claim was subsequently made, it was based on the promises of the written word, and consequently could never have been made if the word had not existed. As a further matter of historical fact, the earthly church has erred repeatedly. The church of Rome, the only branch claiming to possess an oral tradition of truth, has contradicted herself over and over again; and no authority can make two contradictory statements to be equally true. As a matter of fact, therefore, God has not adopted such a mode of preserving truth; and as we cannot impose conditions on God, it cannot be right to argue upon what God has not done, instead of what he has done.

In the same way, God could have established, maintained, and propagated Christianity without the use of inspired writings at all. Had he done so, it would have been our duty to accept such evidences of truth as he might have been pleased to provide. But God has acted differently. As the fact actually stands, we have nowhere and in no form any tradition of Christian truth independent of its inspired documents. All the knowledge of the church has been derived from this source; and no mere extension of an indefinite series of teachers can change the foundation on which their teaching rests. Let the links in the chain be ten or ten thousand, the original authority is the same. Divine Providence has so ordered matters, that we possess no independent and coördinate sources of information. From the moment of the completion of the canon, the Bible has ever stood, and still stands, alone. No authentic documents survive which do not refer their own authority to this source. Either we must accept the knowledge of Christianity we gain from it, or we must be content to be without any knowledge of Christianity at all. In the words already used, Christianity is identified with the Christian Scriptures.

This conclusion may be used in two ways. Either a man may argue that Christianity is true, and that therefore the Bible must be true; and such an argument, although very insufficient, would carry with it a great presumption in its favor. Or a man may argue from the Bible to Christianity; and if he be an opponent, he may say that the Bible is not true, and therefore Christianity cannot be true. Either mode of arguing, however, involves inquiry into the character of the Christian Scriptures. In what aspect do they claim to be regarded, and what authority is there for the claim? The church universal more or less explicitly gives the answer to the first question when she declares her belief that the Scriptures are the word of God. What is the full meaning of the expression "word of God," will come to be considered hereafter. The first thing is to examine the general right of Scripture to such an appellation. By this means alone shall we ascertain how far the assertion sometimes made is true, that the authority of Scripture is independent of the question of its inspiration.

The evidences for its authority are more or less familiar to every Christian. They constitute a necessary stage of the inquiry to which this work is directed, but a preliminary stage only. For the full statement of them the reader is referred to books on the evidences; such, for instance, as the excellent work of Bishop McIlvaine. A slight sketch only of the argument can be given in this place; but it is essential that its outline should be borne in mind, or else the conditions of the question cannot be properly appreciated.

I. The Scriptures are accepted as authoritative because they are the composition of inspired men. These words are apparently very simple; yet, in relation to our present inquiry, almost every one of them requires explanation. A difficulty meets us on the threshold which cannot satisfactorily be passed over; for how do we know that the books of Scripture were written by inspired men, except from Scripture itself? But at the present stage Scripture cannot be brought as a witness, because the character of Scripture, and the amount of authority more or less due to it, is the very question under inquiry. We must first show that it is the production of inspired men, before it can be accepted as a decisive witness. The proof must be found somewhere outside Scripture. Yet if we have no source of information upon the facts and doctrines of Christianity except the Christian Scriptures, and the Christian Scriptures cannot be called to bear witness to the inspired character of their own authors, where is the proof to be found? The difficulty is apparently perplexing, but admits of a very simple answer. It resolves itself into a mere question of historical credibility. For the sake of clearness, I take the case of the New Testament Scriptures only.

We discard for the time all notions about the divine authority of these writings, all questions relative to their religious character and credibility. We take them simply as a collection of ancient books, and submit them to precisely the same process of examination to which all other literature is submitted. What is the time when these books were written, and who were their authors? The existence of the books at the present moment, whatever may be thought of their character, is a fact of common experience, to be doubted by none but a madman. It is equally certain that their existence in their present collected form can be traced backwards as a matter of fact to within a period of two hundred years after Christ, and separate books more than a hundred years earlier, even to the lifetime of the companions of the apostles. In alleging this antiquity for these writings, we rest upon the testimony of enemies as well as of friends—on Celsus, Julian, and Porphyry, as well as on Justin Martyr, Irenæus, Origen, and Jerome. The same testimony affirms that they constituted at that period, as at the present, the sacred books of the Christians. This fact proves them to have been accepted as the undoubted productions of their reputed authors by those who enjoyed personal acquaintance with them, and lived at the times and places when and where the facts recorded in them took place.

These are the undeniable facts of the case, and we proceed to decide from them on the authenticity of the books, just as we decide from evidence of exactly the same kind, although much weaker in degree, on the authenticity of other old books. Is it possible that men nearly contemporaneous with the apostles could have been mistaken on the genuineness and authenticity of these books? For instance, could they have believed the fourteen epistles ascribed to St. Paul to have been really his composition, had the fact been otherwise? Is it possible that the church at Corinth can have believed themselves to be in possession of a letter from St. Paul, attested by his own signature, if it was not the case? That letter professed to come from one who was personally acquainted with them, and to refer to matters lying equally within the knowledge of the writer and of the persons addressed. Is it possible that such a letter should ever have been accepted as the genuine composition of St. Paul, if no such man had ever been at Corinth, if no such events had happened within their knowledge?

What is true of the Corinthians is equally true of the Romans, Galatians, Colossians, Philippians, Thessalonians. The autograph letters addressed to these churches are asserted to have been extant, and open to the examination of all men in the time of Tertullian. I do not say a word at present about the inspired character of these books, or the nature of their contents. I only note that the letters of St. Paul, such as we have them now, were in existence immediately after the times of St. Paul, and were accepted as his genuine writings by his contemporaries and their immediate successors in the churches he is asserted to have founded. It is on testimony of this kind that we accept the genuineness and authenticity of all ancient books. In regard to the apostolic writings, the witnesses are so much more numerous than they are in regard to any secular writings, that if we refuse to accept the testimony in their case, we are much more compelled to reject it in all other cases. If the currency obtained by the Pauline epistles so shortly after the lifetime of St. Paul be no proof of their being really his epistles, then we have no proof of the authorship of any portion of ancient literature. Once let it be admitted that these old books are the genuine and authentic letters of their reputed author, and we have an independent fact from which step by step the historical credibility of the entire gospel history can be deduced.

For then such a man as St. Paul really lived, really exercised an apostleship, really founded churches, really preached Christ, really wrought miracles in attestation of his authority. Then the facts he preached relative to the life, actions, sufferings, death, and resurrection of Christ must have been true; for if they were not true, the apostle who preached them could never have been believed. Then was Paul himself but one of a company of apostolic men, inspired like himself, and like himself, proving their commission as inspired teachers by signs and wonders and miracles.

In short, the facts of Christianity are so linked to each other, that if we can prove any one part of the series, the truth of all the rest must be admitted likewise. The comparative anatomist, when he has found one bone of an animal, can argue from that one conclusively for the existence of all the others necessary to the complete animal, even although he should not actually discover them. He might not be able to determine certainly all the particulars relating to them in the absence of the bones themselves, but he can argue certainly for their existence. In the same way, one independent fact relative to the Christian Scriptures must involve the truth of many other facts. We find this one fact in the existence of the books themselves, and their current acceptation in the earliest times of the Christian church, proved, as we may prove any other historical fact, by the testimony of concurrent witnesses.

But what is true of the writings of St. Paul is equally true of the other New Testament writers—of Matthew, Mark, Luke, John, Peter, Jude, and James. In each case the existence of the old books, and their general currency as genuine productions, are the simple facts of ordinary history, ascertained by an easy train of reasoning, wholly independent of their religious character and inspired authority. Each one of these facts may be made singly the proof of many other associated facts. The result of them altogether goes far to construct the whole fabric of New Testament history and doctrine. They constitute an independent testimony to this truth, at all events, that the Scriptural books were written by miraculously endowed men.

This is the first reason, therefore, for which the

Christian Scriptures are accepted as authoritative ; that they are the productions of men authorized to teach, and themselves specially instructed for this purpose. Their appointment was not made by man, but by God. When an earthly messenger conveys a communication of importance, he may justly be asked for the credentials of his commission, and such as are the credentials, such will be the authority under which he acts. No credentials from a lower authority could authenticate a message professing to come immediately from a monarch. A monarch's commission can only be authenticated by a monarch's sanction. It is equally true, on the other side, that if a messenger brings credentials from a monarch, he is justified in claiming a monarch's authority for his commission. The writers of the sacred books belonged to a company of men claiming a special commission to teach mankind, and referring this commission to the immediate will of God himself. In proof of the Divine authority given to them, they raised the dead, healed the sick, made the blind to see and the lame to walk, and even conferred these extraordinary powers upon others by the laying on of their hands. Such works lie beyond the sphere of any unassisted human powers. The miraculous can only be wrought by God, because the incapacity of man to do it is the element which makes it miraculous. The miracles of the apostolic men were their credentials, open and visible to all men. The credentials were of God; therefore the commission attested by them was of God likewise.

The commission to teach confers authority on the teaching; but this authority does not extend beyond the purpose contemplated in the gift of it. When an earthly ambassador presents the credentials of his commission, he represents the monarch by whom he is appointed in those acts specified in his commission, but in no others. Because a man is authorized to negotiate a treaty, he is not therefore authorized to sell a province or to confer an estate. The dignity of his ambassadorship is attached indeed to his person, but its authority is not attached to all his acts, but only to acts done in accordance with and in virtue of his instruction. He may be a skilful diplomatist, and furnished with every necessary information for his guidance; but he may also be, at the same time, an immoral man in his private life, venal, false, profligate. The private sins of the man would not invalidate the acts of the ambassador. It would be absurd to call into question the authority of his commission in his public acts because of mistakes committed in the sphere of private life. The authority of a commission, therefore, extends so far, but so far only, as the purposes for which it is given.

The sacred writers, in like manner, brought with them an authority to teach; and to their teaching, therefore, and not absolutely to themselves, the authority belongs. The God who gave the credentials must have given the commission, and his authority attaches to the discharge of its duties. What they taught was not theirs, but God's; carried with it not alone their weight, but the weight of God, who authenticated, commissioned, inspired them to teach it. To argue that the sacred writings cannot be infallibly true, because their writers made mistakes in their private life, is to confuse what they did on God's authority with what they did on their own authority. It is the same mistake as it would be to confound the private life of the man with the public acts of the ambassador. There is not a word in Scripture to assert that the sacred writers were secured from all mistakes in every thing they said and did. We are directly taught the very reverse, since Scripture itself makes us acquainted with the quarrel between Paul and Barnabas, and the open disagreement on a point of Christian action, not of Christian teaching, between Paul and Peter. Paul rebuked Peter to his face, not for teaching that a man can be justified by the works of the law, but for giving way to the exclusive habits of the Judaizing teachers. "He withdrew and separated himself, fearing them which were of the circumcision." Gal. 2 : 12. The inspiration of the sacred writers was not therefore absolute and universal, but strictly relative to that special work of communicating divine truth for which they were commissioned.

This limitation is frequently expressed. Thus, when our Lord first sent forth the twelve apostles, their special commission was, "As ye go, preach." Matt. 10 : 7. The promise of his special presence and help exactly followed the commission. On points of ordinary practice they were taught to exercise their own sanctified prudence: "Be ye therefore wise as serpents, and harmless as doves." Matt. 10:16. But in emergencies, their words were to be guided by a special inspiration: "It is not ye that speak, but the Spirit of your Father which speaketh in you." Matt. 10:20. When he gave his final commission, not to the apostles alone, but to his church at large, the instruction was the same, "Go ye, therefore, and teach." Matt. 28:19. In our Lord's deeply mysterious prayer to his Father, recorded in John 17, the same purpose is repeatedly affirmed: "I have given unto them the words which thou gavest me;" "I have given them thy word," "Neither pray I for these alone, but for them also which shall believe on me through their word." When Matthias was elected in the place of the traitor Judas, it was to be as "a witness:" "Thou, Lord, which knowest the hearts of all men, show whether of these two thou hast chosen, that he may take part of this ministry and apostleship." Acts 1:24, 25. When St. Paul was subsequently called of God to be an apostle, "straightway he preached Christ." Acts 9:20. He declared the object of his own calling to be, that he "might preach him among the heathen." Gal. 1:16. In asserting the independence of his apostolical authority, his expressed jealousy is not for any assumed universal infallibility, but solely for the gospel he preached. Of it, and of it only, he asserts, "I neither received it of man, neither was I taught it, but by the revelation of Jesus Christ." Gal. 1:12. In writing to Timothy, he reiterates the same fact: "Whereunto I am appointed a preacher, and an apostle, and a teacher of the Gentiles." 2 Tim. 1:11. In three other passages he uses almost the same words. In the first chapter of the Hebrews, the commission to teach is extended to the writers of the Old Testament; and the teaching is so immediately identified with the teaching of God, that the act of the one is declared to be the act of the other. "God, who at sundry times and in divers manners spake in time past unto the fathers by the prophets, hath in these last days spoken unto us by his Son." Heb. 1:1, 2. And, lastly, St. Peter asserts the same limitation in regard to the holy men of old: they "spake as they were moved by the Holy Ghost." 2 Peter 1:21.

The commission given to the apostles, and the inspiration supplied to qualify them for their work, have thus ever been limited to their teaching, and never been extended absolutely to their persons. In their private lives and conduct, they were left to the ordinary guidance of the Holy Spirit, promised to all believers without distinction. Scripture does not contain a syllable to extend the extraordinary inspiration from the teaching to the persons of the teachers. While they lived, it was embodied in their words. Since their death, it survives embodied in their writings. Had other inspired teachers succeeded them, then the oral teaching of the living apostles would have taken precedence of the written teaching of the dead apostles. But since no such line has ever been perpetuated, and both the miraculous inspiration and the miraculous credentials have ceased together in the church, the written teaching of the dead apostles stands alone. The inspiration of the men is perpetuated in the writings—the unalterable utterance of an authoritative revelation for all time.

Thus St. Paul expresses himself. That inspiration primarily existed in the men inspired cannot be doubted; that, secondarily, it is embodied in their writings, is directly taught. It is the Scripture which is "God-inspired." The words were written towards the close of the apostle's life. With the exception of the two epistles of Peter and the Book of the Revelation—perhaps with the further exception of the Epistle of the Hebrews and the short letter of Jude—the canon of the New Testament was already completed. St. Paul's earlier epistles had already been collected, and were so widely read that St. Peter, writing shortly after the date of the second Epistle to Timothy, could speak of them as familiarly known, "as also in all his epistles." He then proceeds to identify these epistles with the general body of the Scriptures, "which they that are unlearned and unstable wrest, as they do also the other Scriptures." 2 Peter 3:16. This occurs in a letter, not directed to one particular church, but to the general body of believers, "them that have obtained like precious faith with us." 2 Peter 1:1. St. Paul's words to Timothy cannot therefore be restricted to the sacred writings of the Old Testament alone, but must have included the great mass of the New Testament writings likewise. He refers the authoritative teaching of the church, not to the men, but to their writings. The Scripture is "God-inspired," and is "profitable for doctrine"—

not only profitable, but sufficient—"able to make the man of God perfect, thoroughly furnished unto all good works."　2 Tim. 3:16, 17.

But the Scriptures are authoritative, not simply because they are the compositions of inspired men, but because they are the only existing compositions of inspired men.　They stand therefore alone, without any rivals or companions.　Whether other compositions of the same body of inspired men ever existed, and have been lost, is a question wholly devoid of any practical importance.　Its suggestion and discussion serve only to divert attention from the real point at issue.　If it could be proved that these men had drawn up a formal body of truth of which the existing books were but a portion, there might arise a suspicion of incompleteness and consequent insufficiency in the surviving portions: but it will shortly appear that the evidence leans strongly in the other direction.　It is enough for the present to rest on the fact that the books which we have are inspired books, and carry with them the authority due to the commission and supernatural gifts of their authors.　What other books, not in existence, may have been written, is a matter of useless speculation.　As a matter of fact, we can only deal with the books we have.　Their inspired character has been already shown, and no others exist like them.

The care exercised by the ancient church in the formation of the New Testament canon, is evidenced by the number of spurious books rejected as not being the genuine writings of inspired men.　No less than thirty spurious gospels are known to have existed, sixteen books of Acts, and five Epistles. Eighty books have been at various times presented for acceptance into the canon, and have been rejected. These works have not been excluded out of any arbitrary decision that certain writers only should be accepted as inspired, but because they bear upon themselves the manifest proof of imposture, in anachronisms, contradictions, and absurdities which render it impossible that they could be the real productions of their professed authors. The critical tests applied to the canonical and to the apocryphal books are precisely the same. The examination confirmatory of the claims of the one is destructive to the claims of the other. The canonical books are the production of inspired men, and are the only writings of the kind extant.

II. The Scriptures are accepted as authoritative because they are found to constitute in their collected form one complete and harmonious revelation. They have been termed an organic whole. The component parts of this one revelation display every conceivable variety of style, date, circumstances, and personal peculiarity. The Bible contains sixty-six different books from about thirty different writers. Their composition extends over a period of fifteen hundred years. They were written one by one, under circumstances as widely different as can be conceived. Yet when brought together they are found to constitute one book, bridging over the whole course of human history, from the creation to the judgment and the final kingdom of the Messiah. An unbroken historical continuity pervades them all. They are so linked together, that the absence of any one book of the whole would interrupt this order, and make some other portions unintelligible, which, as they now stand, are intelligible and consistent. The same doctrinal truths relative to God and man are found, more or less prominently taught, from the first book of the series to the last. These truths, moreover, are peculiar to this revelation, and stand out in sharply-defined contrast from all the schemes of religious belief existing in ancient heathenism. One consistent scheme of God's dealings towards man runs like a thread of gold throughout the whole, latent in the promises to the patriarchs, shadowed in the types and ceremonies of the law, predicted with ever-increasing clearness by the prophets, and finally accomplished in the eternal substance of the gospel. The progression is as orderly and consecutive as is the progress of the natural sun, as from his rising in the east he marches up the heavens into meridian light and glory. This unity in variety implies the design of an intelligent mind; but as no human intelligence could act over so vast a lapse of time, the mind can be no other than the mind of God. The books must therefore be divine in their origin, and equally divine in their authority.

The conclusion thus formed is only strengthened by the tendencies of skeptical criticism. The whole course of modern thought tends to give to the scriptural books a greater variety of date and multiplicity of authorship. But the more largely we increase the number of writers and the variety of supposed sources of information, the more astonishing becomes the organic and indestructible unity of doctrinal teaching, historical sequence, and intelligent design pervading the whole. If this unity among thirty writers be so wonderful that we can only refer it to the over-ordering interference of God, it must be much more wonderful among a hundred, and consequently still more manifestly divine.

In this particular likewise the Christian Scriptures stand alone. No other sacred books existing in the world exhibit either the same variety or the same unity. The religious books of the Persians, Hindoos, and Chinese do not contain any intelligible or consistent scheme of faith. Comparison between them and the Christian Bible lies beyond the wildest extravagance of skepticism.

It must also be briefly noted that this harmonious scheme of revelation is connected throughout with corresponding events in human history. Its sphere is not in some imaginary cloud-land, but amid the actual events and transactions of the world. At no time has the divine revelation been introduced abruptly, but has filled its appropriate place in the orderly dealings of Providence and the actual wants of humanity. The whole of the Old Testament Scriptures are inseparably identified with the history of the Jewish nation, and constitute the only explanation of its past fortunes and present condition. The New Testament Scriptures are the sequel and complement of the Old, and only complete what would otherwise be fragmentary and imperfect.   As the existence of the Jew establishes beyond a doubt the historical groundwork of the Old Testament Scriptures, so the existence of Christianity and of the Christian establishes the historical character of the New.

Lastly, this unity of design, perceptible through the whole series of the separate scriptural books, supplies the appropriate answer to all useless speculations relative to other supposed works of inspired writers; for if the books we have form one complete scheme, it is natural to suppose that they are all we were ever meant to have.   Providence has ordered that these, and these alone, should be preserved; and divine wisdom has ordered that these should constitute a complete scheme of revelation.   Can it be doubted that the one is as intentional as the other, and that the wisdom overruling the composition of the books and the power preserving them are equally of God?

III.)The Christian Scriptures are accepted as authoritative, because their superhuman contents witness to their superhuman origin.   This argument branches out into several particulars.

(a.) The subjects treated in them lie beyond the possible scope of any human knowledge.   This is true of many of the historical facts, such as the facts of the Creation, the Fall, and the Deluge, of which no human testimony can exist.   It is true throughout of the interpositions of God in human affairs, and of the purposes contemplated in them, alike as regards the events of the past and the prospects of the future.   The mind of God can only be known to God himself, and can be communicated to others only by a revelation analogous to the verbal communications of man with man. It is true especially in regard to the divine nature, and the incomprehensible mysteries of the being of God—mysteries as clearly not contrary to human reason as they are clearly above it; for the human reason can have no knowledge where it has no experience. The contents of the Bible stand, in this respect, in very striking contrast to all human speculations relative to God. The latter are exaggerations, and sometimes caricatures of the nature of man himself, and in their intense humanness betray their earthly origin. The revelation of God in his word, on the contrary, represents his nature as wholly different from our present knowledge, and therefore wholly above our present apprehension. The history, the doctrines, and the morality of the Bible lie equally beyond the sphere of human reason; yet at the same time they furnish the only key to explain the mysteries of human life, the only hopes to supply the wants of human souls, the only motives and influences to sanctify human conduct. Nor is the mode of communication unworthy of the grandeur of the truths communicated. The sublimity, majesty, and beauty of Scripture, and its tone of conscious authority, are confessedly unparalleled in the whole circle of earthly literature.

(b.) The miraculous element of prediction stamps the impress of a divine omnipotence upon the scriptural books. In virtue of the organic unity linking the whole series of writings together, the witness of prophecy to any one part of the series would suffice to reflect its own authority upon the rest. In truth, however, the thread of prediction is wonderfully interwoven throughout the whole. The New Testament at large is the fulfilment of the Old. Many signal predictions of the ancient prophets are fulfilled within the knowledge of our own day, and their accomplishment is found to be the more exact and accurate, the more we know about the circumstances. Egypt, Nineveh, Babylon, Tyre, are as yet but half-deciphered pages, but every line blazes with its testimony to ancient inspiration. The very history of the world is the history of accomplished prophecy. The living Jew, amid all changes of time and circumstance still the Jew, as distinctive and characteristic in his dispersion among every nation under heaven as he was in the days of Solomon or the heroic times of the Maccabees, stands in the full front of the Word, its mysterious and imperishable monument. To know the future is the sole prerogative of Him who orders it. The emphatic stress laid upon this evidence in Scripture itself is very memorable. It is the great argument of the prophet Isaiah; it is the topic of sublime expostulation on the part of God himself, "Who, as I, shall call, and shall declare it, and set it in order for me, since I appointed the ancient people? and the things that are coming, and shall come, let them show unto them. Fear ye not, neither be afraid: have not I told thee from that time, and have declared it? Ye are even my witnesses." Isaiah 44:7, 8. Not, however, on the Old Testament alone is impressed this stamp of Omniscience. The predictions of our Lord himself, the warning declarations of St. Paul relative to the man of sin, and the whole structure of the apocalyptic vision, are full of the same prescience, and have already entered upon the same course of accomplishment.

Thus, from three separate directions is attested the authority of the Scriptures. They are the permanent embodiment of the inspiration of their authors: being dead, they yet speak—yet fulfil their great commission as the channels of a divine revelation. In their collected form, the Scriptures bear in their very front the unity of their Author: the outward world, composed of ten thousand forces and elements, is not more manifestly one cosmos, nor witnesses more eloquently to the glory of its Creator, than the collected Scriptures are one book, and testify to the one Mind which has moulded after his own will such discordant and disordered elements into one completed revelation. The sublimity of its subject-matter and the singular beauty of its composition, attest its higher than human authorship. These lines of argument present to us the exterior of the temple of truth. Full of praise and wonder, we enter into its courts; and what is the voice that fills them but the voice of God, penetrating and solemn as that "still small voice" before which the prophet of Israel veiled his face in his mantle as one who could not look upon God? The three lines of argument concur in one conclusion, blend into one ray of heavenly light, constitute

one diadem of glory, swell into one song of praise.
The Christian Scriptures are a revelation from
God, and come clothed with his authority to the
human heart and conscience.   Nothing less than
this can be admitted—nothing more or higher can
be said.   The Bible is the word of God.

CHAPTER IV.

THE WHOLE SCRIPTURES ARE THE WORD OF GOD.

Presumption that an Equal Authority attaches to the whole Scriptures—Difference of *containing* the Word of God, and *being* the Word of God—Modern Theories—The Inspired Authorship of the Bible belongs to all its Contents without Distinction—Its Historical Details as clearly comprehended within its Unity of Design as its Doctrinal Revelations—Connection of the Detailed Parts of Scripture with its Sublime Doctrines—The Authority coextensive alike with the Authorship, the Structural Unity, and the Doctrinal Revelation.

THE character of a whole must necessarily be the character of its component parts. Any simple and complete object may be taken as an illustration—a piece of sculpture, a painting, a building, a machine. We may judge of one part separately from another part, but we cannot judge of the whole separately either from any or from all its parts, simply because the aggregate of all the parts makes up the whole. Take any one part away, and what is left ceases to be the whole. The statue and the painting may have many exquisitely beautiful parts, and yet another part may be either incorrect in conception or faulty in execution. The architect's design may exhibit features of surpassing excellence, and yet be marred by great defects: it may be exquisite in its details, and yet want breadth of effect; or it may possess dignity of outline, and yet its minor parts may be disproportioned and out of place. The machine may exhibit great ingenuity of construction, and yet some practical defect may baffle the resources of the inventor, and render his ingenuity comparatively useless. There may exist great beauty and acknowledged merits, in spite of defects, and yet in every case, without exception, the standard of excellence attained by the whole is lowered by the defects of the parts. No work can be perfect unless all its parts are perfect; the character of the whole must follow the character of its component parts; and, on the other side, the component parts must partake of the character of the whole. Let it be said that this particular production of art is a perfect statue, a perfect painting, a perfect building, a perfect machine; and the statement involves the absence of perceptible fault in any and all of its parts.

The same mode of speaking must hold good in regard to the word of God. What its exact character and the amount of its authority may be, depends upon further examination. But before the inquirer proceeds to investigate these questions, it is right for him to recognize the presumptive proof already reached, that this character and authority, whatever they may be, will pervade equally the whole Bible, unless some specific reason can be alleged to the contrary. A want of attention to this preliminary probability lies at the root of any difficulties upon the question of inspiration.

Three principal varieties of opinion are perceptible in modern controversy, and contain within themselves many shades and degrees not calling for special notice. The first denies the Divine authority of the Bible, and refusing to recognize it as a complete book, claims the liberty of rejecting its particular portions at pleasure. The second accepts the Divine authority of the Bible, but denies that this authority extends equally throughout all its parts. The third accepts the Divine authority of the whole Bible, without reserve or limitation. The first and the last of these are consistent, because they attach an equivalent value to the whole and to its parts—the one denying the whole, and the other accepting it; the second is inconsistent, because it affirms that the whole Bible is a Divine revelation, and yet denies that all its parts are a Divine revelation. The first of these opinions already falls behind the present course of inquiry, since it concentrates opposition on the three reasons alleged in the last chapter, and denies with equal vehemence the inspired authority of the scriptural witers, the structural unity of their writings, and the supernatural character of their contents. We therefore leave this class of opinion behind, although it will be indirectly touched by the whole course of the argument. The second variety of opinion accepts the three reasons above named, and therefore advances side by side with us to the further discussion of the extent of scriptural inspiration. The conclusions already stated will therefore be assumed to be admitted principles, to which appeal may be made towards the settlement of the specific question, whether the inspiration of

Scripture extends only to parts of the canonical books, or to the whole of them without exception.

But a presumption in favor of its unlimited extension already arises from the grounds of its authority. If this presumption can be clearly established, it will throw the weight of proof on the other side of the question. It will remain for those who accept the general authority of Scripture, but deny its extension to all its parts, to prove the necessity of the limitation, and to establish the positive evidence of it.

The grounds of the authority of Scripture have been already stated to be mainly three. The argument must follow their order, and run on the same lines. To what extent, if at all, are these three reasons applicable to the whole contents of the canonical Scriptures?

I. The authority of the writers clearly extends over the whole of their writings, unless there be some expressed limitation to the contrary. In its absence, the authority must be coextensive with the authorship. We might have possessed books in which fragments by inspired writers may have been incorporated with other matter from inferior pens. In such a case, the authors would have been responsible for what they wrote, and for no more. Where they wrote all, they are responsible for all. Whatever authority the character of the writer confers, extends to every part equally of the writing emanating from his pen and attested by his sanction. It is thus we judge of secular books, and thus, therefore, we ought to judge of sacred. Whatever was written by St. Paul carries with it whatever weight the apostolic commission and inspired authority of the author may be supposed to confer.

The nature of the subject-matter does not affect the identity of authorship in any way. An historical work, for instance, will necessarily contain passages of widely different character, and which tax, in widely different directions and degrees, the resources of the author. On one page we read an eloquent exposition of the character of an age, or a philosophical analysis of the causes concurring in its production. On another page we read an array of details relative, for instance, to the industrial resources of some country, the nature of its revenues, its comparative exports and imports, or the amount of its warlike preparations, the number of its armies, or the exact extent of its available forces in some special crisis of its history. Passages of the first character will have called into play much higher intellectual faculties, and have taxed them to a much greater extent, than passages of the latter kind. The one demands thought, discriminating judgment, careful generalization, and the exercise of the imaginative faculties; the other requires honesty of purpose, diligence of research, and accuracy of statement. Yet for the purposes of the historian, the one class may be as absolutely important as the other; for if the facts were wrong, the conclusions founded upon them would, in all probability, be wrong likewise. The historian is therefore equally responsible for them both. Both classes of statement are equally the fruit of his la-

bor and the production of his pen; both equally
share the authority of his character. The confidence we repose in the accuracy of the facts is as
great as the admiration with which we follow the
progress of his argument; or rather, we are much
more dependent upon the character of the writer in
the one case than we are in the other; for we shall
be less capable of ascertaining the accuracy of the
facts than of testing the soundness of his conclusions from them. Each varying passage exhibits
its appropriate quality in the author, and receives
its corresponding acceptance from the reader. But
the fact of the authorship, and whatever claim upon
our credence may be involved in it, extends to all
the passages alike. The claim may be great or little, but it extends equally to all the parts of the one
work of the one author.

In the same way the contents of the Bible differ
very much in their subject-matter. Thus the Old
Testament contains books of history, books of devotion, books of prophetic teaching. Some of the historical books are remarkable for the subordinate
place occupied in them by the directly religious
element; as, for instance, the books of Joshua and
Judges and the books of Ruth and Esther. In the
last of these, the name of God does not even occur.
The devotional books are replete with the utterances of a personal experience which would have
been wholly out of place in historical narratives.
The prophetic books, professing to contain the application of the divine promises and threatenings to
the religious exigencies of the times of the proph-

ets, are distinguished by the lofty sublimity of their language and the grandeur of their predictions. The style and structure of each book necessarily follows the character of its subject-matter and the objects contemplated in its production. The assertion that all these various books may have been alike issued under the authority of a superintending and inspiring God does not contradict in the slightest degree any principle of human consistency, but may rather be supported by many human analogies. For instance, the architect employs many classes of workmen, and many different men in each class, in the production of the building; through a graduated series of subordinates, he extends the influence of his own mind and will throughout the whole of the workmen, and thus models the entire building into conformity with his design. The influence of his paramount care and authority extends as truly to the ordinary mason who constructs the solid parts of the edifice, as to the sculptor and the painter who contribute its ornaments. But his responsibility for success or failure is co-extensive with his authority. In the same mode, there is no reason why God, in planning and gradually carrying into effect the whole scheme of his revelation to mankind, should not have employed the narrative of the historian as well as the experience of the sacred poet and the genius of the prophet. Every part proceeding from the design of God will, therefore, carry with it equally the authority of God.

The same truth may be applied to the separate books of the Scripture. The books of Moses, for instance, contain portions differing widely from each other in their subject-matter, and consequently in their style. Thus, within the limits of Genesis are comprised the sublime description of the creation and the pathetic narratives of the patriarchal history on the one side, and on the other bare genealogical lists such as occur in Genesis 10 and 11. Similarly, Leviticus contains an enumeration of detailed laws, bearing on questions very minute and apparently trivial; while Deuteronomy contains the last addresses from God to the people of Israel, through the lips of Moses, before they entered into the promised land. In each case the style and diction are appropriate to the subject-matter and to the object contemplated in the revelation; they exhibit variances in these respects precisely analogous to what are found in uninspired compositions. Some critics appear to think that the narrative of the creation, in Genesis 1, ought to have been written with the terse brevity of the *Toldoth Beni Noah* of Genesis 10; or, on the contrary, that this ethnological statement should have been conveyed with the lofty simplicity and graphic vividness of the account of the creation. To suit their views, the enumeration of the legal enactments of Leviticus should either have exhibited the rhetorical force and rich grandeur of Deuteronomy, or the prophetic warnings of Deuteronomy should have been couched in the cold and unimpassioned language of Leviticus. The strict naturalness with which, as the case stands, the language of each portion of the Pentateuch follows the character of its subject-matter, confirms in the strongest manner the genuineness of the whole. There is no more reason why the same man may not have written both Leviticus and Deuteronomy, both Genesis 1 and Genesis 10, than there is why the same Homer may not have composed the list of ships in one book of the Iliad, and the parting of Hector and Andromache in another; or why the same Lord Macaulay may not have composed equally the account of the Loan Bill of December 15, 1692, and the graphic history of the Irish rebellion in 1691, contained in the same volume of his history. But if Moses was the author of these respective passages alike, then the weight of his authority, however it may be estimated, belongs in equal degree to them all. If one is to be believed because Moses wrote it, the other must be believed equally for the same reason. The conclusion must be applied to all the scriptural books. Whatever inspired writers wrote carries with it the weight of inspired authority.

The question is therefore a matter of fact. Are all the parts of the scriptural books equally the composition of their reputed authors? The reply is, that whatever weight of proof exists for ascribing to their authorship a part of them, exists for ascribing to their authorship the whole of them. We have the strongest possible reasons for believing that the existing books of the sacred canon are substantially co-extensive with the original autographs of the Old and New Testaments. The evidence is derived from the outside, since no assertion made in the books themselves could have proved it, while the amount of credit due to the books was the question for decision. God has so ordered the circumstances relative both to the Old and New Testaments, that no alteration of the manuscripts is conceivable so long as the ordinary motives of human action are allowed to have influenced past times as they influence the present.

In regard to the Old Testament, the proof is supplied by the divided and scattered condition of the Hebrew people at the time of the Ptolemies, a time falling within the recognized historical period of the world. The most imaginative of modern writers will not call into question that the books of the Old Testament as we have them now were in existence at the time of the translation of the Septuagint, or that they were acknowledged among the Jews all over the world, or that they were regarded by them with a reverence so great that it ran into superstition, and may almost be regarded as idolatrous. Nor will it be denied that the most ancient portions of these sacred books, the Pentateuch, are still extant in two different forms, the Jewish and the Samaritan; or that these two versions, substantially agreeing, are yet distinguished by characteristic peculiarities of their own; or that the jealous hostility existing from the times of Rehoboam downwards between these two separated branches of the one ancient race must have rendered collusion impossible. All modern criticism has found it much more convenient to ignore the question altogether than to suggest a reasonable and conceivable hypothesis how documents so handed down can have undergone any wilful process of corruption or addition. No other mode of proof can be conceived so free from all possible suspicion or partiality as this which God has actually provided.

It is the less necessary to enlarge on this evidence, because the substantial identity of our present copies with the ancient manuscripts of the Scriptures is not seriously called into question. Modern criticism scarcely dares to suggest more than an occasional interpolation on the part of the transcribers. The grounds on which even these interpolations are asserted are ludicrously arbitrary and capricious. Critics have undertaken to arrange the original manuscripts of the Pentateuch on the authority of a critical instinct of their own; and when any passage has not lent itself easily to a favorite hypothesis, it has been at once accused and summarily sentenced as an interpolation. Such a mode of argument is wholly undeserving of serious notice. But the probability of occasional mistakes in the transcription of the sacred books, and the occasional insertion of notes into the text, may be readily allowed without throwing doubt upon the fact that the autographs of the sacred books were substantially identical with our existing copies, and contained the same admixture of historical narrative and detail with doctrinal teaching and authoritative prediction.

The conclusion therefore remains, that the authority of the inspired writers extends to all that they wrote; and consequently that whatever authority is affirmed for some portions of their writing is really claimed for the whole. The language used in one scriptural book towards other scriptural books confirms this conclusion. They are described by single names, descriptive of the whole of their contents, and which receive, from the known habit of speaking among the Jews, a definite application. Thus the five books of Moses are described under the single epithet, " the Law;" the sixteen prophetical books under the name "the Prophets:" "the law and the prophets were until John," Matt. 11:13. Or more tersely still, the Pentateuch is described by the single name of its reputed author, "Moses;" "they have Moses and the prophets." When we find an independent testimony that the Jews were accustomed to divide the Old Testament books into the Law, the Prophets, and the Hagiographa, it is impossible to give to these expressions any narrower signification. That the threefold Jewish division contained the same number of books as the existing canon of the Old Testament, is known to us positively by the impartial testimony of Josephus.

In accordance with this habit, David in his day applied to the books of Moses expressions of a corresponding kind. He refers with great frequency to God's law, or God's word, or God's statutes, in passages where it is impossible to apply the expression to any one particular passage, or any special immediate message from God; as, for instance, in the analogy drawn in Psalm 19 between the light of the natural sun and the influences of Scripture. The same mode of speaking can be traced downwards to the New

Testament times. When the temple copy of the books of Moses was discovered in Josiah's days, it was described as "the book of the law," 2 Kings 22:8. Isaiah asserts the perpetuity of "the Word of the Lord," Isa. 11:8. Jeremiah declares its preciousness : "Thy Word was unto me the joy and rejoicing of my heart," Jer. 15:16; this expression immediately follows a message of judgment, so that it could not be of the immediate message, but of the general body of the promises, that the prophet spake. Our Lord charged it upon the Pharisees that they made "the Word of God" of none effect through their tradition, Matt. 15:6. St. Paul speaks of "Scripture," and, in a manner parallel to the language of David, applies what may be called corporate epithets to it : "The Word of God is quick and powerful," Heb. 4:12. St. Peter declares it to be "the incorruptible seed," and identifies it with the word just preached, and then written by the apostles : "This is the word which by the gospel is preached unto you," 1 Pet. 1:25. This habitual use of single terms, or of nouns of number, to describe a series of books, supplies a strong attestation to the unity of their respective authorship, and their consequent unity of authority.

II. Beyond the authority given to the sacred books by the inspiration of their authors, a further attestation is given them by their own structural unity. The historical sequence preserved throughout the revelation, the identity of doctrinal truth, and the orderly method of its exposition, can only be the result of intelligence. In the case of books ranging over such vast periods of time, and composed by so many different writers, the intelligence exercised can only be that of God. We have already seen that the contents of Scripture differ very widely in their subject-matter, and comprise history, biography, devotional poetry, prediction, and the dogmatic statement of doctrines at once the most varied and the most sublime in the world. Does this unity of plan include all these various parts, or rather does it require them for its completeness? What has been already said in regard to the authorship is true also of the unity. Whatever stamp of authority is given to the Scriptures by their internal unity extends so far and only so far as the unity extends. If the unity comprises the doctrinal portions of Scripture only, then to those portions only will it give the stamp of a Divine intelligence. But if it comprises the historical, biographical, and devotional likewise, and would itself be destroyed by the removal of any portion of the canonical books, then to these, without exception, does it extend the authority of a revelation schemed in the Divine mind, and, through the agency of human instruments, executed by the Divine wisdom.

The existence of a manifest order pervading the entire series of books from Genesis to Revelation lies upon the surface, patent to the most casual observation. There is not a book which does not contribute something to our stock of information relative to the ways of God with man; not one the absence of which would not produce a gap in the continuity of our knowledge. The complete Scriptures contain an entire history of man in his relation towards God. They take up the wondrous story in the eternity before time, carry it on consecutively over the whole course of time, and only cease with the eternity after time, when the condition of man, his moral trial over, shall again become fixed and absolute as it was before the fall. Throughout the whole of these ages one harmonious plan of redemption marches on towards its accomplishment. The successive steps of the plan are likewise the exact gradations of the record. We are presented with its first beginnings in the promise of a Redeemer, made to man in Eden ; are invited to watch the calling and growth, first of the family, and afterwards of the nation selected to furnish its human instruments. We are made acquainted with their education, their national obligations and sins, their rise, greatness, decline, and fall. Amid the course of the history we watch the development of the Divine plan, and its progressive revelation as the times drew on for its accomplishment. We view its actual execution in the incarnation, life, death, and resurrection, of the Lord Jesus Christ. We watch the commencement of its outward life in the labors of the apostles, and the exposition of its inward life in their teaching. Lastly, we find in the Apocalypse a sketch of its fortunes in the world up to the time of our Master's predicted return, and the consummation all things. Throughout this connected line no one book could be omitted without omitting a link. Nay more, no one separate class of books could be omitted without leaving some crucial and essential point of the history unexplained.

Thus, for instance, no one of the five books of Moses could be destroyed without breaking the links of the historical narrative. If Genesis had been absent, we should have known nothing of the descent, character, and Divine election, of the people who were oppressed in Egypt. If Exodus had been omitted, the giving of the Law upon Sinai, and the history of the forty years' wanderings would have been unintelligible. Without Leviticus we should be ignorant of the details of the law, and, consequently, be unable to explain the phenomena of Jewish history, either in the past or in the present. If Numbers were absent, we should be without information on the history of the forty years intervening between the Exodus and the settlement in Canaan. If Deuteronomy were absent, the purposes of God towards the people, the solemn alternatives of reward or punishment under which they entered upon their mission, and the astonishing attestation furnished to the Divine authority of Scripture by the correspondence between the present condition of the Jewish race and the Mosaic predictions, would have been lost to us. If the Pentateuch had been absent altogether, we should have had a history without a beginning, a superstructure without a foundation, a narrative without a key to its explanation. If the books of Joshua and Judges had been absent, the political and religious condition of the Jews of the days of Samuel and David with the striking changes accomplished since the settlement, would have been inexplicable. If the historical books from Samuel to Ezra had been omitted, the writings of the prophets would have been divorced from the occasions on which they were written ; and in this severance of the historical connection the prophetic books would have been deprived alike of the evidence to their authority, and of the means of their interpretation. Lastly, if the historical books had existed, and the prophetical had been absent, the adaptation of the Divine dealings to the facts of the history, the close relation between the two, and the full development of God's plan of salvation as, amid the decline of the earthly kingdom, the spiritual empire of the Messiah was thrown more and more into prominence, would all have been hidden from the world.

In the New Testament the dependence of the various books upon each other is yet more conspicuous. Had the gospels been absent, the facts of our blessed Lord's life, sufferings, and death, and the consequent fulfilment in them of the Old Testament prophecies, would have remained unknown. In that case, the doctrinal books would have so far resembled the sacred books of Persia and India, that they would have become speculative theories, without any firm foothold on the facts of actual history. How much would have been lost by the absence of any one of the gospels, is seen in the fact that the sublime portraiture of Christ, now possessed by the church, is composed of lineaments contributed by all the four evangelists. The picture is complete in no one of them, and yet, as gathered out of the four, does not present a single incongruous or superfluous feature. If the Acts of the Apostles had not been written, the mode of preaching the gospel 'adopted by the apostles and their contemporaries, and the nature of the opposition it encountered, would have been matters of conjectural probability, not of certain knowledge. Many of the allusions of the apostolic epistles would also have become unintelligible. If the Epistles had been absent, we should have been deprived of an authoritative explanation of the doctrines of the gospel, and their relation to the wants of the soul and the practical necessities of life. Lastly, had the Book of the Revelation been absent, and the church consequently had not possessed its divine warning of the ceaseless conflicts through which Christianity should accomplish its work, there would have been danger of thinking that the gospel had failed, and of regarding the past with disappointment and the future with despair.

Viewing the entire range of the scriptural books together, we see that, had any one portion of them been absent, the wonderful system of mutual reference and connection now perceptible between the Mosaic books and the historical, the historical and the prophetical, the books of the Old Testament and the books of the New, would have become impossible. As the books stand, they present one continuous history. We are able to grasp it as a whole, as vividly as we can grasp the history of any secular people. So closely connected are all its parts, that the break of four hundred years between Malachi and Matthew serves rather to illustrate than to interrupt the continuity. It is also worthy of remark, that during this period secular history came into existence, and serves to throw very considerable light on the history of the dispersed tribes. The information thus gained in a large number of particulars confirms, and in no one single instance contradicts the statements of Scripture, but fits in with an equal harmony to the preceding books of the Old Testament, and the succeeding books of the New.

But the same unity of plan traceable between the various canonical books can be traced likewise between the various parts of the same books. The dependence of the doctrinal teaching of the New Testament upon the historical facts interwoven with it is so transparent, that it suits my present purpose better to take an illustration of the fact from the more doubtful, or rather the less plain and palpable instances of the Old Testament. Of all the portions of the Scripture writings commonly alleged to be traditional and fragmentary, the genealogical lists of Genesis, Numbers, and Chronicles constitute the most conspicuous instances. If I may so say, the weakest part of the case is here. If, therefore, even these can be shown to fill their harmonious place in the structure of the whole, the same conclusion may be confidently claimed in other instances.

To attempt to trace this connection into every minute detail and particular word, would not only be unnecessary, but preposterous; for in human works allowed without dispute to be the product of one mind and one pen, and to be pervaded by one intelligent purpose, no such unity can be traced. It is enough to find its existence in the subordinate section of which particular words form a part.

For example, the detail given by Lord Macaulay of the Loan Bill of December 15, 1692, has already been cited. The object of the writer in noticing this bill is obvious. The national debt of Great Britain, with all the complicated interests involved in it, took its rise in this measure. But it would be impossible to trace an intelligent motive in every detail of the narration. Who could trace any important object in the statement that the duties levied under the act were to be kept separate from all other receipts, and that the rate of interest was to be changed in the year 1700? But these details are added for the sake of accuracy, and constitute the circumstantial character of the narrative. They fill their appropriate place as a part of the whole account of the bill, as the whole account of the bill fills in its turn its own appropriate place in the order of the history. The details are therefore to be judged not as single and isolated statements, but as parts of the whole.

Just thus it is with the Scriptures. The ethnological lists, for instance, in Genesis, constitute a very important part of the narrative. There is a manifest object in roughly tracing out the divisions of mankind in a record where the unity of the human race and its descent from a single pair stands not only as a matter of fact, but as the foundation fact of moral and religious truths of the highest importance. The lists contained in Numbers and Chronicles were of value to the Jews in relation alike to their lands of inheritance and to the descent of the expected Messiah. Their presence gives circumstantial reality to the narrative, and constitutes one of the evidences of its genuineness and credibility. They are closely connected with the genealogical lists of St. Matthew and St. Luke. The purpose of these latter lists in linking together the Old and New Testament histories, and placing upon the head of Jesus of Nazareth the crown of the predicted Messiah, lies upon the very surface of the narrative. But had they been preceded by no information of a kindred kind in the earlier Scriptures, they would have been comparatively useless. There would have been no means of testing their accuracy, in the absence of any corresponding sources of information. The tribal character incorporated into Jewish life and habits appears everywhere in the historical and prophetical books of the Old Testament; recurs in the doctrinal arguments of the New, as, for instance, in the Epistle to the Hebrews; and still colors the habits and institutions of the historical Jew. Consequently, had these earlier lists been absent, broken links would have met us everywhere, and the practical and lifelike characteristics of the sacred writings would have been absent.

We are justified, therefore, in saying that these lists constitute a connected part of God's intelligent design in the framework of his revelation. But to endeavor to trace a design linking every detail to the comprehensive plan of the whole would be absurd. It would be absurd, for instance, to attempt to trace the importance to the plan of salvation of the detailed fact that Joktan had thirteen sons, and that their "dwelling was from Mesha, as thou goest unto Sephar," Gen. 10:30; or that Gamaliel was the captain of the tribe of Manasseh, as recorded in Numb. 1:10; or that Shamed, the son of Elpaal, built Ono and Lod, as recorded in 1 Chron. 8:12. It is enough that they constitute parts of genealogical lists, that these lists form part of their respective books, and that the respective books in their turn form consistent parts of the whole revelation.

But if it would be absurd to carry the proof any farther than this, it is at least equally absurd to rest objections against the unity of Scripture on our inability to do so. To pick out a detail such as those mentioned above, and then triumphantly to ask whether we consider this to be an instance of Divine inspiration, is about the same as to ask whether we consider Lord Macaulay to be a great writer of history, because he records the fact that the memorable law of 1692 passed its third reading on the twentieth day of January. Each part must be considered in relation to its whole. The genealogical lists of Scripture, for instance, form an integral part of the respective books where they are found, and these respective books form an integral part of the whole record. We can trace intelligent design in the entire record, in its component books, and in the genealogical information they contain;

and this is enough. So close a connection suggests a strong presumption that the mind which schemed and framed the whole, schemed and framed the parts. The conclusion appears irresistible, that they all enter into the unity of design pervading the sacred books. Whatever proof of authority this unity of design may be admitted to carry with it, is coextensive with itself. If the design is everywhere, the authority involved in it must be everywhere likewise.

III. A third reason for accepting the authority of Scripture as a Divine revelation rests upon the sublimity of its subject-matter and the superhuman truths it reveals. It may be admitted by us, without the slightest hesitation or reluctance, that these truths are found side by side with matter of a very different kind, and with details of an apparently trivial description. Many persons devoutly accept the Divine inspiration of the one class of passages, but cannot accept it in regard to the other. For instance, they admit that the sublime description of the creation, in the first chapter of Genesis, bears upon it the stamp of Divine authority; but for the genealogical lists contained in the same book they can only admit a human origin. The most important sources of this difficulty must be left for a while, till the positive objections urged upon this ground to what is commonly known as the doctrine of verbal inspiration come to be considered. For the present, some general considerations only must be adduced in support of the assumption, that whatever authority attaches to one part of Scripture attaches to all. It will suffice to show, in the present stage of the investigation, that the difference in the subject-matter of Scriptures constitutes no *primâ facie* objection against the equable inspiration of the whole.

In the first place, we must recognize the intimate relation subsisting between the doctrinal and the historical portions of the word. The doctrinal are admitted to be above human discovery in the nature of the truths revealed, and sublime above human conception in the character of God, and in the hopes proposed to man. But then these doctrines are founded, without exception, upon historical facts. For instance, the doctrine of the person of Christ depends upon the combination of the human and Divine natures in him. The Divine nature involves the eternal generation and the self-existing glory of the Son of God. The human nature depends upon the incarnation; and the incarnation involves the human mother, and the human home, and the human relationships, and the human life, with all its true ordinary sympathies and affections. The doctrine of the atonement depends upon the sinless holiness of our Lord's nature, and upon the free and undeserved character of his sufferings and death. Again, his sufferings and death involve the human agents, motives, passions, and acts. The same connection of the supernatural and the Divine with the human nature and the human sphere of action pervades, more or less, the entire system of doctrine. To take the one element away is to take them both away. The historical facts are therefore interwoven inextricably with the doctrinal truths. Our knowledge of the one is dependent upon our knowledge of the other. If the doctrines are dependent upon the historical facts, and we are not sure that the historical facts are true, neither can we be sure that the doctrines are true. The nature of the Christian revelation and of the doctrines revealed necessitates an earthly platform and earthly associations. Hence the minute facts of the life and sufferings of our Lord do not pull down to their level the associated doctrines of the incarnation and atonement, but the doctrines lift up the facts to their own height. The same remark is true of the whole series of facts recorded in Scripture. However minute and unimportant, they share the dignity and importance of the wonderful events and sublime doctrines of which they form the necessary conditions.

Similar is the relation existing between the biographical and the purely historical portions of the record. The accumulated biographies of the living men of every age would constitute the history of that age, the sole difference of biography being that the events are traced primarily in reference to the character and fortunes of the individual, and only secondarily in reference to bodies of mankind. The biographies of Scripture have, indeed, a twofold character, and both are maintained with an admirable and undeviating consistency. On the one side, the private history of the individual is invariably presented in its relation to the whole revelation of the Divine purposes, and as a link in their completeness. On the other side, the private lesson is itself full of religious instruction : it is at once the illustration of some doctrinal truth, and an example of its practical application. Had all the Scriptural biographies been absent, the whole record would have lost its external reality, and being deprived of its foothold in the common sympathies and circumstances of mankind, would have floated off into the dreamy cloudland of abstract speculation.

Lastly, we must bear in mind the relation of the great to the small. The great is indeed, in human affairs, the accumulation of the small. We speak of God as the moral Governor of the universe, and the conception of the great universe he governs helps us to form some faint conception of the greatness and glory of the Governor. But what is the universe, but the aggregation of innumerable particulars in one complete and harmonious system? This is the case with all things known to us, saving God himself. The self-existent Source is distinguishable from all else in being "without body, parts, or passions."

Not only does the great consist of the aggregation of the little, but through the long series of causes and effects pervading all life the great is dependent on the little. The most trivial events are very often the beginnings of the mightiest results. The dependence of the great upon the small is, therefore, the invariable condition of all human things ; and if the connection had been absent in Scripture, the absence would only have served to isolate the revelation of God's will from all God's other acts, alike in creation and in providence. We should then have failed to see, as we do now, the infinitely little as well as the infinitely great of God's acts; and losing sight of the minute superintendence of the world, we should equally have failed to estimate the omnipotence of God, and to comprehend his omniscience and omnipresence.

Thus it appears that the argument for the Divine authority of Scripture from the grandeur and sublimity of its contents is not weakened by the fact that all its contents are not equally grand and sublime, or by the association of the great in God with the little in man. To argue that because the subject-matter of different portions of the word differs in importance it therefore differs in inspiration, is to confound the subject of the message with the author of the message. All the parts of Scripture are equally true and equally inspired, just as the insect is as much the creature of God as the star; but they are no more equally important than the insect and the star—the insect that perishes unknown, and the star whose destruction would disturb the complicated and delicately-balanced organism of the universe.

Hence on all three lines of argument—the inspired character of the writers, the unity of design pervading the writings, and the sublimity of their subject-matter—the presumption holds good that the authority due to one part of Scripture is due equally to all, because the reasons for it are equally applicable to all. To divide the Bible into two parts constantly intermingled and intersecting one

another, and to say that the one part is divinely inspired and not the other, is to lower the character
of the whole Bible. We might retain, it is true, the
full authority of the parts admitted to be Divine in
one sense, but we do not retain equally the authority of the whole, because the whole contains both
the parts supposed to be inspired and the parts
supposed to be uninspired. The parts supposed to
be marked with Divine infallibility, and the parts
supposed to be marked by human fallibility, are included in the same revelation. Hence the character of the whole must be lowered, and the security
for the truth damaged, by the rejection of any of
its parts. The parts and the whole composed of
them must correspond. Whatever authority over
human belief is claimed and assigned to one portion
of Scripture, is equally claimed and must be equally
assigned to all. If the Scriptures are the word of
God, it follows that the whole Scriptures are the
word of God.

CHAPTER V.

DOES SCRIPTURE BEAR WITNESS TO ITSELF ; AND HOW ?

Does the Bible assert its own Authority and Infallibility ?—Various Answers to this Question—Cause of the Misapprehension—Arbitrary Nature of the Proof demanded—Reasons why Reiterated Assertion of its Inspired Character should not be expected—The True Proofs of Credibility—How afforded by the Inspired Writers to their Contemporaries, and by their Writings to Ourselves—The Clear Inferences of Scripture as Authoritative as its Direct Assertions.

It has been shown, in the preceding chapter, that whatever claims of authority are asserted for one part of Scripture, are really asserted for the whole. This conclusion rests on the identity of inspired authorship pervading the entire body of Scripture, the structural unity connecting the whole, and running undiminished through all the variations of its subject-matter, and the essential dependence of its great facts and sublime doctrines on minute details, historical, biographical, and genealogical. The express claim advanced in one specific portion is not confined to that individual portion, but extends to the whole of which it forms a component part. In ordinary matters, the principle is accepted without dispute. The mind and authority, and therefore the responsibility, of the architect extend to every part of the building; that of the artist, to every part of the painting or the sculpture; of the mechanician, to every part of the machine; of the author, to every part of the book. The possible employment of subordinate agents upon the coarser portions or on separate parts of the whole in no degree affects this responsibility, since the authority of the higher and controlling agent takes up into itself the action of the lower and subordinate. In the same way, if the Scriptures be a revelation from God, the authority, whatever it may be, attached to a Divine revelation extends to all its parts, and includes all the subordinate agencies employed in its communication.

We are now, therefore, prepared to ask to what this authority amounts. What is the character of the Bible? what influence must be allowed to it upon the belief and conduct of mankind?

These questions cannot be determined by theory, but must be settled by an appeal to Scripture itself, and a careful examination alike of its facts and of its principles. All parties to the controversy agree in this. The variations of conclusion arise only from the adoption of different modes of conducting the inquiry. For instance, the rationalist considers that when he has proved the variety of books contained in Scripture—the diversity of their dates, authorship, and subject-matter—and has shown the probability that particular books contain older documents incorporated into themselves—that he has disproved the existence of a Divine inspiration. He forgets that there are two sides to the question, and that both must be taken into account. Arbitrarily affixing the charge of narrowness of thought to all dogmatic assertion of scriptural authority, he limits his own view to one class of Biblical phenomena, and to one alone. Thus he loses sight of the fact, that if diversity be a characteristic of Scripture in one point of view, unity is no less a characteristic of it in another. His process of breaking up the Scripture into fragments only strengthens the argument for the inspiration of Scripture. His disintegrating process leaves the unity just where it was before, and renders it the more wonderful in proportion to the variety of details comprehended and over-ordered by the one superintending Mind.

The rule of discarding all theory upon what we think Scripture ought to be, and confining ourselves to an inquiry as to what Scripture really is, cannot be too rigidly maintained. To take facts as they are, and not as they might conceivably have been, is a rule never to be forgotten. On this specific ground we have been led to the conclusions of the previous chapters. It has been shown that Christianity is inseparably identified with the Christian Scriptures, that these Scriptures contain a revelation from God, and that they are invested throughout with an equality of authority co-extensive with the identity of authorship and unity of structure.

In settling the amount of this authority, we must neither go beyond, nor must we fall short of, what Scripture claims for itself. But we must take care that the appeal is not made in a false and one-sided manner. We must not establish any arbitrary standard of our own, and say that Scripture ought to assert its own authority in one way, and in one way only, and that if the assertion be not made in this one way, we will not accept it in any other. The nature of the assertion and the mode of making it belong to the Giver of the revelation, and our duty is simply to examine the facts. Whether the mode of assertion may be agreeable to our views or not is a mere matter of theory, and of no importance. What does Scripture assert? is the one practical and all-important question.

The objection has been often made, and reiterated even to weariness, that the Scriptures contain no assertion of their own infallibility. How contrary the objection is to the facts of the case will appear shortly. Meanwhile the meaning of the objection must be considered, and the fallacy involved in the arbitrary demand of one particular mode of proof exposed. The objector means that the assertion of an infallible truthfulness is not made in so many words. We reply to him by quoting passages in which the assertion is plainly made, or by an immediate inference necessarily involved. For instance, we allege the words of David, "Thy word is true from the beginning;" "The testimony of the Lord is sure;" "Thy law is the truth." Or we refer to the language of St. Paul, where he declares the Scripture to be profitable for doctrine, reproof, correction, and instruction; or to expressions like that of our Lord, "The Scripture cannot be broken;" or to the words of St. John, in the concluding book of the canon, "These are the true sayings of God." Psa. 119:160; 19:7; 119:142; 2 Tim. 3:16; John 10:35; Rev. 19:9.

But the objector immediately replies, that these epithets are applied to certain particular portions of the Bible, and not to the whole Bible. For instance, the language of John refers to the declaration relative to the blessedness of the holy dead. Our Lord refers to the Old Testament application of the word "gods," and makes an appeal to men familiar with Old Testament language, and treating it with almost superstitious reverence. In the same way St. Paul refers to the ancient Scriptures, and David to the books of Moses only.

However confidently this rejoinder may be urged, the conclusion reached in the previous chapter refutes it. We are justified in extending the character claimed for one part of the Bible to all the other parts issued under the same sanction, contained in the same plan, and united as the greater and lesser links in the same chain of truth.

But the objection enables us to appreciate the kind of proof the objector demands. If no evidence but immediate verbal assertion is enough, and the demand is to be pushed to its full limits, it would be necessary that each individual sentence in the entire Scriptures should be sealed with an assertion of its infallible truthfulness, either fully expressed or at all events comprised in some acknowledged formula, such as the significant and oft-repeated scriptural phrase, "It is written." The statement of such a demand suffices to show its absurdity, and yet nothing less could stop the loopholes against possible scruples. Or if men were not so unreasonable as to ask for this, the objection would at least demand some such verbal and reiterated claim at the beginning or the close, or both, of each individual book of the canon. It is therefore important to see that, had such a verbal claim existed, it would have been absolutely useless, and would have proved literally nothing.

For such a verbal claim would carry with it the credibility due to the writer, and no more. Where the amount of this credibility is the point of dispute, as it is between the Christian and the skeptic, it could not be taken into account. Familiar experience shows that we do not believe persons on their assertion of their own credibility. We expect some positive evidence of trustworthiness; and then, but not till then, we believe them. Otherwise we may make two replies, according as we think the speaker to be deceiving or deceived. We may say, "I do not believe your statement, for I consider you to be an impostor;" or we may say, "I do not doubt your own honest belief in the truth of your statement, yet I do not believe the statement, because I consider you to be deceived, either by your own ignorance and fanaticism or by the duplicity of others." In either case the speaker's own assertions, if unsupported by evidence, would not carry with them a feather's weight. Thus, on one or other of these grounds, according to individual opinion, we repudiate the self-assertions of Mohammed, of Joanna Southcott, and of the prophet of the Mormons. We disbelieve them, not because they fail to advance claims on our belief, but because the claims advanced are unsupported by evidence.

The same mode of arguing would have been as applicable to the sacred as to secular writers. If they had been fond of reiterating their own claims, and had appended to every book or to every sentence of every book, the affirmation of their own infallible authority, not only would such assertions have been perfectly ineffectual to establish their credibility, but they would have been effectual to throw doubts about it. The very redundancy of claim would have awakened suspicion. Why this constant protestation, it would have been argued, if there did not exist some secret consciousness of weakness and of the absence of valid claims upon belief? Our Lord himself did not scruple to assert the vanity of claims that rest only on the words of the claimant: "If I bear witness of myself, my witness is not true."

The assertion, therefore, that the scriptural writers do not assert their own inspiration or their own infallibility, is only true in this sense, that they do not make it the subject of formal declarations to any great extent. For instance, we search in the other books in vain for assertions corresponding to the language used by St. John in regard to his account of Christ's death: "He that saw it bare record, and his record is true: and he knoweth that he saith true, that ye might believe;" or to the declaration appended to his gospel: "This is the disciple which testifieth of these things, and wrote these things: and we know that his testimony is true." 1 John

19 : 35; 21 : 24. These passages stand alone in Scripture; but we do not expect a truthful man to be always parading his own truthfulness. He contents himself with the delivery of his testimony, and falls back upon his known character for its credibility.

On this principle the sacred writers evidently acted in their own personal ministry. They carried their attestation with them to the generation among whom they lived. The word written was in the first case the word spoken, and the credentials of the speaker consisted in his own prophetic office and supernatural gifts. Thus Moses was accredited to the Hebrews of his own day by the miracles of the exodus, and the forty years' sojourning in the wilderness. When his commission from God was called into question, as by Miriam, and afterwards by Korah, Dathan, and Abiram, direct appeal was made to God to show whom he had chosen, and the answer was given by some outward and visible miracle. The prophetic office of Samuel was known to all Israel, for "the Lord was with him, and did let none of his words fall to the ground." The commission of the later prophets was attested by their office in general, and special signs in particular; as by the prescient visions of Isaiah, the special deliverance of Jeremiah, the mysterious call of Ezekiel, and the wise interpretations of Daniel. Our Lord's ministry was accredited by the miracles which, like flashes of the indwelling Deity breaking through the veil of the flesh, proved Him to be more than man. "The works that I do they bear witness of me." The apostolic company exhibited the same credentials: "God bearing them witness both with signs and wonders, and with divers miracles, and gifts of the Holy Ghost." Heb. 2 : 4. To men thus divinely accredited, the verbal assertion of their right to teach would have been as unnecessary to those who recognized their character as it would have been useless to those who denied it.

As the inspired prophets acted in their personal ministry, so it is natural that they should act in their writings. Their claims did not cease with their lives, or with the generation for which they wrote. It is perpetuated by the historical fact that their books have been received in the canonical Scriptures. This reception could not have been obtained unless the inspired authority of the books had been the subject of contemporary belief, and this belief can only have been founded on the credentials attached to the living men. It could not have been founded on their own assertion; for, as our opponents object, the formal and reiterated assertion is not found in their written words, and therefore may be concluded to have been absent from their spoken words. It must have been founded on their personal office and character, because this was the only kind of proof available, and to it the writers themselves consistently appeal. Whatever authority was due to the spoken teaching of the living men is therefore perpetuated in the written teaching of the dead men. The personal history and the official authority rest on the same historical evidence, and are sealed by the unbroken descent of their writings and their continuous position among the canonical Scriptures down to the present day.

That this is the true account of the matter, is evidenced by the exceptional circumstances distinguishing those books of the New Testament which were for a time called into question. These are enumerated by the ecclesiastical historian Eusebius as being the Epistle of James, the second Epistle of Peter, the second and third Epistles of John, and the Epistle of Jude. At the beginning of the fourth century the persecution of the emperor Diocletian against the church, and his determined effort to destroy the Christian Scriptures, led to a very searching examination of the books belonging to the canon. On the close of the persecution, those who had given up their books to be destroyed were called "traditores," and were excluded from the church. Hence it became a matter of great importance to decide what were and what were not inspired books. It was evidently the interest of persons compromised by such a denial of their Christian profession, and actuated more by considerations of personal safety than by the sense of religious duty, to limit to the utmost the number of books, the betrayal of which constituted a traditor, and was punished by exclusion from the church. The epistles above enumerated were found, on examination, not to be universally received as authoritative. But even this exception was but of short duration, for in the middle of the same cen-

tury the whole of our present books were enumerated by Athanasius as belonging to the New Testament canon. The large number of spurious books
rejected, proves the severity of the inquiry. The
fact that it issued in affirming the inspired character of all the books now received without exception,
supplies an historical testimony of the highest value
to their genuineness, authenticity, and credibility.

The authority of Scripture, therefore, as a revelation from God, does not rest upon its self-assertion, but on independent credentials inherent in the
character and office of the writers. The indirect
assertion of such an authority pervades, however,
as I shall proceed to show, the whole language of
Scripture, and is ingrained into its very structure.
What is true in regard to the general authority of
Scripture, is specially true in regard to its inspiration and infallibility. They all rest on the same
foundation, and must stand or fall together. If the
only sufficient proof consists in formal and reiterated assertion, then we must give up not only the
plenary inspiration, but the authority of Scripture
altogether, for no such formal and reiterated assertion exists. The fact that such assertions would
have been worthless, had they existed, proves the
absurdity of setting up any capricious standard.
We must accept whatever evidence is available,
although it should not be direct, but indirect; not
formal, but inferential; not couched in the shape
of distinct propositions, but involved in its moral
claims, its subject-matter, and its professed defects.
The conclusions so reached, if founded on a solid

chain of reasoning, are as much founded on facts, and not on theory, as they would be if every chapter and verse of Scripture contained the assertion of its own authority. They are founded on fact, because they rest on the statement of Scripture itself, and not on any human conjecture formed beforehand relative to what Scripture should be or should not be. Those who deny the authority of the Bible altogether as a Divine revelation, will consistently reject its assertions regarding itself, as they reject its assertions upon other matters; but those who accept it as a Divine revelation, and believe its teaching on other matters, must equally believe its teaching relative to itself. It cannot alter the case in the slightest degree, whether the teaching is implied or expressed. The necessary inference carries the same weight as the formal assertion.

CHAPTER VI.

THE TESTIMONY OF SCRIPTURE TO ITS OWN CHARACTER.

Testimonies of Scripture to its own Character classified—I. A Revelation from God as well as of God—II. Accredited with his Formal Authority—III. Given for the Purpose of Religious Instruction, and Sufficient for the Purpose intended—IV. Provided to supply the Defects of Natural Light and Conscience—V. True alike in its Recorded Facts and in its Revealed Doctrines, and claiming to be implicitly believed—VI. Unbelief in them declared to be a Sin, and deserving the Punishment of Sin.

THE testimony of Scripture borne to its own character is exceedingly copious and varied. Having shaken off the trammels imposed upon inquiry by the supposed necessity of direct and reiterated self-assertion, we enter upon a sphere of evidence so wide, that the only difficulty is to embrace the whole in one consistent view. For this purpose it is necessary to classify the statements of the sacred writers relative to the authority of their own books. They may be resolved into six propositions having immediate bearing on the question of inspiration.

I. The Scriptures are a revelation from God. The entire mission of Moses to the Hebrew people was performed under this commission: "Thus shalt thou say unto the people of Israel: 'I Am' hath sent me unto you." Exod. 3 : 14. The book of the Law, believed by those who accept the Divine authority of the Pentateuch to be identical with the five books of Moses, was written by the express commandment of God. Exod. 24 : 4–7. We are taught that the lawgiver perpetuated in this written form not only doctrines and laws, but likewise historical facts. Exod. 17 : 14. The mantle of Moses descended upon Joshua. He was "full of the spirit of wisdom, for Moses had laid his hands on him." The book called by his name opens with the assertion of this Divine commission : "The Lord spake unto Joshua." His last solemn charge to the people before his death was prefaced with the words, "Thus saith the Lord God of Israel." The historical books contain no such positive affirmations; indeed, their form does not admit of them. Their contents describe God's direct dealings—the immediate interferences of his wisdom and power in the fortunes of his people. These books, from Judges to Nehemiah, are a narrative of facts. To their accuracy we have the direct testimony of David and Samuel. The seventy-eighth and one hundred and sixth Psalms are founded upon their narratives. But we have yet more specific testimony. St. Paul quotes the language of the Book of Kings as "the Scripture." 1 Kings 19 : 14; Rom. 11 : 3. A passage from the Second Book of Samuel, 7 : 14, is adduced in the first chapter of the Epistle to the Hebrews as God's words towards his Son : "I will be to him a Father, and he shall be to me a Son." Heb. 1 : 5. Of Samuel himself we are told, "The Lord revealed himself to Samuel in Shiloh by the word of the Lord." David refers his own language to the express authority of God: "The Lord said." "The wisdom of God was" in Solomon. The books of the prophets are composed almost entirely of direct messages from heaven. Isaiah refers his commission to an immediate vision of the Almighty. "The word of the Lord came to Jeremiah the prophet," and to "Ezekiel the priest." "A vision appeared" unto Daniel, and an archangel was sent to interpret it. Hosea, Joel, Jonah, Micah, Zephaniah, Haggai, Zechariah, and Malachi, claim to be divinely employed; in the striking phrase of Jeremiah and Ezekiel, "the word of the Lord came to them." Amos and Obadiah open their prophecies with the solemn phrase, "Thus saith the Lord." To Nahum "the Lord gave commandment," and on Habakkuk laid the charge, "Write the vision, and make it plain."

If these testimonies appear to be in any degree defective, the language of our Lord and his apostles supply the void. Thus our Lord quotes from four out of the five books of Moses, from David, Isaiah, Malachi, and Zechariah, with the formula "It is written." St. Paul quotes in the same way from the other book of Moses not quoted by our Lord, from David, Isaiah, and Jeremiah. "The Prophets," as a well-known division of the Jewish Scriptures, are referred to as authoritative on matters of faith. The author of the Epistle to the Hebrews states that "God spake by the fathers;" and St. Peter, with a special reference to unfulfilled prophecy, that "holy men of old wrote as they were moved by the Holy Ghost."

This is the attestation of our Lord and his apostles to the authority of the Old Testament Scriptures; but what of their own authority? Our Lord himself, in his prayer to his Father, declares of his teaching in general, "I have given unto them the words which thou gavest me," John 17:8. So far, then, as the gospels contain the actual teaching of our Master, they are affirmed to be the words of God. Not only so, but the same authority is ascribed to the books in general containing these words. Our Lord's statement contains a threefold chain, in which each link in the descent is equally strong, from the Father to himself, from himself to his apostles, therefore from the Father to his apostles through him. Accordingly, a special promise of the presence of God the Holy Ghost was given to them: "It is not ye that speak, but the Holy Ghost," Mark 13:11. Or if these words appear to be limited to definite occasions, we do but turn to the broader promises; such as, "The Holy Ghost, whom the Father will send in my name, he shall teach you all things, and bring all things to your remembrance, whatsoever I have said unto you." In the fulfilment of this promise, St. James did not scruple to declare, at the first council at Jerusalem, "It seemeth good to the Holy Ghost and to us." In a similar spirit, St. Paul, over and over again, referring the gospel he preached to an immediate revelation, identifies his own words with the words of the Holy Ghost: "Which words we speak, not in the words which man's wisdom teacheth, but which the Holy Ghost teacheth." In another striking passage St. Peter first asserts the inspiration of the Spirit for the ancient prophets, "Searching what or what manner of time the Spirit of Christ which was in them did signify, when it testified beforehand the sufferings of Christ, and the glory that should follow." Then, in the words following, he asserts the the same Divine influence for himself and his fellow-apostles: "Unto whom it was revealed, that not unto themselves, but unto us, they did minister the things which are now reported unto you by them which have preached the gospel unto you with the Holy Ghost sent down from heaven," 1 Pet. 1:11, 12. Finally, St. John declares the book of his prophecy to be "the revelation of Jesus Christ which God gave unto him."

Thus, in various forms, the contents of the Scripture are declared to be a communication from God. They are a revelation not only of God, but from God, in the truest and closest sense—in which the authority of a message depends not upon the character of the messenger, but upon the character of him by whom he is commissioned.

II. The Scriptures assert themselves to be accredited with the authority of God, as of a higher power claiming by right acceptance and obedience. It is conceivable that a superior authority may deal with an inferior in the way of condescension as a friend with a friend, giving advice, but neither claiming nor exercising control. It is the characteristic of Scripture, that it not only comes from one invested with an authority so absolute that no human relation can furnish a parallel, but that it is itself

invested with this authority. It is formally enuncia-
ted as a proclamation from a King, who as Creator
has a right to command creatures who, by virtue of
their dependence, are under obligation to obey.
Thus the books of Moses were issued as containing
the will of an autocratic Lawgiver. The Scriptures
laid up in the ark by the order of Moses were "the
book of the Law." Its details of enactments are
designated in the New Testament "the law of the
Lord." Ten out of sixteen of the Old Testament
prophets use the same word "law" with reference
to their own special communications. The terms
"statutes" and "ordinances" carry the same force of
an obligatory revelation, and are nearly coextensive
in their use with the word "law." Thus David, speaking of the Scriptures extant in his day as the word of
God, declares, "The law of the Lord is an undefiled
law .... the statutes of the Lord are right." To
the legislative power of the Lawgiver is added the
administrative power of the King. The very words
"the commandments" express alike the form of authority maintained in the language, and the sanction of authority given to the enactments. Our
blessed Master, by his own repeated use of the word,
placed the seal of his own witness to this character
of revelation. Our Lord asserted it as strongly for
his own teaching as he attributed it to the teaching
of the fathers, "He that hath my commands and
keepeth them," John 14:21 ; nor did this authority
cease with his personal ministry, but by virtue of
his commission extended to the ministry of his apostles. "The things that I write unto you," declares

St. Paul, "are the commandments of the Lord." "The commandment of us, the apostles of the Lord," is the language of St. Peter. The apostle of love reëchoes the language, "This is his commandment;" and towards the close of the apocalyptic vision he seals up the record with the words of Christ in his glory, "Blessed are they that do his commandments."

III. The Scriptures affirm themselves to have been given in the specific character of a revelation, and for the specific purpose of communicating a knowledge of salvation. Of the Old Testament writings in general St. Paul affirms that they are profitable for "instruction in righteousness, that the man of God may be perfect," and that they are able to make "wise unto salvation." In the Epistle to the Corinthians he declares that the narratives of the Mosaic books "were written for our instruction;" and more generally still he teaches the Roman Christians that "whatsoever things were written aforetime were written for our learning." That the word "whatsoever" is coextensive with the ancient sacred writings, and neither exceeds nor falls short of them, is proved by his applying to them the recognized and generic name, "the Scriptures;" for the passage continues, "that we through patience and comfort of the Scriptures." Our Lord declared, "He that believeth my word hath everlasting life." The commission to his apostles was to "go and teach," and the object of the teaching is defined in the baptismal formula to be belief in the Father, Son, and Holy Ghost. The official titles of the apostles bear the same meaning; they are termed "messengers," "evangelists," "teachers," "prophets." Of the preaching of the gospel at large, first by the prophets and subsequently by the apostles, St. Paul affirms that it was "according to the commandment of the everlasting God made known to all nations for the obedience of faith."

Two remarks must be interposed at this place. 1. It is admitted that whatever God does he does perfectly; that is, not perfectly according to any arbitrary standard of our own, but perfectly according to the designs of his own will. What God designs to do lies beyond the competency of our judgment, and can only be revealed by himself. The texts quoted above supply the information. The object is to make "wise unto salvation." Hence we must believe that in giving information for this purpose he has given information sufficient for the purpose. The assistance bestowed upon every chosen agent of God is specifically related to the work to be done, and adjusted alike in kind and in quantity to that work. When God inspired Bezaleel and Aholiab "with the Spirit of God in wisdom, and in understanding, and in knowledge," that inspiration had special reference to the workmanship of the tabernacle, to "make all that I have commanded thee." For the purpose intended it was sufficient. "Bezaleel . . . made all that the Lord commanded Moses." But it was not an unlimited inspiration; it was not, for instance, an inspiration to teach, but only to make. When "the Spirit of the Lord came mightily upon Samson," it was an inspiration for a specific purpose, as in the case of Bezaleel, but the purpose was different. It was declared by the angel to be that he should "deliver Israel out of the hand of the Philistines." It was adapted for this purpose, and was sufficient for it. "Thou hast given great deliverance into the hands of thy servant," was the language of Samson himself. But this inspiration did not give skill in workmanship, as it gave to Bezaleel, but astonishing strength of body. It included exactly what was necessary for the work, but no more. In the same way, when "holy men of old spake as they were moved by the Holy Ghost," the inspiration was specific to the work to be done. This work was to teach, and to the work of teaching their inspiration had strict reference. It neither gave skill in workmanship as to Bezaleel, nor strength of body as to Samson; but he gave them what the work required, "a mouth and wisdom." This the apostle repeatedly affirmed. "We speak wisdom," "we speak the wisdom of God," God "abounded towards us in all wisdom and prudence, having made known unto us the mystery of his will." As the skill of Bezaleel was sufficient for the workmanship of the tabernacle, and the strength of Samson was sufficient for the deliverance of Israel, so the knowledge and wisdom bestowed upon the sacred writers were sufficient to make them "teachers of the Gentiles in faith and verity."

2. The Scriptures are the only provision asserted to have been made by God for the purpose of making men wise unto salvation. This character is

never affirmed of our Lord's person, or said to have formed the purpose and design of his incarnation, suffering, and death. He was not himself a revelation of God, given for the specific purpose of teaching, as the Scriptures are.

Doubtless he did himself teach, and is the Prophet as well as the Priest and King of his church. Thus, in the synagogue of Nazareth, he applied to himself the language of Isaiah: "The Spirit of the Lord is upon me, because he hath anointed me to preach the gospel;" and we know that he fulfilled the prediction, for "all bare him witness, and wondered at the gracious words that proceeded out of his mouth." We are repeatedly told that he went about "preaching the gospel;" he was "the Word" of God, and all our knowledge is derived from the "Light of the world." The entire ministry of the church is derived from his authority. His ministers are "ministers of Christ," "messengers of Christ." "God hath in these last days spoken unto us by his Son." And that this message is identical with the gospel preached by the apostles, we are expressly told in the context of the same passage. The great salvation "began to be spoken by the Lord, and was confirmed unto us by them that heard him." In the same spirit St. Luke describes his gospel as being a record "of all that Jesus began both to do and teach until the day in which he was taken up." The whole of his personal teaching was but the beginning of a prophetic office perpetuated in the living church.

But this teaching of our Lord is so far from

standing in contrast with the Scripture, that it is contained in this inspired record, and is absolutely unknown to us from any other source. It is an integral portion of the sacred record, and to us has no existence apart from it.

When therefore the assertion is made that the Scriptures are the only provision made for teaching the church, the verbal teaching of our blessed Lord is included, not excluded. But our Lord, apart from his teaching, was not in himself and in his life a revelation in the same sense as the Scriptures are. We are told indeed that we see the glory of God in the face of Jesus Christ; but it is in Jesus Christ as personated in the written word, "We preach not ourselves, but Christ Jesus the Lord. For God hath shined in our hearts, to give the light of the knowledge of the glory of God in the face of Jesus Christ." 2 Cor. 4:6. Our Lord himself was the object of the gospel, its subject, its end, its everlasting theme; but he was not himself the revelation of the gospel, nor, apart from the spoken or written word, is he ever so presented. His office, as prophetically described, was to do the Father's will, so he himself declared: "I came from heaven not to do mine own will, but the will of him that sent me." "I have finished the work which thou gavest me to do," was the language of his prayer to the Father. What was this work his own words express: "The Son of man is come to seek and to save the lost;" and still more specifically, "The Son of man is come to give his life a ransom for many." Thus he is ever presented in the apostolic writings as "the Lamb of God which taketh away the sin of the world." The whole presentation of his person, work, and offices, is hereby summed up in the language of St. John: "We have seen and do testify that the Father sent the Son to be the Saviour of the world." 1 John 4:14.

IV. The Scriptures affirm themselves to have been given to supplement the light of nature, and to supply that knowledge of God which neither the witness of the outward creation nor the teaching of inward conscience was competent to give. Thus the language of Moses, reëchoed by St. Paul, states the possession of the Scriptures to be the grand and elevating distinction of the Jews, making them illustrious over the rest of mankind "as a wise and understanding people." The benighted ignorance and moral corruption of the Gentiles are described in the most vivid language. The prophet depicts the heathen as sitting "in the valley of the shadow of death." The psalmist declares them to be ignorant of the "judgments" of God. Psa. 10:20; 147:20. St. Paul designates them as "having the understanding darkened, being alienated from the life of God through the ignorance that is in them, because of the blindness of their heart." Again, he exhorts the Thessalonians not to live "in the lust of concupiscence, as the Gentiles which know not God." Our Lord, by his description of his own office, throws into contrast the hopeless condition of mankind without him: "I am the light of the world; he that followeth me shall not walk in darkness, but shall have the light of life." John 8:12. The song of Zacharias declares it to have been the object of tho mercy of God "to give light to them that sit in darkness and in the shadow of death." St. Paul, at Athens, vividly describes the best condition of the Gentiles as that of men who "seek the Lord, if haply they might feel after him and find him," and then places the past and the present in sharp contrast: "The times of this ignorance God winked at, but now commandeth all men everywhere to repent." Acts 17:30. The entire argument of the first chapter of the epistle to the Romans turns upon this. The apostle expresses his readiness to preach the gospel both to the Greeks and to the barbarians; and he proceeds to give his reason, as if anticipating the modern rationalism which considers Christianity to have nothing to give to the heathen. He declares that the light of nature was in itself sufficient to teach the primary truths of the eternal power and Godhead of the Creator, but that, nevertheless, the guilty ignorance of man was incapable of learning even this lesson, and was without excuse; "they became vain in their imaginations, and their foolish heart was darkened."

God's word was therefore given, because God's works were insufficient. Hence the formal revelation made in Scripture must be clearly distinguished from the revelation given in nature. In a secondary and figurative sense, we say that outward nature witnesses of God, because to a thinking mind it points upward to its great Architect: "The heavens declare the glory of God, and the firmament showeth his handiwork." But it is a book the lessons of which depend upon men's intellectual and moral capabilities of learning; and Scripture itself declares them to be insufficient. To argue, therefore, that because mistakes and errors are made by man in his interpretation of God's book of nature, therefore God may be expected to have left fallible elements in his own book of revelation, is to confound two things between which God himself has drawn the separation. Doubtless God's works are as perfect as God's word; the error is not in the book, but in the interpreter. But it is because man has failed to understand the book of nature that God has given him the book of revelation. The primary object of nature cannot be properly said to be teaching; but God has given revelation for this specific purpose of teaching, and has therefore made the teaching as complete as was consistent with his own ordained permission of man's moral action. The elements of error still remain, but in the interpreter, not in the book. Even in regard to the interpreter, God has reduced them to the lowest degree consistent with his declared purpose of human probation.

V. The Scriptures affirm absolute credence to be due to their contents, by virtue alike of the God from whom they come and of the evidence by which they are authenticated. Thus both elements are combined in the witness God gave to Moses when he came down to him "in a thick cloud" upon Sinai: "That the people may hear when I speak with thee, and may believe thee for ever." The words of Jehoshaphat, addressed to the people during their solemn act of devotion in the wilderness of Tekoa, asserted the same claim : "Believe in the Lord your God, so shall ye be established ; believe his prophets, so shall ye prosper."   Our Lord rebuked the want of faith in the two disciples at Emmaus : "O fools, and slow of heart to believe all that the prophets have spoken."   The unbelief of the Jews was the frequent subject of denunciation.   "If ye believed Moses, ye would have believed me, for he wrote of me ; but if ye believe not his writings, how shall ye believe my words?"   St. John twice states the object of his gospel to be, "that ye might believe."   St. Paul declares that "the god of this world hath blinded the eyes of them that believe not."   And the angel in the Apocalypse, rejecting the proffered worship of the apostle, declared himself to be a member of the church of God, under the striking epithet of "them that keep the sayings of this book."

It is in strict accordance with this that the apostolic writers appeal to the Old Testament as authoritative upon all questions of faith : "What saith the Scripture?"   This appeal is made, not only to declarations of doctrine, but to narratives of facts. Thus our Lord refers to the order of the creation, to the events of the forty years' wanderings, and to the story of David.   St. Peter refers in the same way to the history of the creation and of the deluge; while St. Paul appeals so copiously to the facts of the Old Testament history as to render detailed references unnecessary.

VI. The Scriptures assert their own claim to a believing acceptance to be so authoritative that the absence of it is a sin, and will be punished as a sin at the last day. Thus our Lord asserts the rejection of the Old Testament to be the result of such a hardness of heart as to be beyond the reach of hope : "If they believe not Moses and the prophets, neither will they believe though one rose from the dead." In regard to his own teaching, he imputes the unbelief of the Jews to their sinful love of the world : "He that rejecteth me and my words hath one that judgeth him. The word that I have spoken, the same shall judge him in the last day." St. Peter finds in their contempt of the Scripture, and their wilful disbelief of God's creation of the world and its subsequent destruction by the deluge, the characteristic of the scoffers of the last days. He first urges the authority of the Old and New Testament Scriptures. Of the Old, "Be mindful of the words that were spoken before by the holy prophets;" of the New, " And of the commandment of us, the apostles of the Lord and Saviour." In this immediate relation, he predicts the rise of " scoffers walking after their own lusts, and saying, Where is the promise of his coming?" Then he traces their sin to disbelief of the Scriptures: "This they willingly are ignorant of, that by the word of God the heavens were of old." In the close of the same chapter, he puts his seal alike to the canonicity of the Pauline epistles and to the authority of the entire word : "Which they that are unlearned and unstable wrest, as they do also the other Scriptures, unto their own destruction." What destruction is intended, may be gathered from the language of St. Paul: "The Lord Jesus shall be revealed from heaven with his mighty angels, in flaming fire taking vengeance on them that .... obey not the gospel of our Lord Jesus Christ: who shall be punished with everlasting destruction from the presence of the Lord."

These assertions might be variously stated, and largely increased in number; but the texts quoted suffice to show how freely Scripture speaks of itself, and asserts its own authoritative character. It does not deal, indeed, with direct and reiterated assertions of its Divine origin and authority, because such assertions would have been equally incongruous and useless. But in a large variety of forms, and in a great many direct passages, it assumes to itself the qualities, and makes upon others the demands, which belong to a Divine origin and authority, but would be utterly out of place in writings owning an exclusively human authorship, or tainted with a human fallibility. Instances of these direct assertions have now been given. It remains to put them all together, and to see what conclusion is necessarily involved in their accumulated and consentient testimony.

CHAPTER VII.

THE SCRIPTURES ARE THE TRUE WORD OF GOD.

Force and Meaning of these Claims—The Bible neither a Speculation, nor a Fiction, nor a Blunder, nor a Fraud—Assertion of Scripture of its own Absolute Veracity—This Veracity not Limited, but Universal—The Theory that the Bible is partly True, partly Untrue, measured by these Claims—The Scriptures not only Truly the Word of God, but the True Word of God.

IT has been shown in the preceding chapter, that the testimony of Scripture in regard to itself may be reduced into six varying, but consistent assertions. These assertions must be recapitulated in order that, bearing them distinctly in mind, we may the more fully appreciate their force and combine their consentient testimony. These passages are independent of the direct and formal affirmations of positive truthfulness appended to some portions of the word. They supply the data for further conclusions; and these conclusions, if they can be shown to be necessary, will have the same authority as their data; that is, they will be matters of revealed fact, not of human theory.

The first assertion in the natural order of the argument is, that the Scriptures constitute an immediate communication from God to man. (2.) They are invested with the supremacy of their Divine Author—not speculative propositions for discus-

sion, but royal ordinances for acceptance and obedience. (3.) They are not simple statements, but
communications immediately addressed to man,
with the specific object of teaching him the truths
necessary for salvation. (4.) They have avowedly
been given to supplement such sources of information as were independently available from the light
of conscience and the outward works of creation;
because, in the estimate of God, his fallen creatures
were incompetent to gather from them what they
needed to know. (5.) They claim to be believed as
"faithful sayings, and worthy of all acceptation,"
not only in those parts which deal with the sublime
mysteries of God and of his will, but in those parts
also which recall earthly transactions and human
conduct. (6.) They are so authenticated as to leave
unbelief without excuse, and to constitute it a sin
for which God will call men into judgment, and
which he will punish when the dead "shall come
forth, they that have done good unto the resurrection of life, and they that have done evil unto the
resurrection of damnation." It has been shown
that each of these six assertions is made of the
entire series of the Scriptures: they sweep the
whole course of revelation, from its beginning in
the books of Moses to its conclusion in the vision of
St. John.

It is impossible to conceive any claims more solemn, any sanctions more tremendous, than these
assertions involve. Their grandeur and dignity,
when placed in contrast with the more familiar objects of human life, would almost startle the mind

into incredulity, if the testimony authenticating them were less ample and cogent. We are almost inclined to ask, "Can all this be true?" Yet they are as harmonious alike with God and with ourselves as any thing can be conceived to be. If there be a personal God, what more natural and what more blessed than the possession of his revealed will? The Most High has not vacated his throne of government, nor dropped out of his mighty hands the reins of active power. The Lord is in his holy temple, and these Scriptures are the utterances of his will. The dignity of the monarch who speaks in them, the sublimity of their subject-matter, the breadth of universal man included in their application, the tremendous interests of heaven and hell involved in them, the responsibility resting upon man if they are true, and the hopeless darkness brooding over him if they are not true, invest them with an awfulness almost oppressive, and an importance without a parallel in all the other spheres of human life and action.

Whether they are true or not in our judgment does not constitute the immediate subject of inquiry. The present question relates to the character given by the revealed word to itself. It has been shown to assume certain characteristics, and the question is, what quality or qualities are necessarily involved in their assertion. It may all be summed up in one word; and this word expresses the whole gist and substance of the controversy relative to the Christian Scriptures. This word is their *truth*. They assert themselves to be not only truly the word of God, but the true word of God—the word of God, and therefore true.

Into the exact nature of truth and truthfulness it will be necessary to look more closely in a subsequent chapter. For the present, it is enough to fall back on the common acceptation of it. It is one of those words which it is alike easy to understand and difficult to define. Our trust, credence, confidence, assurance, rest on truth; it is the pillar which bears up the entire fabric of human hope, and round which is clustered every form of human action.

Truth is asserted in contrast with unreality. The imagination may conjure up many an idle form floating in the cloudland of the fancy, but having no foothold on the actually existing things of life. Delirium and madness people the world with shapes which have no being save in the disordered brain. The dream presents to the eye and mind of the sleeper scenes, and acts, and persons, which actually affect the feelings for the time, but which, when the sleeper awakes and resumes the mastery of his mental and moral self, are found to have gone, and to have no reality save in the sensations excited by them. The inspired type of vanity is "as a dream when one awaketh." "A hungry man dreameth, and behold he eateth; but he awaketh, and his soul is empty: a thirsty man dreameth, and behold he drinketh; but he awaketh, and behold he is faint." But truth abides independently of all subjective sensations. It is truth still, when it is forgotten as when it is remembered; when it is denied as when it is believed; when it is accepted as when it is rejected. The dream was, indeed, used by God as a means of communication with his prophets; but the reality and perpetuity of his own words are expressly contrasted with the idle fancies of heathen dreamers. "Hearken not to dreamers," was warning of Jeremiah; and Jude, warning the church against the foes of "the faith once delivered unto the saints," designates them "these filthy dreamers."

Truth is asserted in contrast to fiction. Works of imagination, as they are called, do not profess to be the narratives of actual events accomplished under the conditions of time, place, person, and connection in which the fiction presents them, but only to have that kind of verisimilitude about them which enables them to touch the feelings and awaken the sympathies. They are the unreal reflection of real things; they do not appeal. to belief, or claim the acceptance and authority of history. It has been suggested that the Bible, or at least portions of it, such as the Pentateuch, are only a work of fiction, a kind of religious romance. A very strange and wild suggestion it is; since the Bible, instead of reflecting, as all fiction does, a real world outside, has revealed a new real world of its own, and a consentient body of such grand truth, that our highest human knowledge only consists of scattered rays from this sun. When we assert the Bible to be true, we assert the contradictory of this. It is not a fiction—not even a fiction composed by God himself, like some of the parables of our Lord; but it is the actual record of real things existing either in the heavenly or in the earthly sphere. Thus, by the mouth of Isaiah, God repeatedly asserts his own supremacy from this argument, that he had shown to his people "the former things" before "they came to pass," and that he would show them "things to come." Thus, St. John declares, "The things that we have seen and heard declare we unto you." And St. Peter expressly repudiates this suspicion of a fiction: "We have not followed cunningly devised fables."

Truth is asserted in contrast to errors and mistakes. These may occur in any statement consistently with the honest intention of a narrator, but they prove imperfect information and inaccuracy of statement; they are wholly inconsistent with Divine attributes, and constitute the distinctive proof of human fallibility. It has been already shown to be the declared object of Scripture to correct the mistakes into which man had fallen regarding God. St. Luke declares his own purpose in writing his gospel to be, that Theophilus might know "the certainty" of the things in which he had been instructed; and the ground of the assurance was, that the writer himself had "a perfect understanding of all things."

Truth is asserted in contrast with fraud. Fraud is the deception practised by wilfully representing circumstances to be different from what they really are. It involves a design to deceive. Such an accusation was actually brought against our Master by the Jews of his day: "We remember that this deceiver said." On the other hand, the Spirit pro-

phetically vindicated Christ's perfect truthfulness:
"Neither was there any deceit in his mouth." The
prophetic witness is reëchoed in the apostolic description : " Who did no sin, neither was guile found
in his mouth." St. Paul presents the charge
brought by the world and its contradiction, side by
side, in a brief and startling paradox when he describes himself and his fellow-apostles as " deceiv-
ers and yet true." The charge of intentional deceit brought in former days against Christ and his
apostles has been abandoned by modern skeptics
as plainly untenable. The question yet remaining
concerns not themselves, but their words. Could
the authors be honest, and yet intentional fraud be
charged upon their words?

Truth involves, therefore, the reality of the
things recorded, the earnestness and gravity of the
narration, the absence of intentional errors, and the
freedom from intentional fraud. If any one of these
things can be proved to exist in any book, the book
cannot be true. In saying that the six characters
claimed by Scripture for itself involve the assertion
of truth, we say that Scripture is neither a speculation nor a fiction ; that it is as free from error in its
details as it is above the possible suspicion of imposture in the motives of its authors. There is no
third quality between truth and untruth ; the proof
of the one involves the exclusion of the other. If
the Scriptures be true, there must be absent from
them any element of unreality, or fiction, or ignorance, or fraud. If they are untrue, they must be
tainted either with unreality, or ignorance, or fic-

tion, or fraud. Are either of these qualities consistent with the assertions of Scripture relative to itself? I answer unhesitatingly in the negative.

Can we conceive that a revelation from God should be tainted either by ignorance or fraud? Can God either be supposed to make mistakes, or to represent things in aspects inconsistent with external reality? On this question, infidelity, at all events, gives a most decided negative. It replies, that the first attributes conceived to belong to a perfect Being are truth and truthfulness; the one being the knowledge of things as they are, the other the statement to others of things as they are. It argues that there are certain statements in the Bible which are proved not to be true; therefore it concludes that the Bible cannot be a communication from God. The second or minor premise in this argument, namely, that the Bible contains things proved to be untrue, is equally rash, hasty, and devoid of proof. But, supposing the charge to have been just, the conclusion that the Bible, containing mistakes, cannot be the word of God, appears to me to be unanswerable. Any other conclusion shocks the natural instincts of reverence, and imputes to the Divine Being the very defects and imperfections which the Scriptures indignantly repudiate. A Christian can scarcely entertain a lower conception of the attributes of God than a skeptic. One who studies his character as displayed in the sufferings and death of his atoning Son, can scarcely frame lower conceptions of him than one who knows him only from the witness of external nature.

Let the possibility be tested by an earthly illustration. Let us conceive the case of a message sent from one human being to another on a subject of the highest conceivable importance, and touching the mutual honor of both parties. The message is a written one, for this is the analogous case. That the inspiration was first seated in the men, does not at all affect the fact that it is now incorporated in the writings, "the Scripture is God-inspired." Such a written message from man to man might undoubtedly contain mistakes; but what would be their origin? There are only three alternatives—ignorance, carelessness, or untruthfulness.

Ignorance is plainly inconceivable in God, because he filleth all in all. His creative care is over all his creatures, and does not overlook a single one of the countless myriads of living things which people the earth and the air and the seas. But can carelessness be predicated of God? We can understand that a human creature may intrust a message to another, and may either fail to superintend its correct transmission, because his own attention is otherwise engaged, or superintending it, may fail to notice some wrong word or some inaccurate expression. But God is as wise as he is omnipresent, and his Divine activity is as infinite as his goodness. It would be blasphemy to ascribe to him either lassitude of mind or defects of attention. But we can no more conceive that God can be untruthful, than we can conceive that he can be ignorant or careless. That he would say what is untrue, directly or indirectly, or would in any way

be a party in inducing his creatures to believe what
is false, is directly contradictory to the character of
"the only true God." "Yea, let God be true, and
every man a liar;" "just and true are thy ways,
thou King of saints." It is, therefore, incredible
that any communication sent by God can be untrue.

But every successive step of the argument makes
the incredibility still more incredible. The Scriptures are the formal proclamation of a King to his
subjects, claiming obedience by virtue of their allegiance, and on pain of his displeasure. What should
we think of an earthly monarch who should pledge
his royal word for some ingenious fiction, and give
the weight of his royal authority to a romance?
The Bible professes to contain the sovereign will of
the King of kings and Lord of lords. It is directed, indeed, to mankind, but reaches farther and
higher than the race of Adam—to angelic intelli-
gencies. St. Paul, speaking of his own letters and
of their teaching, declares it to be the purpose of
God that unto "principalities and powers might be
known by the church the manifold wisdom of God."
St. Peter, speaking of the great truths conveyed by
the preaching of the gospel, adds, "Which things
the angels desire to look into." The angel who
appeared with John in the Apocalypse declared his
own membership in the written promises: "I am of
thy brethren the prophets, and of them that keep
the saying of this book." The Scriptures constitute
therefore a royal proclamation, made before the
universe, and sealed with the yea and amen of Him
that cannot lie. This is what Scripture says of

itself; and is it conceivable that such a proclamation should not be true?

Again, Scripture is given for the very purpose of teaching. Its declared object is to make wise. How can it fulfil this purpose if its contents be not true? If it teaches what is untrue, it undermines the very basis of all wisdom, and becomes the instrument of demoralizing deception. What would be thought of an earthly master who should put into the hands of his pupils a manual of instruction made up of fact and fiction, and should teach them an imaginary and fictitious history instead of the record of the world's actual events? Such an act would rather unteach than teach. Shall we suppose that the all-wise God, of his sovereign mercy towards mankind, has voluntarily professed to supply us with a text-book of religious instruction, and yet that it is not true?

Scripture is the latest and most special instrument for making known God's will. First, God made man in his own image, and in the intimate intercourse of Paradise met him face to face. Man fell, and lost in the fall this immediate access to God. He carried with him indeed into his banishment from Eden the knowledge already received in his unfallen state. But for the preservation of this tradition of truth, and its extension to succeeding generations, he became dependent on his reason and conscience, and the teaching of the outward world. The spring of truth was no longer gushing forth unceasingly from its Divine fountain-head. But reason and conscience proved inadequate.

"They became vain in their imagination, and their foolish heart was darkened; professing themselves to be wise, they became fools." Wherefore God ceased to strive with them. "As they did not like to retain God in their knowledge, God gave them over to a reprobate mind." He still retained a good seed in the world, a remnant according to the election of grace. He still made himself known by prophets beyond the Abrahamic line, such as Melchisedec and Jethro and Balaam, and the old prophet of Bethel. But this oral teaching was proved to be inadequate for the ever-deepening darkness of the Gentile world. God therefore made use of one other means for the declared purpose of maintaining a truth which unassisted human nature had failed to preserve, and this other means consisted of a written revelation. But if this written revelation itself contained mistakes, and was darkened by the reflection of human ignorance, its very objects were frustrated. It would not only fail as other agencies had failed, but it would aggravate the evil. Containing errors under the form of a revelation from God, it would enlist human reverence on behalf of the false, not on behalf of the true, and would perpetuate the darkness it was intended to remove.

But, further, the Scriptures demand human belief, not alone to their doctrines, but also to their facts. But such a claim would be monstrous if its assertions were accompanied by the consciousness that the teaching claiming belief was not true. It would be contrary to the first instincts of justice to insist upon credence in the absence of sufficient grounds for it; for the higher nature of man clings to the true, and rebels instinctively against the false; its noblest faculties and purest affections stand up in arms against a lie. It is unimaginable that a holy God should have endowed man with a capacity for knowing and loving truth, and then should expect him to contradict his heaven-given nature by believing what is untrue. The New Testament writers, men miraculously endowed with the extraordinary gifts of the Spirit, quote the Old Testament Scriptures as the final court of appeal, the conclusive and unanswerable arguments for truth. Yet, if the contents of the Old Testament Scriptures be not true, we are shut up to this conclusion, that God moved his servants to appeal to the unerring certainty of a standard which he knew all the while to be erring and deceptive.

The alternative thus presented is yet further strengthened when the last of the six specified assertions of Scripture relative to itself is taken into account. This is, that disbelief in Scripture is a sin, and will be punished as a sin. It becomes as strong an argument for the absolute truth of the revealed word as can possibly be conceived; for the absence of such a truth would charge the conduct of God (I speak the very words with awe and fear) with the highest conceivable injustice. It amounts to nothing less than this: that if the Scriptures be not absolutely true, God must have sent a communication to mankind clothed with all the sanctions of his own authority, and sealed ostentatiously with

his awful name, and that he has declared his purpose
to punish mankind for not believing it, though false—
that is, for not obeying a revelation of his will, intentionally made through human messengers, and
which, either through a defect of power or of will,
(it matters not which alternative is adopted,) he has
not preserved from being mixed with idle fancies,
weakened by fiction, distorted by mistakes, or tainted
by fraud.

It follows, therefore, that Scripture does assert
its own absolute veracity, and does it in the mode
most consistent with the self-consciousness of an
inspiring Deity. Reiterated affirmation of truth
attached to each writer or each book, or each statement in each book, would have been equally useless
and incongruous. The claim is asserted in the majestic attitude and Divine character of revelation,
and cannot be separated from them. Absolute truth
is the immediate and necessary inference, or rather,
perhaps I should say, the essential condition involved in all the statements of Scripture relative to
itself. Six separate lines bear the same independent testimony; their voices combine in one harmonious and consentient witness, like the voices of
angels proclaiming trumpet-tongued the spotless
excellence and abiding authority of the everlasting
gospel.

But the same argument avails to extend with
great force the assertion of this quality of truth to
all and every part of Scripture. The Bible not only
contains some true things, but it contains no untrue things. All its contents are true, according to

the nature of their truth. Its deep mysteries, its grand promises, its records of the past, its predictions of the future, its majestic history, its graphic narratives, its ethnological and genealogical details, all are true. Let us not shrink from accepting the only legitimate conclusion in all its length and breadth. None will deny that errors have taken place in transcription, that dates have been inaccurately copied, that glosses have been interpolated. We leave the determination of these questions, and the settlement of the true text in those minute details on which alone existing copies differ, to the ordinary resources of criticism. We take the text as thus settled, and for this text, thus identified with the original autographs, we affirm that it contains truth, and nothing but truth. We base the assertion, first of all, on the Divine character of Scripture as a revelation from God; and secondly, on the positive statements of this divinely-revealed Scripture as to its own character. As they involve the truth, so they involve also the universal truth of their contents. We have already seen how strong presumption of this equality of character arises from the nature of the attesting evidence. We now gather the same conclusion from its positive teaching.

Let the conditions of the case be again borne in mind. The Scriptures are a revelation from God, sanctioned with his authority as Creator and King, and for the express purpose of teaching us the things that belong to salvation, intended to correct the defects and mistakes of what is called natural religion, claiming absolute credence alike for its statements of facts and revelations of doctrine, denouncing disbelief as a sin, and pronouncing upon it the severity of God's wrath. Now let us place side by side with these claims the supposition that the Bible is partly true and partly untrue, and note what would be the consequences.

Several theories have been advanced as to the source and extent of this admixture of truth and error in one and the same book. It has been said that its doctrines are true, but not its historical narratives; and yet the narratives are so interwoven with the doctrines as to make a separation practically impossible, and reduce the attempt to an utter absurdity. It has been said by others that those portions are true which immediately affect salvation, but not those portions which affect details of character and conduct; and yet the minute maxims of the Bible are all corollaries from its fundamental principles. It has been said that its teaching, so far as it affects questions lying beyond the range of the human intellect, is true; but not its teaching on matters falling within the legitimate range of human discovery and knowledge; and yet it is an unsettled question what subjects are discoverable by man and what are not. Some think that the human intuitions are able to discover infallibly even God himself. Some think that human knowledge cannot deal infallibly even with the minutest fact; and certainly of the two the weight of experience inclines very decidedly towards the latter.

But for the present let either theory be adopted; the Scripture then is partly true and partly untrue.

Part of it may be accepted with the most implicit and unreserved faith; part needs to be scrutinized with the most jealous suspicion, and part to be rejected with the most unhesitating promptitude. The embarrassing difficulty lies in the intermixture of these portions. If each of them occupied its own distinctive and distinguishable sphere, so that it could be taken bodily out of the rest, and being regarded as a whole of itself, could be either accepted or rejected as the case might be, the task would be comparatively easy. But, unfortunately for such a supposition, the two are intermingled everywhere, lying side by side, and even compacted together as the fine metal and the earthy dross may be. Nor is there any thing on the surface to guide the mind in distinguishing them. The same air of validity and verisimilitude surrounds the whole. They are all framed into one consecutive and harmonious revelation; they fit naturally into each other; they are surrounded by the same external sanctions. The case is not that, upon the theory of skepticism, the Bible is like a mass of rock, with the glittering gold intermingled with the baser material in one conglomerate, but so sparkling and bright in contrast with the dross that the eye can immediately and certainly distinguish it; but the case is, that the Bible is like an ore which needs to be submitted to the furnace, and from which the purifying fire alone can separate the precious metal from the worthless admixture.

Hence, to distinguish the true from the untrue is a work of admitted difficulty. Upon the theory of the skeptic it requires an intuitive critical instinct, accurate scholarship, and unflagging industry, assisted by all the resources of a criticism perfected only in the course of four thousand years, and disciplined by many years of exercise; and when the study has been pursued for a life, the result attained is indefinitely variable and uncertain. An individual critic will speak of his own conclusions, it is true, with the utmost confidence; but it is scarcely possible for other men to accept them with the same feeling, both because of the frequent changes of the individual opinion, and the utter contrariety of view existing between him and others of the same craft. Modern critics are like an army, where every man's hand is against his fellow. The utmost approximation to certainty in such a case does not exceed a probability. But if within the charmed circle of critical experts this is true, what must be the hopeless condition of the outsiders? A large proportion of mankind have neither time nor ability for such studies, nor interest in such questions. How can such men discriminate the true and the untrue, mingled as they are asserted to be in the same books, the same chapters, and the same verses? The position of an educated man, with the ordinary resources of an average education at hand, is not much more favorable. For which of the critics shall he take as his master, Schleiermacher, or Paulus, or Strauss, or Renan? At whose feet shall he sit as an obedient disciple, Eichhorn or Vater, De Wette or Ewald, Donaldson or Colenso? To cast lots among them, and allow what men call chance to settle the question, would perhaps be as reasonable a mode, and as likely to be satisfactory, as any other that can be suggested.

Thus the picture presented to us on the supposition that the Scriptures are partly true and partly untrue, is a Bible not blended of sharply contrasted colors, but bearing a thousand hues and tints and shades; a mass of confusion hopelessly and inextricably blended together, making inquiry doubtful and certainty impossible.

Yet, according to the positive statements of Scripture, life and death, obedience or disobedience, a blessing or a curse, heaven or hell, hang upon the solution of that problem. If any partiality of feeling, any self-love, any personal prejudice or hostility, blind a man's judgment, he may incur the awful risk of setting himself against God on the one side, or of imputing to God what never proceeded from him on the other. If indeed a man could rest secure on the consciousness of an unclouded purity of intention, an unsullied love for truth, an unmixed and unfailing wish to do right, and only to do right, he might venture to throw himself upon the unknown mercies of God, and trust to be pardoned for his involuntary and inevitable mistakes. But the position even of such a man as this would be a very awful one in face of the severe warnings and unqualified denunciations of the Word—awful as if he walked amid the thunders and voices of Sinai, and nigh to the quivering sides of the mountain which none might touch and live. As to the certainty of the Bible, its clear guidance and the security of its teaching, why, what David described as a lamp would be either a flickering spark struggling amid the darkness, or a false meteor luring men to their death.

But such a conclusion cannot be avoided, if, on the one side, Scripture makes these six assertions relative to itself, and if, on the other, its contents be not all true. I believe that no mind whatever can accept such a conclusion, can believe in such an alternative; and if we are thus shut in on one side and on the other by results equally tremendous and incredible, what remains but that we should follow the one open path, and adopt the one natural and consistent belief, that the contents of Scripture are true, and all true? The conclusion is no matter of theory, but one of positive and revealed authority. The word of God claims certain characters for itself. It is God's own voice, with his own solemn utterance affirming his word to be truth without admixture of error. On this assurance let faith calmly rest, and before this warning let speculative theories be hushed into obedient silence— "Thus saith the Lord."

CHAPTER VIII.

A REVELATION IMPLIES TWO PARTIES, AND THEREFORE TWO ELEMENTS.

Skeptical Denial of the Truth of all Scripture—Must be settled by Appeal to Facts—Preliminary Settlement of the Standard to be followed—Misapprehensions relative to the two Elements of Scripture—Their Existence Inevitable and Agreeable to all God's Mode of Working—Both must be maintained, and yet not separated—No Inconsistency between them—Analogy of the Personal Word—The whole of Scripture Human, and the whole of Scripture Divine.

It has been shown in the two preceding chapters that the Scriptures assert their own plenary authority and absolute truth. The loftiest epithets supplied by human language are not too strong to express its aspect and attitude. The immediate sanctions of a Divine authorship, the solemnity of a royal proclamation, the sufficiency of an inspired teaching, the claims of an unerring veracity, the obligations of a moral duty, and the sanctions of an everlasting reward or punishment, invest it with a character alike solemn and unique, like the vestments of power upon the shoulders of a manifested Deity. This is the account Scripture gives of itself. Is this account to be accepted as conclusive, or do other considerations imperatively modify it?

Whatever authority belongs to the Christian Scriptures in general belongs equally to their assertions relative to themselves in particular. It has been shown that they fill a position peculiar to themselves and without a parallel. The inspired character of their human authors, attested as it was by signs and wonders—the organic unity characteristic of their contents, and by the very diversity of the human authorship and date suggestive of a Divine intelligence planning and superintending the whole—the sublimity of its contents, and its revelation of mysteries far transcending the utmost powers of the human intellect—attest with one consentient voice its supernatural character. It is scarcely possible for a mind which accepts this evidence to demur to the authority of its teaching, whether it has reference to the character of Scripture itself or to any other portion of the Divine dealings with mankind, if the teaching be sufficiently definite and precise. Do we rightly interpret its own language? will be, to a devout Christian, the only open question.

The proofs already alleged appear to be sufficiently precise. Yet, if the assertions ostentatiously made and paraded by modern skepticism be true, there must be some mistake, since it is inconceivable that God should allege claims not substantiated by the facts of the case. It is asserted that the contents of Scripture are not all true, and have been proved to be not all true. Its facts are alleged to be inaccurate, its recorded events incredible, and some of its revealed doctrines monstrously at variance with man's first conceptions of a pure and holy God. Could these assertions be substantiated, it would inevitably follow that the contents of the

Bible could not be all stamped with Divine infallibility. With regard to the special claims quoted in the preceding chapter, two alternatives only would remain. Either we should conclude that these passages did not really involve the claim of absolute truth, however plain and cogent the inference may apparently be, or that these passages contradict the claim to a Divine authorship; since, in their proved untruthfulness, they must only be the extravagance of a human fanaticism, and not the utterances of a Divine word.

Having, therefore, examined the claims asserted by the Bible, as it is, and regarded it as a whole, relative to its own authority, it becomes a matter of the highest importance to examine the evidences on the other side, and ascertain how far they invalidate the force of the positive claim. Have inaccuracies, mistakes, and contradictions been proved to exist in Scripture? We need not fear to enter upon the inquiry with the utmost frankness. From the investigation, faith in the Divine authority of the Scriptures will but emerge trebly armed. In the face of all modern argument, its ingenious speculations and elaborate inquiries, we need not fear to maintain with unabated confidence, and deeper conviction than before, the inerrability of the word of God, and that its contents are all, in the fullest and plainest sense of the word, true.

The critical tests applied to the solution of this question are, however, variable, arbitrary, and capricious in the extreme. The mode of forming a conclusion is frequently so replete with misapprehensions, alike as to the real nature of the question at issue and the actual facts of the case, that it is necessary to clear the ground somewhat farther before we enter upon its discussion. By carefully marking the road as we advance, we shall avoid those ambiguities of language by which the question of inspiration has been most seriously embarrassed.

The conclusion already reached is, that the Scriptures are not only truly the word of God, but that they are the true word of God. Their characteristic is not only their truth, for this they may possess in common with many human works, but their guaranteed truth. The very signature, as it were, of God himself is upon his written word. Human books may be true or may not be true, because the human mind is fallible, and its highest exercise affords no demonstrative evidence of veracity; but the word of God must be true, because it is the word of God. The assertion of its truth involves, therefore, the assertion of its inspiration, and the assertion of its universal truth the assertion of its universal inspiration. The two things must be correlative and coextensive; for we mean by the word inspiration that Divine side of the Scriptures by virtue of which they are the word of God.

The specific question of inspiration thus comes before us in its natural and its Scriptural order. The course of the argument has not been that the Scriptures are inspired, and that therefore they are the true word of God, but that they are the true word

of God, and therefore are inspired. This is the
natural order; for what is first in the act of God is
necessarily last in the knowledge of man. We begin with the facts nearest to ourselves, and trace
them back to their original and originating cause.
It is the Scriptural order; for although Scripture is
comparatively silent in the assertion of its universal
inspiration, it has been shown to be particularly full
and specific in the assertion of its Divine and authoritative character. A further advantage gained
by this order is, that the stress of the controversy
is not laid upon the word "inspiration." Much has
been said of the usage of the word, alike in ancient
times and in the formularies of the churches of our
day. It is unnecessary even to discuss such a
question; for it can only affect our employment of
a word, not our acceptance of a truth. That the
almost unanimous voice of all Christian theology,
alike in the primitive days and in the times of the
Reformation, has asserted the predominant authority and absolute truth of Scripture, cannot be denied. Whether the word inspiration be the best
word to express the Divine element by virtue of
which Scripture possesses these qualities is a matter of very secondary interest. We use the word
because it is a convenient term, and the term most
closely corresponding in our language to the apostolic θεόπνευστος; but the object near to the heart of
the Christian is not the defence of a word, but the
vindication of the truth expressed by it.

The expression that the Bible is the true word
of God is, perhaps, the most absolute assertion of

the Divine element that can be made in words. It therefore serves to illustrate the impossibility of stating the claim without including a human element as well as a Divine. Much discussion has been raised as to the existence of a human element. The term itself has been employed with singular uncertainty and ambiguity of sense, and the belief in a plenary or verbal inspiration has been represented as necessarily involving the denial of its existence. The discussion is little better than a conflict about words. There must be two elements in a revelation, because there must be two parties concerned—the party by whom the revelation is made, and the party to whom it is made. If the second party be absent, it ceases to be a revelation, and becomes a mere act of self-consciousness on the part of God. It is impossible to state the facts of the case in words which do not involve a human element; that is, human action in the composition of Scripture. The very description of the word is human in the terms, in their construction, and in the sense conveyed. If we say that the Bible is the true word of God, the term "word" involves the human element, for it denotes at once the fact of a communication and the channel through which it is made. If we say that the Bible is "God's word," we express it yet more distinctly in the further term, "written;" written how but in human words, by human hands, through human materials, and for human readers? To talk of a revelation devoid of a human element, is to use words devoid of sense. Such an element must exist; and no theorist, however extreme, can ever have intended to deny its existence. All discussion is needless here. The question remaining to be settled is, In what sense, or more accurately, To what extent it exists in Scripture? For if there be nothing to qualify its extent, it must evidently involve the possibility of human error, as well as the employment of human words and the agency of human minds.

The answer is to be found in the very fact of the existence of the two elements; for if they are two, they must be distinct from each other; if they are not distinct, they become one; if they are elements, then they are constituents of some common whole. The two are consequently ever distinct, but never separate. Let us keep them so, neither confusing them together nor allowing either one to absorb the other, and the question will be found to be answered. The perfect Divine element is to be maintained on the one side; the perfect human element is to be maintained on the other; but the Divine is neither to absorb the human, nor is the human to derogate from the Divine.

In holding this equipoise of the two, we are assisted by the analogy of the personal Word of God. In him "two whole and perfect natures, the Godhead and manhood, were joined together in one person, never to be divided." Article 2. Here, therefore, is distinction, but not separation. If we say that the two natures were mingled so that there was a third something made up of both, but itself neither Godhead nor manhood, then we destroy both natures, " confounding the substance." If we separate the two natures, so that Christ was at one time and in one act simple Godhead and in another simple manhood, then we destroy "the unity of person," and make two Christs instead of one. Scripture asserts him to have been perfect God and perfect man, and we therefore accept him as both in one, although the point of contact between the two and the mode of their union are beyond all human comprehension. Truly, "Great is the mystery of godliness : God was manifest in the flesh." 1 Tim. 3 : 16.

We must learn to think and speak in exactly the same mode relative to the Divine and human elements in Scripture. If we attempt to confound them together, and say that Scripture is neither human nor Divine, but something made up of both, we are corrected by the plain facts of the case, for the distinct human element is palpably there in the language, imagery, and style ; and the distinct Divine element is also there in the all-pervading unity of design and sublimity of subject. We can no more suppose the former to be Divine than we can suppose the latter to be human. To confound the two together is only to destroy both.

Nor are we any more able to separate the two elements than we are to confound them. For if we say that part of the Scripture is Divine and part of it human, we are again contradicted by the facts; for in the part we acknowledge to be Divine the human element still survives. We can indeed say, if we like, that the whole is human, for this is perfectly conceivable. But in saying so we are met by the other class of facts specified in chapter III., which prove that it cannot be all human, since the supernatural is ingrained into its very structure, and stamped as with a visible signet alike on its external and internal evidences.

The only alternative, therefore, left open to us is to maintain both elements, distinct and yet inseparable. The whole of Scripture is Divine, and the whole of Scripture is human; none the less Divine because it is human; none the less human because it is Divine. To argue that because it is Divine it cannot be human, or that because it is human it cannot also be Divine, is practically to argue that the Divine and the human cannot be united. No believer in the hypostatical union of the two natures in the one person of Christ can with any consistency adopt such a plea. The glorious person of Christ is the living protest against it; for if the two can be united in the personal Word, why may they not be united equally in the written word? The agent of the union is the same in both cases, even God the Holy Ghost. In the personal Word we believe that he was "conceived by the Holy Ghost"—here was the Divine side of the one person; and that he was "born of the Virgin Mary"—here was the human side. In regard to the written word, "holy men of old wrote"—here is the human side; "as they were moved by the Holy Ghost"—here is the Divine. Yet both meet in the same word, as the two clauses are but the constituents of one sentence: "Holy men of old wrote as they were moved by the Holy Ghost." 2 Peter 1:21.

We must therefore maintain the Divine element of Scripture in all the infallibility of its truth, and all the authority of its source. We must no less maintain the human element in all its fulness and essential characteristics. Whatever is peculiar to human writing is there; whatever is peculiar to Divine authority is there. The sole limitations are supplied by the union of the two. We must neither so press the Divine as to exclude the human, nor so extend the human as to exclude the Divine.

CHAPTER IX.

THE HUMAN ELEMENT OF SCRIPTURE IN ITS RELATION TO THE DIVINE.

Man's Part in the Composition of Scripture to be maintained in all Particulars Essential to Human Agency—The Personal Peculiarities of the Writers—The Human Point of View, and the Human Mode of Thinking and Speaking—Opposite Theories of the Capability of Man to receive Divine Knowledge—Imperfection of Human Language, yet Reality of Divine Truth—Peculiarities of Human Language—Structural Identity of Inspired and Uninspired Compositions.

I HAVE said that the human and the Divine elements are distinct on one side, and yet inseparable upon the other. Neither of them can therefore be considered by itself, but must ever be viewed in connection with its correlative. To regard the case otherwise is to violate one of its ascertained conditions. Thus, in examining what is meant by the human element, and the extent of agency exercised on the part of man in the production of the Scriptures, we must view it from the standpoint of the Divine element, or of God's part in the accomplishment of the same work. In the same manner, in examining into the extent of the Divine element in Scripture, and the characteristics involved in it, we must view it from the standpoint of the human, maintaining alike their distinctive attributes and their inseparable union.

I. Thus the Divine element is not to absorb the human. God, in giving his revelation, employed human agents as his messengers. There was no other mode consistent with the recognized principles of his moral government over the world conceivable by our minds for the purpose, except this use of human instruments. The only mode of testing this fact is to exhaust the alternative methods, and then to see what would have been the necessary consequences of their adoption. This has been fully done by the writer in a previous work, and it is unnecessary to recapitulate the argument. On the supposition that God deals with mankind as creatures invested with moral responsibility, and in whom therefore the work of Divine redemption must be conducted in harmony with the constitution he has given us, there is no possible method of making a revelation of God's will to man except through the vehicle of human language. This language, moreover, must have been used according to its known and ordinary laws, and not employed in a mystical and secondary sense, contrary to its familiar usage. Moreover the human language could only be used through human agents with a recognized standing-ground of their own in the working world, and amid the ordinary activities of human life. The caution must be borne in mind that these conclusions do not exist in the form of a fatalistic necessity imposed from without upon the freedom of the Divine action, but arise out of the sovereignty of the Divine choice, and the principles avowedly adopted in his moral government over the world.

God employed human agents as the messengers of his will; they must be accepted therefore, and judged as regards the manner of fulfilling their commission as human agents. They do not themselves become Divine, because they are used by a Divine wisdom, and made the channels of a Divine revelation ; they lose none of their human characteristics, but retain them to the full. All that is human belongs to them to the utmost limits imposed by the concurrent action of the Divine. There is a wonderful harmony in this very fact ; for as the truths revealed are intended to incorporate themselves as it were into human life, and to pervade as a blessed leaven the whole mass of practical thought and action, so they are brought closely into contact with it by the familiar sympathies, habits, and speech of the messengers who conveyed them. It is no more possible to draw a sharp line of demarcation between the principles of language used by inspired writers and the principles of language used by uninspired writers, than it is possible to separate the mental faculties of religious men from the ordinary faculties of irreligious men. Human nature is elevated and sanctified by grace, but it is not changed in its essential qualities. The inspired writers acquired from the Holy Spirit, working in them and through them, qualities not possessed by uninspired writers ; but they never ceased to be human or to use the ordinary modes of communication between man and man, however much these modes may have been elevated into more than ordinary force and beauty by the Divine agency. They continued to be human instruments throughout, and as human therefore they are to be judged.

Thus the inspired writers retain their respective peculiarities alike of intellectual gifts and moral character. The effect still survives in their writings, which are just as characteristic of the respective authors, and of their times and circumstances, as are the productions of uninspired writers. The mode of viewing and stating truth, with the method of its illustration, the selection of the appropriate language, the use of illustrative figures and their specialities, the manner of argument, and the literary style, and even the influence produced on all the foregoing, by the moral qualities of the writer and his constitutional temper and tendencies of feeling, constitute the patent features of the scriptural books. This portion of the human element is acknowledged by all parties to this controversy, at least as fully and distinctly by the advocate of a verbal inspiration as by others, if not more fully than by others. The only peculiarity of his view is, that he maintains this human element as one constituent only of the composition, and not the whole, keeping it alike distinct and inseparable from the concurrent element of Divine inspiration. To charge him with denying or forgetting it, is either a blundering misapprehension of his belief, or a libellous perversion of it.

II. But we enter upon more difficult ground when we take another step, and assert for the inspired composition the essential peculiarities of all human thought. Here we need to steer our course between two extremes. On the one side of the scale stands the avowed claim of rationalism to be the competent and self-sufficient judge of all truth, even that relative to the nature and will of God. On the other side stands the mistake of supposing that we are incapable of knowing any truth relative to God, and that the teaching of revelation itself does not present to us the truth of things, but only such an adumbration of them as alone the highest faculties of the human intellect are competent to receive. The just and scriptural view holds the mean between these extremes. Against the rationalist it maintains that the human mind is wholly incompetent to find out God for itself, and that even the conceptions it gathers from revelation are inadequate to comprehend the full majesty of the facts. At the same time it maintains that although the revelation of God contained in his word is limited by the capacities of a finite intellect and the capabilities of a finite language, it is real and true as far as it goes—not a mere shadow of truth, but truth itself. What we know is but a small part of the whole; but it is real and true so far as it extends.

The claims advanced on behalf of the competency of the human reason to judge of Divine things, involve a controversy much wider than the question now under discussion. It is remarkable that the claim is based on no process of the reason, but on the intuition. It is, therefore, tacitly acknowledged in the very form of the argument, that we possess no data from which the reasoning faculties are competent to argue about God, and that those quick, subtle, sudden flashes of truth, which lie so wholly beyond the range of definite argument,

that we call them intuitions, are alone supposed to
be capable of discovering him. But the utmost possible distrust must attach to processes of the reason which do not admit of reasoning. It may be
justly suspected that these flashes of unconscious
truth are no more than the reflections of revealed
knowledge, principles so absorbed in the process of
education, into the very texture of our mental selves,
that we become unconscious of the source whence
we obtain them, and attribute to some latent divinity in the mind itself, what are really the reflected
rays of an external revelation. So far are the intuitive conceptions of the intellect from being competent to supply the place of a revelation, that they
are themselves its witnesses and fruits.

With this argument, however, the question of inspiration is only concerned in a secondary degree.
It concerns us more closely to note that human
language can only correspond to human ideas,
and that human ideas are only coextensive with
human objects. If any thing exists—and doubtless
in the wide universe there are many such things—
totally dissimilar to any thing that has ever fallen
within our own range of knowledge, it would be
neither possible for us to conceive it in the absence
of the appropriate ideas, nor to describe it in the
absence of appropriate words. This would be the
extreme case. But in proportion as any object differs from the lessons of our own knowledge, we lose
our power of comprehending it; and only so far as
it resembles them can the description of it be
framed into words.

7*

Now, the rationalist assumes that God must be wholly like man, and is therefore to be reckoned among the things knowable by man. The philosopher, at the other extreme, avers that God is totally unlike man, and therefore is unknowable by man. We turn from both to the Scriptures, and there we find the Deity described, in some respects, as absolutely beyond the power of our understanding, and in other respects within it.

Thus God's natural attribute of omnipotence, omnipresence, omniscience, his self-existence and nature, lie wholly beyond our comprehension. But why? Because we have no experimental knowledge of such attributes in ourselves, and therefore we cannot understand them in another. We use the words, and understand that there must be attributes corresponding to them; but we cannot understand the attributes themselves, because they are the natural attributes of Deity, and the nature of God must be wholly different from that of man. But it is otherwise with God's moral attributes and relations. These are repeatedly described in Scripture as the objects of our human knowledge, and the model for our imitation. Thus, in our Lord's words, "This is life eternal, to know thee, the only true God, and Jesus Christ, whom thou hast sent," John 17:3. Again I ask, Why? Because we have experience of similar attributes in ourselves. Our human qualities, at best, fall infinitely short of the glories of the Divine perfection, and are, moreover, so corrupted by sin as almost to have lost their original stamp; yet they are in themselves the moral reflection of the Creator. We know what love and pity, kindness and benevolence, approbation and sympathy, are in ourselves, and we can therefore understand what they are in God. For where but in our moral nature are we to find the image of God, in which we were created, and into which the operating power of the Holy Ghost again renews the regenerated soul? Thus St. Paul exhorts his Ephesian disciples "to put on the new man, which after God is created in righteousness and true holiness," Eph. 4:24. To the Colossians he writes, "Put ye on the new man, which is renewed in knowledge after the image of Him that created him," Col. 3:10. The Spirit, by St. Peter, uses this remarkable language: "By these ye might be partakers of the Divine nature," 2 Pet. 1:4. There is therefore in the moral nature of man a similitude to God, defaced by the fall, but again renewed by the work of the Holy Ghost. We possess qualities similar in kind to the qualities of God. From this experience, consequently, we gather the appropriate ideas, and from the ideas the appropriate language, through which a true knowledge of the Divine Being, and of his relation towards us, and our relation towards him, may be communicated.

When, therefore, we say that the Divine element in Scripture is to be so understood as not to swallow up the human, the principle accounts for the employment of human conceptions and human methods of thinking, since by no others could we receive truth. In every case the revelation is as complete as the most perfect use of human language—confessedly an imperfect instrument, at the best, to express our thoughts, much more the thoughts of God—could make it. As regards the distinctive attributes of Deity, they are presented through human analogies. Thus the knowledge of God is depicted by the all-seeing eye; his power by the all-mighty hand; his acquaintance with our thoughts and words by his open ear; his majesty and power by the illustration of crowns, and thrones, and sceptres. But the illustrations are at the same time accompanied by explanations which prevent all imputation of carnal ideas to God, and teach us to regard the outward images as no more than the vivid delineation of the spiritual God to the faculties of a sensuous creature. The truth is there, but we are warned of the imperfection of its representation. The same inadequacy of our conceptions applies in part, but in part only, to the moral attributes of God and our relation towards him. Our ascription of various qualities to God is a human thing altogether, and a mode of speaking exactly analogous to what we use in speaking of his eye, his hand, his ear. God is one, "without body, parts, or passions." But we can only understand him by analogies drawn from ourselves; and so we transfer to him the notion gathered from our own experience of various qualities subsisting in one person. But when we come to the qualities themselves, we drop the use of figures altogether, and speak and think of God no longer mediately, but immediately. In receiving the revelation of his love towards us, of our original relation to him, of our separation by sin, of our restoration through an atonement, of our regeneration after his image, of our position as sons by adoption, and of the promise of present peace and future glory, the corresponding ideas in our own experience enable us to understand the revelation and grasp the truth without the necessity of intervening illustrations. Still, in both cases it is a revelation to human thought, and therefore through human methods of thought and all the distinctive peculiarities of human thought. They are part of the human element; and without the human element there could not be a revelation at all.

III. Lastly, the Divine inspiration not only leaves untouched the peculiarities of human language, but makes use of them as the appropriate vehicle of truth. Thus the construction of sentences, the method of argument, the admixture of expostulation and appeal, the use of poetical phrases, the employment of imagery, and, what requires special notice, the free adoption of all the recognized figures of speech, necessarily follow the ordinary standard of language. So far from shrinking from this plain principle to its utmost extent, we should find it difficult to conceive how it could be otherwise. Once admit the use of human language, and it is impossible to frame any other limit of its ordinary usages than is supplied by its contact with the Divine inspiration. Within this range there can be no restriction, or the language of Scripture will have ceased to be the ordinary speech of mankind. Why should the liberty of a sacred writer to use the full resources of language be restrained within narrower limits than the liberty of a profane writer? The broad principle must be maintained, that whatever modes of expression are consistent in an uninspired writer are equally consistent in an inspired one.

Thus we see the futility of an objection sometimes urged against a belief in verbal inspiration, that modes of expression found in Scripture are inconsistent with the majesty of a Divine Author. The plea is only gained by separating some one detail in the plan of revelation from the other parts of the same scheme, and then leaving out all the intermediate links, and bringing into sharp contrast the individual word or phrase and the omniscient Mind which framed the entire plan. The objection is mainly urged against the hyperboles of Scripture; as when, for instance, it is predicted that the seed of Abraham should be as the sand upon the seashore for multitude. It is much the same as if a man objected, on a similar ground, against the gift of the Spirit of God to Bezaleel and Aholiab. These men worked under a special inspiration, directed not alone to the quality of the workmanship, but to the correspondence of the work to the divinely-given pattern. How absurd, it might be said, to suppose that God gave his Spirit to Bezaleel in order to enable him to carve a pomegranate or make a candlestick. Let the whole be considered together, and it is not absurd, for the entire tabernacle was a visible prophecy of no ordinary grandeur, and the little details were but the essential conditions of the whole design. A similar argument might be used with regard to Samson, if reverence to the inspiring Spirit did not teach us caution in coupling his immediate inspiration with the minor acts of the Israelitish champion, such as tying together the tails of the foxes, or eating honey out of the jaw of a dead lion. Doubtless God's Spirit did really move Samson to these very acts; for the difference between great and little which impresses our minds can really have no place in the mind of God. Samson was raised up for a special work in delivering Israel, and of that work each little detail was an inseparable part. Thus it is in the present case. God has been pleased to give a revelation through human language; and of this human language figures of speech constitute an inseparable part. We must learn to follow principle with greater decision than is ordinarily the case. When we have found a truth, let us not shrink from accepting it, and from following it out to its full legitimate results.

The Divine element in Scripture is, therefore, to be maintained in consonance with its human element. It is not to be so understood as to destroy the peculiarities of the individual writers, the properties of human thought, or the characteristics of human language. All these are essential to the human element, and must therefore be maintained in their utmost integrity and freedom.

CHAPTER X.

THE DIVINE ELEMENT OF SCRIPTURE IN ITS RELATION TO THE HUMAN.

God's Part in the Composition of Scripture to be maintained in all
Particulars Essential to Divine Agency—The Selection of the
Sacred Writers, and their Education for their Work—The Sub-
ject-matter of their Writings communicated, verified, select-
ed—Intelligent Comprehension of their own Writings on the
Part of the Inspired Authors, with its Limitations and Excep-
tions—The Language of Scripture, and its Importance—A
Revelation from God to the Prophets not Identical with the
Communication of Revealed Truth from the Prophets to us—
What the Accurate Transmission of Truth involves—The Abso-
lute Truth of Scripture Inseparable from Divine Agency—The
Relation of the two Elements, that of Superior and Inferior.

THE principle already applied to the adjustment
of the human element in Scripture must equally be
applied to the Divine. Whatever is characteristic
of Divine action must be maintained, and only
modified, on points nonessential, by the concurrent
action of the human intellect and will. It has been
shown that the Divine element must not be allowed
to swallow up the human: it must now be shown
that the human must not be allowed to derogate
from the Divine.

It must not be said that because the mode of
conception or expression in Scripture is characteristic of man, that therefore it cannot be inspired.
The human and the Divine elements exist together,
and the existence of the one is consequently no dis-

proof of the existence of the other. As on the one side every essential of the human is to be maintained in its union with the Divine, so on the other side every essential of the Divine is to be maintained in union with the human.

I. The authoritative character of the Scriptures, as being a formal communication from God to his creatures, is not lessened by the employment of human instruments as the channel of conveyance. Not only is the will conveyed the will of God, but the manner of its conveyance—the times, places, and persons—the literary structure and doctrinal proportions of the revelation—were planned by his sovereign wisdom, and executed under the supervision of his omniscience. In pursuance of his own eternal plan he selected the men by whose means he would reveal himself, living at such an especial period, placed under such peculiar circumstances, endowed with such definite gifts of intellect and qualities of heart, as were accordant with his purposes. Thus he selected Moses to be his agent, not in the full flush of his manhood and vigor of his courage, but tempered and matured by age, and sobered by experience. "Come now, therefore, and I will send thee unto Pharaoh," Exod. 3 : 10, was the charge laid upon him against his will by the God of his forefathers. Samuel was established from his childhood to be a prophet of the Lord. David was taken from the sheepfolds. Isaiah received his commission in a special vision of the glory of the Lord. Jeremiah was warned by God himself: "Before I formed thee in the belly I knew thee; and before thou camest forth out of the womb I sanctified thee, and I ordained thee a prophet unto the nations." Jer. 1:5. The vision of God by the river of Chebar prepared Ezekiel the priest for his prophetic office. Daniel was the "man greatly beloved" of God. Dan. 10:11. "The Lord took" Amos "as he followed the flock." Amos 7:15. Jonah accomplished his mission against Nineveh under the immediate compulsion of a chastising Providence. The apostles were chosen by Christ: the latest of them, as one born out of due time, was "separated from his mother's womb." Gal. 1:15.

Thus the writers of the Scriptures were specially selected for their work. They were not taken at haphazard, but immediately chosen; and it cannot be doubted that the choice involved the special adaptation of their constitutional gifts and qualities to the work they were called to do. As an earthly architect selects his subordinate agents with direct reference to their special qualifications, so the sacred writers were in the hands of God but as clay in the hands of the potter. He called them into existence, gave them their special faculties, ordained their place and circumstances, and then employed them, each to do his special part in that general scheme of a revelation, the whole order and purpose of which was known to the mind of God alone.

It is farther evident that God provided for his chosen instruments a special training, alike intellectual, moral, and religious. The forty years' banishment of Moses, the military experience of Joshua, the education of Samuel under aged Eli, the adventurous youth and enterprising manhood of David, the visions of Isaiah, Jeremiah, and Ezekiel, the early trials and training of Daniel, constituted their preparatory discipline for their subsequent ministries. In the history of St. Paul this adaptation of the early experience to the particular work subsequently intrusted to him, is especially remarkable. His early life, his associations, his education, his own religious struggles, his fanatical attachment to the law of his fathers, and the mode of his conversion, bear palpably upon them the signet of an overruling Providence. They equally combined to give intensity to his natural force of genius, depth to his religious experience, definite direction to his teaching, and influence to his personal example.

The God who gave the sacred writers their work, first fitted them for it. The language prophetically applied by Isaiah to our Lord may be used to describe the prophetic office in general, and is indeed used by the writer primarily of himself. " He hath made my mouth as a sharp sword; in the shadow of his hand hath he hid me ; he made me a polished shaft." Isa. 49 : 2. In these matters the human qualities of the writers so little interfered with the Divine power and authority of the ultimate author of the Revelation, that they formed the material which they moulded and the instruments through which they were declared.

II. The same harmonious suitability exists in the further action of the Divine Spirit in conveying to the human instrument the knowledge of the will and purposes of God. Here the subject-matter of the revelation divides itself into two parts. On the one side is the knowledge lying wholly above the reach of the unassisted human faculties; and on the other the knowledge lying within it. The teaching of Scripture falling under the first head, that, namely, relative to the nature of God and of unseen things, to the history of the past and the prospects of the future, and to the purposes of the Divine mind towards mankind, can only have been known to the writers through an immediate revelation, "Who hath known the mind of the Lord? or who hath been his counsellor?" Rom. 11 : 34. Inspiration here includes the whole communication of the truth to be conveyed to the mind of the earthly writer.

In regard to the second head, much information must have been naturally acquired through the ordinary processes of experience and observation prior to any action of the Divine Spirit. Nevertheless the sphere of inspiration remains here as clear and specific as elsewhere. It would act in two directions. In the first place it would complete and authenticate the information already possessed, and supplement it on points where personal knowledge must necessarily have been wanting. For instance, Moses must have possessed a personal acquaintance with a large number of facts relative to the exodus, but he has recorded others with which he could have had no immediate connection, and which he could only have known through the testimony of other men. I do not allude to the early history of

Genesis, which belongs properly to the class of things naturally unknown and immediately revealed; but I allude to such facts as those relative to Korah, Dathan, and Abiram, and to the narrative of Balaam and Balak. Moreover we find in Scripture not alone a narrative of men's acts, but an explanation of their motives, and these could not be known save to the Searcher of hearts. Exodus 14 : 5; Numb. 14 : 2–4; 2 Kings 2 : 17. The same remark applies with still greater force to the actions recorded of God himself, an element very largely and prominently pervading the whole of Scripture; for in imputing motives and acts to God, the writer must either have guessed them out of his own imagination, or have learned them from God himself. In the first case the narrative would possess no higher character than a human fiction, which we have already seen that it is not. The knowledge of them must have been communicated by God himself. In regard, therefore, to matters falling within the range of possible human knowledge, inspiration acted in completing, correcting, and verifying information which was or might have been otherwise possessed.

But it occupied also a further sphere in directing what portions of the facts should be recorded and what should not. Facts may be in themselves exceedingly trivial, and yet may have very important bearing on some special form of religious temptation. An instance of this is found in 2 Timothy 4 : 13, a favorite quotation on the part of those who object to the plenary inspiration of the word. The subject will only be slightly alluded to here, because an admirable answer will be found in Prof. Gaussen's "Theopneustia." His vindication serves to illustrate the principle that inspiration was exercised in directing what should be recorded and what not; but it by no means exhausts the teaching of the passage in question; for, in addition to the touching picture presented of the apostle's loneliness and bodily privations, we have the farther illustration how completely the inspired apostles were men like ourselves. There is great religious danger in conceiving of them as men of another mould, and by natural constitution of a more heroic type than ourselves—thus depriving ourselves of the comforts of their experience and the force of their example. With what vividness is the danger met by the simple portrait of the man so preoccupied as to have forgotten his cloak and papers, and subsequently distressed by their absence. It identifies the great apostle by a single vivid touch with our ordinary human nature and its familiar wants and weaknesses.

But this function of inspiration extends not alone to the selection of individual acts to be recorded, but to considerable passages, and even to the construction of entire books. This has been frequently forgotten, and as a result men have fallen into mistakes which would be ludicrous were it not for the gravity of the subject and the unhappy effects flowing from the misapprehension. For instance, God has been charged with uttering sentiments in the book of Job formally condemned in the very same book as not being in accordance with God's mind. Is not, then, the book of Job an inspired book? Certainly; but the inspiration covers the accuracy of the account, not the justice of the sentiments. It is true, indeed, that three passages from this book are quoted in the New Testament; but these passages derive authority not from Eliphaz the speaker, but from the inspired apostle who quotes and applies them. For of Eliphaz in general, in common with Bildad and Zophar, we have God's immediate condemnation: "My wrath is kindled against thee, and against thy two friends, for ye have not spoken of me the thing that is right." Job 42:7. It would therefore be as unjust to charge upon inspiration the sentiments it records to have been uttered, as it would be to make a human historian responsible for all the bad deeds and unrighteous sentiments recorded in his history.

In all the historical and biographical portions of Scripture the relation of God towards the matters recorded is exactly the relation of an historian towards the materials of his history; his responsibility is for the relation, and not for the things related. . . . . .

How natural this province of inspiration is, may be seen by the analogy of human things. Suppose a superior, not employing an amanuensis, for that would suggest the erroneous idea of a mechanical dictation, but superintending the composition of a narrative; what more natural than that his suggestions and corrections should produce the concurrence of two minds in one and the same composition?

This subject must not be dismissed without a further caution. The communication of truth to the intelligence of the sacred writer appears to have been the ordinary rule. But, as if presciently to guard against the supposition that the Divine element in Scripture closes with this, some notable exceptions have been recorded. That the prophets did ordinarily understand the messages they embodied in words, and were as far as possible removed from mere machines bereft of intelligent consciousness of what they were doing, is evident from the effect produced by the message in certain specified cases upon the feelings of the writer. Thus Ezekiel, divinely warned of the unbelief and opposition of Israel, and amazed at the picture of human sin and Divine vengeance presented to him, "remained astonished for seven days." Ezek. 3:15. Thus Daniel was "astonished" at the vision by the river Ulai. Dan. 7:27. In the same way, Habakkuk "trembled" at the knowledge of the Divine indignation against his people, and gave utterance to his own unshaken confidence in God amid the sorest national calamities: "Yet will I rejoice in the Lord." Hab. 3:18. There was, therefore, an intelligent apprehension of the messages conveyed; not, perhaps, to the full height of their meaning, but as to their general character. On the other hand, we are warned that the prophets themselves did not always understand the entire purport of their own revelation. St. Peter asserts distinctly that the prophets "inquired and searched diligently what or what manner of time the Spirit of Christ which was in them did signify." 1 Peter 1:11. He also teaches that "no prophecy of the Scripture is of any private interpretation." Why? Because "the prophecy came not in old time by the will of man, but holy men of God spake as they were moved by the Holy Ghost." 2 Peter 1:21.

Here, as in other instances, both sides of the teaching must be combined into one common truth. On the one side, we are taught that inspiration was no mechanical influence, acting solely from the outside, as if it were possible to conceive that the living Spirit, the Spirit of life, its Lord and Giver, could pass over a living man's intellect and heart without stirring it into activity to the utmost capacity of its finite powers. On the other hand, we are warned against the opposite extreme of measuring the meaning of the Divine message by the meaning given to it by the human messenger. Not what the man intended, but what God intended, should be the object of our inquiry. As if to make this lesson as distinct as possible, we have not only the prediction of Caiaphas, but we have the inspired explanation of it. As understood by the wicked speaker, his words were an iniquitous encouragement to murder. As overruled by the Holy Spirit, they conveyed an interpretation of the profound mystery of the atonement. "This spake he not of himself, but being high priest that year, he prophesied that Jesus should die for (ὑπέρ) that nation, and not for that nation only, but that also he should gather together in one the children of God that were scattered abroad." John 11:51.

III. This undeniable instance of a verbal inspiration suitably introduces the farther element of Divine authority underlying the patent human agency. God not only chose the writers, prepared and disciplined the writers, supplemented and verified their information, but he also acted concurrently with them in its conveyance. Leaving in all their natural peculiarity the human elements of style and manner of thought and expression, or rather employing them as his foreintended instruments, the Spirit of God yet so far concurred as to secure that the truth should be accurately conveyed and expressed just as God willed it to be expressed. This will be seen if we consider that the existence of a divinely given knowledge in the minds of certain men could be of no possible good to any one else but themselves, except so far as it is made known. It is, therefore, as important to know whether the message has been accurately given by the sacred writers to us, as it is to know that it was accurately given by God to the sacred writers. The introduction of error, whether in the process of transmission from God to them, or in the process of transmission from them to us, would be equally fatal. We stand at the farther link of the chain; and if a failure exists in any part of it, it matters not in the slightest degree in what particular link it exists. If the chain snaps next to the hand that holds it, it is the same to us as if it snapped at the farther end. It must be secure throughout, or it cannot be secure at all. If the Divine will has not been accurately conveyed to us, then we have not got a revelation.

The sacred writers had it, and they have given us their conceptions of it; but as these conceptions are simply their own, and as we are specifically taught that they did not fully understand their own predictions, an indefinite element of contingency and doubt is introduced fatal to all absolute certainty and truth. For what then, if truth comes to us in this shape and in this only, becomes of the lofty claims advanced by Scripture, and of the tremendous issues of life and death asserted to hang upon our acceptance or rejection of it? Surely we must be judged by the revelation as it is received by ourselves, not as it was received by men, the latest of whom died nearly two thousand years ago. But if the Divine authority stopped with the transmission of the revelation to the writers, and did not extend to its transmission from the writers to us, then we have only the human description of a Divine revelation, and not the Divine revelation itself.

But the whole question becomes so indefinitely complicated and embarrassed by limiting the Divine agency in this manner, that it becomes impossible to frame any consistent conceptions of inspiration at all. If it had been possible to bring the human mind in any way into immediate contact with the inspired minds of the prophets and apostles, without the intervention of any secondary instrument, then we might have received the Divine revelation with no farther sources of error than are inherent in any case in the intellectual and moral weaknesses of man; but of such a possibility the wildest visionary does not dream. What they received from God we can only receive from them through the vehicle of words, and nothing can alter the fact that the veracity of the truth transmitted must be equivalent, neither more nor less, to the accuracy of the words which convey it.

But, further, it is generally admitted that the scriptural writers were inspired men. Is it meant that they were inspired only to receive, and not inspired to communicate? If so, then, so far as the act of putting into words the teaching of God is concerned, they were not inspired. The inspiration ceased with the act contemplated in it; that is, with the receiving of truth from God. So far as concerns their writings, they were inspired men no longer; they were, therefore, ordinary men, and no more— liable to ordinary human weaknesses and mistakes. If it be replied that they were inspired men all through, in the act of transmitting to us as well as in the act of receiving from God, then this is all we contend for; then the inspiration extended to their writing, and the authority of God is coextensive with the inspiration; that is, it extends to the writing. Accordingly, it is of the writing, not of the men who wrote, that inspiration is directly affirmed. The specific word occurs but once, and then is applied to the thing, not the persons. The Scripture is God-inspired; but the Scripture is not the sense. The soul possesses no orthography. The words expressing the sense are written, but not the sense separate from the words. Unless, therefore, by the inspiration of the writing we are to understand the mere act of moving the pen, the inspiration must be the inspiration of the words, since the words, and the words alone, are written. The language of the Bible undeniably suggests an immense presumption in favor of the inspiration of the words. The reiterated use of such phrases as "thus saith the Lord," "the word of the Lord," or in the plural, "the words of the Lord," as the term is employed with great frequency in the New Testament, when the plural word cannot possibly refer to any thing but to the separate words making up the one communication—can bear no other meaning than that of a verbal inspiration, if the language has a meaning at all. Whatever reason we have for believing the Bible to contain a true revelation from God, we have equally for believing in the inspiration of the words which convey it, and through which alone it is known to us.

The human element, therefore, is not so to be understood as to derogate from the action of God in his word, as selecting, preparing, and teaching the writers, and by a concurrent act protecting the transmission of the message from verbal inaccuracy and mistakes.

IV. But, further, the Divine authority carries with it the guarantee of unerring veracity. Scripture is the product of two constituent elements, the Divine and the human. But it is formed, not by their fusion together in a third something, neither Divine nor human, but by their coincidence and co-operation. Hence it follows, as already stated, that both the elements are to be maintained complete. This can only be done by retaining what is essential on either side—all, without reserve, necessary to the existence of the authority of God on the one side, and the intelligent instrumentality of man upon the other. It follows that the human element does not derogate from the absolute truth of Scripture. When the words "human element" are used in the sense of necessarily involving in the composition of Scripture the mistakes characteristic of secular compositions—in other words, as implying that, because there is a human element in the word of God, there must also be mistakes in it—their use involves not only ambiguity of language, but a fallacy of thought. Man is as clearly fallible as God is clearly infallible. But to be fallible, or capable of making mistakes, is not the same as making mistakes; the liability must not be confounded with the act. To be wrong is a separable accident, not an inseparable property of human nature. If it was of the essence of humanity, then man never could be right, but must be universally and invariably wrong; but man is sometimes right, sometimes wrong. Many human narratives are wholly true; a thing may be wholly human, and yet not untrue. To be wrong, therefore, is not essential to the human element; and the fact that the Scriptures were written by human instruments does not prove the existence of mistakes in them; all it proves is, that in the absence of any other influence to prevent it, there might be mistakes in them. But this corrective influence is supplied by the Divine element; for to be right is an essential of the Divine nature. It is not even conceivable that the Omniscient should be capable of ignorance, the All-wise capable of mistake, the All-holy capable of fraud. What is not essential to the agency of man may therefore be omitted, without affecting the true human element. What is essential to the agency of God must be maintained, or else the perfection of the Divine element is lost. There is no reason on the human side why there should be errors in Scripture; but there is the most conclusive reason on the Divine side why there should not be. The Divine authority, therefore, carries with it the Divine veracity.

Thus the two elements are each maintained in their fulness and integrity. How they were united we can no more explain than we can explain the union of the Godhead and the manhood in the one inseparable person of Christ. But we assert the fact on the authority of a revelation bearing a Divine stamp on its very front. If we cannot explain how it can be, neither is any one competent to say that it cannot be, since our human experience supplies repeated analogies to prove its possibility. We maintain the fact of the union, without propounding any theory to account for it. Both elements exist together everywhere. The Divine element does not destroy the human individualities of character, thought, style, and language; the human element does not derogate from the authority of a revelation from God, or necessitate the admixture of error with the all-embracing knowledge and unerring wisdom of the Omniscient. Every part of the Bible is human, and every part is Divine. There are two concurrent elements, and the result is the

word of God, that "liveth and abideth for ever."
1 Pet. 1:23.

But while there is concurrence between the two,
there is likewise a manifest subordination.   The
spring of all the revelation, as the spring of all life,
is in God, and man is but his instrument.   No other
relation than this is conceivable, when the Creator
and the creature are brought together in a community of action.   In entering upon the study of the
Scriptures, it is with the human element that we
are brought first into contact; for this is the link
of the chain nearest to ourselves.   The earthly
messenger, with his earthly language and personal
peculiarities, is the first object presented to us.
But we must not stop with him, but must trace the
revelation upwards, through its secondary instruments, to its originating cause.   The voice is no
longer human, but Divine.   We pass into the immediate presence of Him whose sovereignty invests
the written word with authority, and whose wisdom
bestows upon it the attribute of perfect and unmin-
gled truth.

CHAPTER XI.

WHAT IS TRUTH?

What is meant by saying that Scripture is True or Untrue—Adjectives of Intensity and their Meaning, "Strictly True," "Literally True"—Adjectives of Quality, and the Ambiguous Sense in which they are used, "Logically True," "Scientifically True"—Nature of Truth the Same in all Cases—The Objective Fact or Facts—The Subjective Account of It—The Intention of the Narrator—The Selection of the Language involves no Change in the Truth of the Fact—Logic and its Forms—The Pauline Epistles—The Professed Character and Object of the Scriptures.

Misapprehensions arising from the ambiguous use of the terms "Divine element" and "human element," have been corrected in the previous chapter. It has been shown that the two are concurrent constituents of Scripture, and that they must be maintained everywhere distinct, and nowhere separate.

Another class of misapprehensions is next to be considered. These arise from an uncertain use of the word "truth," and from the addition of epithets to the word, as if there were degrees of truth, or kinds and qualities of truth, and as if truth were not itself invariably and universally the same.

Two classes of expressions require to be considered. The one consists of adjectives of intensity and force, as in the phrases, "strictly true," "simply true," "absolutely true," "literally true." The other arises from the use of adjectives of quality, as, "logically true," "scientifically true," "historically true." These are generally employed to express doubt in the veracity of Scripture, and in its inerrability, or freedom from all error. The expressions are themselves highly ambiguous. Upon a theory of universal doubt, they might be consistently employed; but such a theory finds its refutation in the common sense and conscience of mankind. On any other theory, they can only serve to conceal the real nature of the objection they are intended to convey, and its actual bearing upon the authority of Scripture.

In the first place, care must be taken not to confound what is meant by truth with the word truths, as commonly used. Truths are simply statements that are true. There may, therefore, be a great variety of truths, for they may be found in every branch of human knowledge. There may be historical truths, scientific truths, moral truths. The common word "truths" is applied to them because they have this common quality—that they are true. The question now to be settled is, What is that common quality we express by the word "truth?"

Truth is the correspondence of a representation with the thing represented. This correspondence must be measured by the avowed purpose of the representation. Thus the term may be applied to a picture in two ways. The painting may be true to some reality of actual life, or it may only be true to an ideal existing in the mind of the painter. A portrait is an instance of the first kind. What is called a fancy landscape, or a grotesque representation of fairies, sprites, and ghosts, are instances of the second kind. It would be very unjust to measure the ideal picture by the standard applied to the portrait. It would be vain, for instance, to object to it, that it was not true to the reality, or that such forms as are presented on a canvas can never have existed. The answer would be, that the painting was never intended to be true to an existing reality, but only to represent forms existing in the fancy of the painter. To the intention of the artist the picture would be true, and only untrue to the blundering misapprehension of the critic. The professed purpose of the representation must, therefore, be taken into account in judging of its accuracy or inaccuracy.

When, therefore, it is said that truth is the correspondence of a representation to the thing represented, the statement involves three things: (1) It involves the actual existence of the things to be represented. (2) It involves the accuracy of the representation. (3) It involves the intention on the part of the agent to represent certain things, and no others. A painter does not intend his picture to represent any thing or every thing a critic chooses to make it; but he intends it to represent certain defined objects, and by its correspondence with their reality, its truth or otherwise must be measured. No opinion can be formed on this point without knowing the reality as it exists on one side, and keeping in view the avowed purpose of the representation on the other.

This is as true of a representation made by words to the understanding, as of a representation made by form and color to the eye. The familiar experience of ordinary life may readily suggest an illustration. Let it be supposed that some event has taken place, a disastrous accident, a great public spectacle, a hotly contested battle. Let it be supposed that some person is giving to another a narration of the event. Such a circumstance may occur every day. Let it be recalled, and a very little consideration will show that belief or disbelief in the story involves all the three conditions abovenamed, namely, the occurrence of the facts, the correspondence of the narrative with the facts, and the intention of the narrator.

If the facts never occurred, the story could not be said to be either true or untrue, since it would become a mere fiction. If the facts took place, and the narration corresponds with the occurrence, then it would be true; if it does not correspond, it will not be true. But this correspondence must be measured by the professed object of the narrator. Suppose a person to object that the story was not true because it omitted some of the facts, the objection would only hold good if the narrator professed to tell all the facts; otherwise it would still be true, although a part of the facts were omitted because they did not fall in with the design of the narrator. For instance, a man has lost his life in some fatal accident. It is the object of an eye-witness to narrate to his relatives the mode in which he perished. Would his narration be untrue unless he included in his tale the entire series of facts connected with the whole of the accident? Thus, whenever truth is in question, the question involves the reality of the thing narrated, the correspondence of the narration, and the purpose of the narrator.

In discussing whether Scripture is true or not true, all these conditions must be kept in mind. We can only say that it is untrue when, from our knowledge of the realities, we can compare the Divine narrative with them, and ascertain the correspondence or otherwise. In regard to many facts of Scripture, such as relate to the nature of God, his actions and will, and the unseen and future world, we have no independent knowledge of our own, and therefore no means of measurement. But in regard to many other facts of Scripture, we possess sufficient independent information to judge, and are therefore able-positively to affirm the truth or untruth of the sacred narrative. The question will be, not whether all the facts of the case have been accurately recorded, but only whether that portion of them has been accurately recorded which it was the purpose of the sacred writers to record.

Here, therefore, we find the answer to the skeptical question whether there is such a thing as truth, or whether any thing is true which men believe to be true. Thus one school of infidels have said that the Bible is true; only meaning by the words that it accurately describes the religious belief of mankind at different periods of the world. Others have said that " every truth is a falsehood," which is an absurdity; for what is false cannot be a truth. The words can really mean no more than that what one man believes to be true, some other man believes to be false.

Is there nothing absolutely true—nothing absolutely false? The definition already given supplies an answer. Truth is the correspondence of the representation with the thing represented. Do things exist independently of our conception of them, or do they only exist because we conceive them, and cease to exist when we cease to conceive of them ? The latter would be an absurdity indignantly rejected by men's plain sense. Every instinct of reason and conscience decides otherwise. We owe allegiance to a real God; we live in a real world; we form part of a real system ; we are affected by real events; we are real ourselves, with real bodies and souls; and there is a real eternity for which to provide, however idly men may dream of such matters. But if there are existing things to be represented, then it must be possible that the representation should correspond or should not correspond with the reality of the thing. In the one case it is true; in the other it is false. Things are not, therefore, what men make them, true to one man and false to another, but they exist in themselves fixed as the Creator; "by whom are all things, and for whom are all things." Heb. 2 : 10.

There can therefore be no degrees in truth. Either the description corresponds, or it does not. When we meet with the phrases "partly true" or "perfectly true," "simply true," "entirely true," we must understand that they refer to degrees of extension or application, not to degrees of truth. By partly true, we mean that part of it is true and part untrue, not that the same part is in one sense true and another untrue. By "perfectly true," "simply true," "entirely true," we mean that the whole is true without exception, and that every part of the representation corresponds to the thing represented. With regard to each individual part there can be no degrees, no gradations; it is either true or it is not true.

The same rule should be applied to the second class of phrases—logically true, scientifically true, historically true. Their only proper meaning is, that those parts of the Bible referring to logical arguments, to matters of science, or points of history, are true or not true as the speaker may intend to say. But this is not the sense in which they are ordinarily used. They are employed to disguise the naked alternatives of truth or falsehood alone open to our adoption, and to suggest that there are different kinds of truth, so that the Bible may be in one sense true, and yet in another sense untrue. They are employed to soothe the sense of reverence towards the word of God, and to put it off its guard. Their use disposes men to give up their belief in the truth of the Bible without experiencing a shock to faith, or perceiving the full meaning of the charge they are bringing upon its Divine Author. The interests of Christianity demand that the question should be fearlessly faced. The authority of the Christian Scriptures must stand or fall with their truth. We cannot lose the one and yet in any degree maintain the other. If their contents are not true, they cannot be the infallible word of God. If they are true, no false distinctions must be allowed to detract from their full and plenary authority over the human intellect and conscience. If they are true at all, they are logically true, scientifically true, historically true—in every sense true.

For these words denote no variety of truth, but only variety in the mode of its statement, and in the character of the language chosen to express it. This language necessarily varies with the standpoint from which the subject is regarded. An object may be one in itself, and yet may be regarded in many relations and from many points of view. The sun is but one; but it may be regarded with reference to its office as light-bearer to our world, or to the influence of its genial warmth in quickening nature, or to the solar system of which it is the centre, or in its relation to the other portions of the universe, or with reference to its own substance, or with regard to its office of irritating into motion the luminous ether, or as to the chemical qualities of its rays, or as to their component parts, or as to their relation to color, or in other points which an ingenious mind may easily suggest. The one object may thus enter into the inquiries of half a dozen different branches of natural science, and each one of them would have its special point of view, and a technical language of its own. To combine all these modes of conceiving, and consequently of speaking, into one, would be impossible. It is necessary, therefore, to select the aspect in which it is to be regarded; whether it shall be viewed with the eyes of an ordinary observer, or of a poet, or of a philosopher, or of an astronomer, or of a geographer, or of a chemist.

Yet all this variety of view would make no difference in the object itself; the difference would be only in the thinker and speaker, and the common phenomena would remain absolutely unaltered by the verbal differences of description. The statement might be equally true in any case, and the varieties of description would not be degrees of truth, but only diversities in the mode of presenting it. The same thing is true of groups of objects as of single objects, of trains of thought, and of processes of argument. No subject can be submitted to the action of the human mind which does not admit of being viewed in different relations, and consequently of being described in different forms of words, without compromising in any of them the perfect correspondence of the representation with the thing represented on that side of it which alone enters into the purpose of the writer.

With this plain principle applied to the phrases now under discussion, it will appear that the truth of any statement is independent of the mode of its expression; and that, however widely the expression may vary, the truth remains the same so long as the representation continues to correspond with the thing represented. The use of one class of terms in preference to another varies the form of the statement, but not the truth of it. When it is objected that one part of Scripture is not logically true, another not scientifically true, another not historically true, the phrases mean no more than that they are not couched in the technical forms of the logician, expressed in the technical language of the man of science, or framed after the technical methods of the historian.

The first two of these phrases require a few additional remarks; the last will need a more extended examination, and will consequently be postponed for another chapter.

1. It has been objected that some of the reasonings in the Pauline epistles are not "logically true." But logic has no special kind of truth peculiar to itself. It simply professes to give an account of the necessary laws of thought—laws invariably observed in all correct reasoning, however unconsciously they may be used by the reasoner himself. If reasoning be correct, it follows these laws; if it does not folfow these laws, it is not correct. All reasoning consists of premises and a conclusion, the premises being what are popularly called the reasons on which we rest the conclusion. If the conclusion properly follows from the premises, then it is logically correct, although the special terms and peculiar forms adopted by logicians may be wholly absent.

Hence an argument may be stated in many different ways, and may be amplified in this part of it or in that, according to the mental habits and tendencies of the arguer. Or parts of the train of reasoning may be omitted, and it may be left to the intelligence of the reader to supply it. Or the mode of arguing may deal in abrupt transitions and complicated connections, or connections apparently complicated, because we do not hold the explanatory thread of reference which existed in the hands of the original writers and readers. Or it may admit of rhetorical interruptions, vehement appeals, impassioned outbursts, or lofty description. These peculiarities belong wholly to the minds of the writers, and they are perfectly familiar to us in all branches of human knowledge. No two men will state an argument in precisely the same way, because their mental gifts are not precisely similar; yet the argument itself, when reduced to logical form, may be identical and as absolutely conclusive in the one form as in the other, each form being adapted to some special tendency of mind.

Now all these peculiarities are to be found in different parts of the Bible, and many of them are very prominent in the writings of St. Paul. They belong to the human element of Scripture, for it has been already shown that the personal individualities of the writers are essential to it, and only so far belong to the Divine side as God saw fit to use the agency of men gifted with these peculiar tendencies of thought and utterance. To have reduced the whole of Scripture into a series of digested syllogisms would have been to make it unintelligible to the mass of mankind, would have destroyed its power and sublimity, would have rendered the writings of inspired men wholly dissimilar to the writings of uninspired men, and would have absolutely contradicted in this one sphere of God's action the principles of moral discipline maintained by him in every other sphere without exception. Technical precision is happily as absent from Scripture as is loose inconclusiveness. Logical truth is as universally present as logical forms are universally absent.

2. It has been objected that parts of Scripture are not " scientifically true." The stock objection of infidelity to the standing still of the sun in the days of Joshua is still urged by modern writers, and may therefore be used as an illustration, although it has been refuted even to weariness. I do not discuss the possibility of the miracle, for that belongs to a different branch of inquiry altogether, but only the language in which it is described, and the objection brought against the inspiration of Scripture from its alleged want of scientific accuracy. That the language is that of the ordinary spectator, and not that of the man of science, is most true; but it is the language of the ordinary spectator of every age, and no more peculiar to the fourteenth century before Christ than to the nineteenth century after Christ. An uninspired writer recording the fact in our own day would use exactly the language used by Joshua. The event is described from the optical point of view, as it appeared to the eyes of the spectators. But this mode of description is as accurate in this point of view as the most precise language of the astronomer would be in his point of view. The truth or otherwise of the fact does not come into question, and must be decided on perfectly different grounds, namely, as a matter of evidence. The only possible question that can be

raised is whether Joshua's mode of describing the miracle is the best. When men are writing with a view to ordinary life, they use the language of ordinary life, just as Joshua did. I open a modern almanac, and I find it stated that on the 14th day of May the sun will rise at 4h. 13m. Is not the statement true, and scientifically true, since science attests its accuracy? And yet it is not expressed in scientific language. In the same way, and for precisely the same reasons, those portions of Scripture which speak of the phenomena of the natural world are not written in scientific language, and yet they may be true, and scientifically true, nevertheless.

The language used in any book, whether inspired or uninspired, must ever be selected with reference to the object contemplated by the book and to the readers for whom it is intended. To write a poem or a history in the language of science would be ridiculous. Equally ridiculous is it to object to the inspiration of Scripture, that it is expressed in language appropriate to the times, circumstances, and personal peculiarities alike of the authors and of the readers. Would it be expected that God should employ human language as the channel of a revelation for mankind, and yet so employ it as to make it absurd? We need to watch against being misled by our own descriptions of parts of Scripture when we speak of some portions as poetry, some as history, some as biography. All these and other portions are but parts of one great plan, and themselves share in the characteristics of the plan. To

take separate parts, and judge them separately from
the design of the whole, is only to mistake the conditions of the case. The Bible at large is not a
poem, nor is it a work of science, nor is it a history,
nor is it a manual of biography; and therefore it
cannot be measured by the rules applicable to compositions belonging to the sphere of poetry, or science, or history, or biography. The Bible is a revelation given for the declared purpose of making
men wise unto salvation. In constructing the whole
marvellous book, God has used poetry, and history,
and science, and biography, just so far as he saw
each of them to be appropriate to the contemplated
object and harmonious with the general design of
the whole. To measure the whole by its parts, and
not the parts by the whole, would be a strange perversion indeed of our ordinary modes of arguing.
The Scriptures constitute a revelation adapted in
its separate stages to the ages when it was given,
and in its totality, adapted to universal humankind.
We may venture to apply to it the test which our
Lord applied to the Sabbath, and to say that the
Bible was made for man, and not man for the Bible.
Its Divine congruity with human habits and methods of speech is not less remarkable in the diversities entering into its human element, than in the
overshadowing authority inherent in the Divine.

CHAPTER XII.

HISTORICAL TRUTH.

History distinguished from Biography—The Partial Character of all History—Its Diverse Branches and Objects—A Human Transcript of the Divine Knowledge Impossible—Events and Their Causes—Principles and Their Evidences—I. What Historical Truth does not require—II. What it does require—The Genealogies of St. Matthew and St. Luke—Historical Truth not involved in Their Reconciliation—The Object and Character of the Genealogies.

"The books of Moses are not historically true." So says the modern objector. What then is historical truth, and in what respects does it differ from any other truth? I reply that it differs in no respect. The words are but a euphemism to disarm suspicion, and to soften down by gentle words what might otherwise appear as a harsh denial of the veracity of Holy Scripture.

History constitutes a separate branch of human literature. It may therefore have methods of its own, and a mode of speaking belonging to itself. This is not the case at present; for what professes to be historical criticism, is as yet little more than the arbitrary opinion of individual men, guided by no settled principles and working by no recognized rules. But let us suppose that historical science should acquire a shape as distinctive as logic, or astronomy, or geology, it would in that case acquire

a language and form of its own, in the same way as
these have done.   In such a case, the phrase historically true might be used, as the phrases logically
true or scientifically true are used, to express one
particular mode of viewing truth and one particular mode of expressing it.   And the objection, the
Bible is not historically true, would mean, its statements are not couched in the historical form ; or
if not this, it would have no definite meaning.   But
such an objection is really no objection at all.
Scripture no more professes to be a human history,
or to be a formal history at all, than it professes to
be a book of human poetry or a compilation of human biography.   It contains history, and poetry,
and biography, but only as parts of something
higher than them all.   Scripture professes to be
a Divine revelation of saving truth, conveying a
knowledge of the facts of the past only so far as
they are necessary to the duties of the present and
the prospects of the future.   As it bears a character
different from all other books, so it must be measured by a different standard ; as it springs from the
highest of all authority, it cannot be subject to laws
inferior to itself.

History consists of a record of the past, with
this limitation, that it concerns itself primarily with
the fortunes of some society or body of men, and
subordinately only with individual men.   The latter is the province of biography.   History occupies
the wider circle of groups of men.   Hence it was
said by Dr. Arnold, History " is the biography of a
society : it does not appear to me to be history at

all, but simply biography, unless it finds in the persons who are its subjects something of a common purpose, the accomplishment of which is the object of their common life. History is to the common life of many what biography is to the life of an individual."

History will therefore consist of two parts, the explanation of causes and the statement of facts. Its highest object is, to record the great events of the past, and to trace their producing causes. The mere outward circumstances of mankind will constitute its least important portion ; the mental, moral, and religious circumstances its most important portion, since the outward events of the world have ever been shaped by its moral influences and conditions. A mere disjointed accumulation of detailed facts will not constitute a history. It is necessary that they should be regarded in their mutual order and relation towards each other, and be presented, not only in their true succession of time, but in their proper sequence of cause and effect. The past has not consisted of a series of abrupt disconnected and isolated facts, but of a series of events where each one has been as closely united to what went before and what has followed after, as are the links of an unbroken chain. The record of the moral causes that have operated on the fortunes of mankind is the highest purpose of history. But these causes can only be explained by a knowledge of facts in detail; and history therefore deals, in the second place, with their investigation, analysis, and accurate narration. But these facts are the proofs or

evidences of the causes, and must therefore correspond with them. It is the object of the historian
to record, not all the facts of the past—for it will be
seen that such a record would be simply impossible—but those classes of facts which elucidate the
principles of the history, and belong to that special side of it which it is his object to narrate. The
selection of the facts will consequently follow the
professed purpose of the record. Such as are the
causes the historian desires to explain, such will be
the facts selected to prove their existence and illustrate their action.

Now a historian may write from any one of
many standpoints, or for one of many purposes.
In each case the facts narrated will correspond with
them. He may chronicle the history of some particular race or of some special tribe, and the origin,
progress, and downfall of that particular body will
constitute the limits of his history. Or he may
enlarge the area of his labors, and deal with groups
of nations; as, for instance, Mr. Alison has done in
his " History of Europe." On this wider sphere,
many persons and many events which stood prominent on the narrower stage of one particular people will naturally disappear amid the broader interests, and another set of persons and events take
their place. On the other hand, new sets of facts
altogether will be introduced, bearing on the mutual relations of separate nations towards each other,
their affinities and conflicts, and the international
interests of the larger whole constituting in this
case the primary object of the historian. Or, again,

the writer may take a bolder flight, and select the history of mankind in general as his theme. Here again, as the point of view is varied, so will the topics be varied and the correlative facts be varied likewise. He will deal less with national peculiarities of race, constitution, country, and climate, and more with facts, and qualities, and moral influences belonging to all men in common. The very character and moral color of his picture will be varied by the variation of his standpoint. Perhaps at the very period when the historian of some particular nation would have to dip his pen in the gloomy hues of national disaster, the historian of mankind at large may depict a condition of advancing civilization and progressive prosperity.

Still wider diversities of object and standpoint in the work of the historian may arise in other directions. Thus he may propose to himself to write the history of literature; and then the literary men of the world, its great thinkers and writers, stand out at once into the foreground. Or he may wish to write the history of human thought; and then its various schools of philosophy will occupy the page, and the reader will pass into a class of subjects so different from what he finds in the pages of the ordinary historian, that it is like stepping into a new world. Or again, he may undertake to record the history of the industrial arts and manufactures of mankind; and here a new set of words and phrases, a new order of facts, and a new series of events and circumstances, will supply the materials of his story. Or he may take upon himself the more intricate and difficult task of writing the history of its scientific discoveries in the various but closely-related provinces of astronomy, geology, chemistry, botany, mineralogy, etc. Or his sphere may be a more familiar one; and he may deal with the domestic and social habits of mankind, widely varying as they have done in different lands and climates, and during different stages of civilization. Still, when these have been enumerated, the varieties of human history are not nearly exhausted. Their possible number almost defies enumeration. The history of government, of religion, of representative institutions, of ecclesiastical affairs, of laws, of architecture, of trade and commerce, of wars, of military and naval affairs, are further instances of the almost endless diversity of object and standpoint from which human affairs may be regarded.

These varieties are not imaginary. Actual histories exist under each of these separate heads. Grote's "History of Greece," Gibbon's "Decline and Fall of the Roman Empire," Rollin's "Universal History," Pritchard's "Physical History of Man," are illustrations. Hallam's "History of Literature," Brucker's "History of Philosophy," Whewell's "History of the Inductive Sciences," Merryweather's "Domestic Habits of the Middle Ages," Delolme on "The Constitution," Neander's "Ecclesiastical History," Ferguson's "Handbook of Architecture," Napier's "History of the Peninsular War," James' "Naval History of Great Britain," or Kinglake's "Crimea," may be enumerated, and the list might be indefinitely increased.

But without entering on a wider range, seventeen different kinds of history have been enumerated, sharply distinguished from each other in the classes of facts recorded and the character of the language employed. If these are even cursorily compared, it will be found (*a*) that whole classes of facts are included in one history, and omitted in another; (*b*) that where the same classes of facts are recorded, the details widely differ; in regard to particular events, circumstances will be found to be recorded with the utmost particularity in one case, which are passed over in total silence in another; (*c*) that the same facts are stated in different proportions, the stress lying from one point of view on facts which, from another point of view, become wholly unimportant; (*d*) instances are found of facts recorded by different writers which appear to be directly contradictory to each other, but which a third fact incidentally noticed proves to be perfectly consistent and harmonious. In some instances the contrasts presented by different histories to each other are so strong as to call into play a different set of faculties on the part of the reader, and to constitute a totally distinct line of study.

Yet a moment's reflection will show that the subject-matter of all these various histories is but one and the same throughout. Mankind has only had one history, and not a dozen different ones. It has not lived the same stage of its existence over and over and over again. Its life has been but one, its order of events one, its progress one. It is but the same human nature in the same world viewed from different standpoints, and from different parts of the united whole. The diversity is not objective in the history, but subjective in the historian. He selects those portions of the whole which accord with his particular object and fall in with his special purpose; but in the occurrence the entire history of mankind has progressed together, the individual nations and the collective whole, their literature, philosophy, arts, science, habits, government, religion, laws, and commerce, have advanced side by side, the distinct but inseparable parts of one aggregate whole.

Suppose therefore that some skeptic should take his stand on some one branch of history, and making this the standard of all other branches, should object to the credibility of all the others, because they do not harmonize with that one, he would do exactly what is done when men object to the plenary inspiration of Scripture on the ground that its contents are not "historically true." The answer is the same in both cases, because the mistake would be the same. The diversity is not in the truth or otherwise of the facts, but solely in the mode of its narration. It does not represent degrees of truth, but only varieties of the standpoint from which it is regarded.

These considerations render it easy to lay down the conditions which historical truth does not require and which it does require.

I. It does not require (*a*) that no facts should be omitted, since such a condition would be impracticable. In the infinite complexity of human affairs,

and the variety of causes concurring to bring about
the events of human history, it is a natural impossibility that human knowledge should comprise
them all, or if they were known, that human understanding should be able to unravel them all. The
only mind capable of knowing all, without omission,
is the mind of the Omniscient. But human history
is not a mere transcript of the Divine mind, nor
can it be so. "We cannot by any amount of research know all that all the successive millions
forming a community have thought, said, done, suffered, or seemed; the facts that we can know, or
that knowing we can visibly take into account, are
at least in every case but a miserable percentage of
this ideal aggregate. . . . The real question is, since
all cannot be known and remembered, What is it
best to know and remember? Since the facts out
of which we must construct our histories in idea
are but a small proportion, a mere remaining shred
of that enormous intertwined infinity of facts which
actually went into the histories while the web was
being woven, are there any kinds or orders of facts
which more than others it is desirable for the purposes of history to secure and keep hold of?" (En-
cycl. Brit., art. History.) The mere omission of
facts out of a series is therefore no failure of historical truth. It is open to an objector to allege
that such and such facts should not have been
omitted; but the mere fact of omission is no ground
of objection. Omission somewhere is inseparable
from the defects of the creatures to whom God has
given the revelation.

(*h*) Historical truth does not require that in several narratives of the same events the facts recorded should be absolutely identical. One part may be given and another omitted. Or the facts given may be viewed from different points, corresponding either to the objects or to the personal character of the narrator. Such variations furnish a strong evidence of the veracity of the writers, and not a disproof of it, since they show their independence of each other, and therefore present as many witnesses as there are writers. These variations only become contradictions when the different statements are so palpably opposed to each other, that one and all cannot equally be true. Thus, in regard to the admitted variations in the evangelical narratives of the New Testament, as, for instance, in regard to the blind men cured at Jericho, the skeptic must prove that both accounts cannot be true. The Christian advocate has to show that they may both be true. He is not called to prove any particular mode in which they are true. If half a dozen conceivable modes of reconciling them present themselves, this very variety only presents the stronger disproof of the skeptical assertion that they cannot both be true.

This may be illustrated by the passages referred to. It is objected that St. Matthew speaks of two blind men who addressed our Lord as he departed from Jericho. St. Mark speaks only of one at the same spot; and St. Luke, of one as our Lord "was come nigh unto Jericho." Luke 18:35. Hence it is argued that the narratives are not "historically true," and therefore cannot be inspired. We reply that there is no necessary contradiction between the narratives, and that therefore they may all be equally true. Mark mentions by name one of the two referred to by St. Matthew, and many conjectural reasons may be assigned for his doing so, such as that Bartimæus was personally known to St. Mark himself, or to those into whose hands his gospel was first placed. Luke states one blind man to have been healed as our Lord entered Jericho, and Matthew two to have been healed as he left it. We do not know what pause our Lord made in Jericho. We are told indeed, not only that he passed through Jericho, but that he "entered and passed through it;" and the expression seems to imply a pause more or less. That the words "passed through" imply direction only, and not continuous and unbroken movement, is shown by the fact that the same word is used of journeys which could not have been accomplished without pauses for rest and sleep. Thus St. Luke records (ch. 17, ver. 11) that he "passed through" the midst of Samaria and Galilee, a journey occupying several days. If our Lord made a pause in Jericho, what more natural than that the tidings of the cure wrought on entering the city should become known throughout the community of the blind in Jericho, and that others should have sought the same help as he left the city, and should have asked it purposely in the words which had effectually attracted the attention of the wonder-working Son of David in the case of their companion. Or the apparent difficulty may be solved in another direction altogether, for at the time of our Lord there existed two Jerichos, the ancient city and the new, situated in proximity to each other, and in coming out of the one our Lord and his apostles would have been drawing nigh unto the other. Thus variation is not contradiction. Historical truth neither requires the absence of omission nor the absence of variation in the narrative.

II. But it requires (*a*) that the facts should have taken place as they are recorded to have taken place; that they should be real facts attested by persons qualified to bear witness to their occurrence; (*b*) that the facts should correspond with the statements they are adduced to illustrate, as when St. John states the object of his gospel to be "that ye might believe that Jesus is the Christ, the Son of God; and that believing ye might have life through his name," John 20:31—where it is involved that the facts narrated in his gospel are sufficient to prove the divinity of the Son of God and his atoning efficacy.

No better illustration can perhaps be adduced of these conditions than is afforded by the two genealogies of Christ. A great deal of learned ingenuity has been expended in reconciling them, and at least two hypotheses have been suggested, either of which sufficiently meets the facts of the case, since, as already said, the Christian apologist only needs to show that they may be reconciled, and not to decide absolutely upon the mode of reconciliation. I refer to the supposition that the genealogy of Matthew contains our Lord's legal descent through Joseph, and the genealogy of Luke his actual descent through Mary, and to the alternative supposition that the one contains his official and the other his personal genealogy. The question is one of very considerable interest to the biblical student, and is especially valuable as leading us to realize more than we are accustomed to do, the peculiarities of Jewish genealogy as they sprang out of the peculiar enactments of the Law and the tribal divisions of the Hebrew people. But the solution of an interesting problem must not be confounded with the question of the truth of the genealogies. This is quite distinct, and would be wholly unaffected by our absolute inability to reconcile the two accounts, if such an inability really existed.

We must view the details with reference to the proposition they are intended to prove. This is stated in the first words of St. Matthew: "The book of the generation of Jesus Christ, the son of David, the son of Abraham." The proposition to be proved is that Jesus Christ was the lineal heir of David, as David was the lineal descendant of Abraham. Now, supposing the facts to be true, they undoubtedly prove this, since they trace an unbroken genealogical line from Abraham down to Christ. If the names recorded by St. Matthew represent successive descent in the same line, then the proposition is proved. This would not be affected in the slightest degree by the fact that the genealogy of St. Matthew is avowedly artificial, that it is so arranged in an artificial form under three divisions of fourteen each, and that some names have been omitted in order to bring it into this shape. The use of these artificial forms is known to have existed among the Jews as a common practice, and instances are furnished in the genealogical list of Philo, who divides the generations from Adam to Moses into two classes of ten descents, and one of seven. A Samaritan poem arranges the descents of the same period into two sets of ten, and for this purpose omits six of the least important names. Thus omission does not invalidate the accuracy of the descent. For instance, in the second list of fourteen given by St. Matthew, three names—Ahaziah, Joash, and Amaziah—are omitted between Joram and Ozias; but the omission of the three intermediate links does not alter the fact that Ozias was the lineal descendant and heir of Joram, and this is all that the historical truth of the genealogy requires. Thus, in the third list, Eliakim is omitted between Josias and Jeconias; but this does not alter the fact that Jeconias was the lineal descendant and heir of Josias. It is the fact of this unbroken descent by blood which alone is expressed in the technical phrases uniting the successive stages of the descent together. Whether, in the descending scale of St. Matthew, the expression employed be that A begat B, or, in the ascending scale of St. Luke, it be that B was the son of A, the truth expressed is the same fact of lineal descent, and is wholly unaffected by the mode of its expression. That this class of phrases was used with much more latitude among the Jews than it would be used among ourselves, is proved by a variety of instances. Thus, in the Old Testament Jehu is described as the son of Nimshi, 1 Kings 19:16, whereas he was the son of Jehoshaphat, who was the son of Nimshi. The special form of speech employed must in every case be interpreted by its known usage. The names specified in the lists of St. Matthew and St. Luke lay in the natural order of generation and descent, and if so, they prove what they were intended to prove, and the genealogy is historically true.

Now there is not the shadow of an evidence to impugn the fact of this lineal descent in any one case specified in either genealogy. The objections raised by skeptics from an early age of the Christian era downwards, have been solely founded on the internal variations of the genealogies themselves. Into their discussion it is not my purpose to enter, because, however interesting, I regard them solely as a question for curiosity. The only point with which I concern myself is to show that both genealogies may be true, and that there is nothing in their variations to impugn their truth.

The proposition which they are employed to prove is our Lord's lineal descent, either by natural or by imputed filiation. The proposition itself is made in order to prove that the predicted marks of identity, by which the Messiah of the prophets was to be recognized, met in the person of Jesus of Nazareth. Whether the two genealogies are both the genealogies of Joseph, or whether they represent the one a legal heirship, and the other a natural descent; or whether, thirdly, the one is the genealogy of

Joseph, and the other the genealogy of Mary—in either case the conditions of the question remain the same. There are two ends, so to speak, to be united by a chain of descent, and these, too, cannot be altered. But the chain of descent might almost indefinitely alter. For the line of descent might conceivably be traced, not only through two, but through half a dozen varying channels, yet the first named and the last would remain the same, and the lineal descent uniting them be as close, and real, and true, in any one of the six different lines as in any other of them. When a genealogy extends through such great periods as the two thousand years from Abraham to Christ, it must inevitably have been divided into many collateral branches, parallel streams beginning at the same fountain-head, and debouching into the same estuary. This is not a matter of conjecture, but of historical fact.

Instances might be indefinitely multiplied, but one is as good for the purpose as a hundred. The lineal descent of Henry VIII., from king John, may be traced in two perfectly distinct lines, containing thirteen links in the one case, and eleven in the other, and they do not touch each other at any intermediate point. On the other side, the descent of James I. from Henry VII., also traceable in two lines, conjoins five successions in each line, and the five successions touch at two points, namely, Mary Queen of Scots, and Margaret, daughter of Henry VII. The descent is equally true in either case, and the truth would not be affected by any prolongation of the descent, so long as each link is connected by descent or inheritance with the links preceding or succeeding. The descent of our Lord from Abraham by lines of descent, converging at one point and diverging at another, is entirely consistent with known experience, and therefore with historic credibility. The exact genealogical tables which are known from Josephus to have been carefully kept in the temple of Jerusalem, and which perished at the destruction of the city, must necessarily have been exceedingly complicated, and must have admitted of variations in one and the same descent, much more intricate and various than are contained in the two evangelical genealogies. The reasons which may have guided the construction of these particular tables along one line rather than another, may be referred to considerations clear and intelligible to the Jews of that day. But in the absence of the facts, it would be a wanton waste of ingenuity for us to endeavor to supply them.

We must, however, bear in mind that the peculiar habits of the Jews, and the reference of all their institutions to the coming of the predicted Messiah, must very largely have increased the causes of intricacy existing in a similar case among ourselves. Thus it was the invariable habit of the Jews to trace their genealogies in the male line; and therefore to account the next of kin, or the husband of a sole surviving daughter, as standing in the place of a son. The whole system had reference to the indefeasible tenure of the land, the division of the tribes, and the privileges of the houses of Levi and David. That, according to Jewish usage, the links of a genealogy implied descent and heirship only, but not always the strict relation of a child to a father, is. abundantly illustrated in the genealogies of the Old Testament. Thus, Ephraim and Manasseh, the sons of Joseph, were reckoned among the other patriarchs, as if they had been sons, not grandsons of Jacob. Gen. 48:5. The list of the sons of Benjamin, (Gen. 46:21,) in the same way, contains grandsons as well as sons, and even the names are given differently in 1 Chron. 7:7 and 8:1. The imperfect acquaintance, which alone we possess, with the details of this subject, shows the absurdity of attempting to test, by an arbitrary and conjectural criticism, the details of lists so peculiar in their construction, so complicated in their details, and so removed in their facts from the possible reach of modern knowledge.

To object against the genealogies of our Lord, that they are couched in a Jewish form and framed according to Jewish habits, would only be to object against a human element of Scripture in the teeth of the fact that without a human element a revelation would have been impossible. Taking the human element as it exists, and making the necessary allowances for the peculiarity of form it has impressed upon the Scriptures, the genealogies are internally consistent, and bear upon their front the signs of genuineness and authenticity. There is not a solitary tittle of evidence to impugn their historical truth, or, therefore, to call into question the inspiration which directed the selection of these particular lists, and the accuracy of their details.

I have dwelt the more fully upon this instance in order to illustrate the mode in which Scripture must be dealt with, in fully maintaining alike its human and its Divine elements. Such a mode of interpretation sweeps away an immense mass of speculative objection. Historical truth is the same as all other truth, and has relation to the correspondence between the description and the thing described. It neither limits the point of view taken nor the character of the language selected, but only its accuracy. Whether the form of expression adopted be prosaic or poetical, didactic or devotional, popular or logical, optical or scientific; whether it be the language of ordinary biography or the stately diction of history, are considerations equally consistent with the human element in the personal peculiarities of the writers and with the Divine element in the sovereign wisdom which selected and employed them. Varieties of expression touch the mode of conveying truth; not the truth conveyed. Of this truth there are no degrees, no variations of kind. Truth is but one, and the written word of God is its Divine embodiment.

CHAPTER XIII.

THE TRUTH OF SCRIPTURE PROVED BY THE TESTIMONY OF FACTS.

Circumstantial Accuracy of the Sacred Narratives—Immense Range of its Facts—Corroborations of Profane History—The Governing Nations of the Ancient World; their Manners, Customs, and Government—Egypt as depicted in Scripture, and as represented on the Monuments—Particular Instances of Historical Accuracy in the Old Testament—Instances in the New—The Persons and Places of the Evangelical History.

THE question has sometimes been suggested, What would be the effect on the doctrine of inspiration of discovering errors in Scripture? To such a question I shall reply by simply declining to entertain the suggestion; and this upon the principle repeatedly explained in the foregoing chapters, that our duty is to deal with facts as they are, and not to speculate about facts as they might have been. The discovery of mistakes in Scripture would alter the conditions of the case altogether, and when the alteration takes place it would be time enough to estimate its effects. The facts of the case are the groundwork of our argument in regard to revealed truth as much as in regard to natural truth. It is, therefore, as useless to attempt to reconcile our belief in inspiration with facts which do not exist, as it would be to reconcile the theory of gravitation with some altered condition of the physical world.

We take the case as it is, and resolutely decline to go beyond its limits.

We maintain that no mistake has ever been discovered in Scripture, and we believe that it never will be discovered. We ground this latter conviction on the astonishing correspondence found to exist between the narratives of the Bible and the ascertained facts of history and geography as illustrated by modern archæological discovery. These correspondences are so minute and frequently so latent, so ingrained into the very structure of the narrative as to constitute an authentication of the claims advanced by Scripture for itself of the same kind as the miracles of the Christian period afforded to the authoritative commission of our Lord and of his apostles. This conclusion is confirmed by our knowledge that many passages charged with inaccuracy or manifest error have been proved on fuller information to be exactly and minutely true. We rest our position on the matter of fact that no mistakes have been proved to exist in Scripture, and on the reasonable conclusion, founded on its proved accuracy on the one side and its own positive statement on the other, that no mistake will be found to exist in it in the future. To the elucidation of these points the present chapter will be directed.

The Christian advocate rejoices to bring the question to this test. In passing out of the sphere of abstract argument into the sphere of facts, he passes from ground already strong into ground still stronger. He places his feet on that solid rock of historical truth against which every skeptical attack has hitherto beaten as vainly as waves that shiver themselves to pieces against the side of some immovable cliff.

These circumstantial evidences divide themselves into two branches. On the one side we need to show the positive proofs in support of the veracity of Scripture; on the other side we need to examine the grounds on which this veracity has been impugned, and show that no evidences exist of an opposite character, and consequently that the positive proofs stand clear and unassailable.

. In stating the positive evidences for the veracity of Scripture, we enter upon an immense field of inquiry. Attention would be distracted in so wide a sphere, unless some special line be adopted. I purpose, therefore, briefly to intimate the general character of the evidences at large, and then to substantiate it by entering more fully into some individual instances.

The professed object of Scripture is the revelation of the Divine will; but the communication of it is grouped round the history of the chosen race. Revealed truth was formally intrusted to their keeping, and out of their line came the Saviour of the world. The most ancient books of Scripture consequently contain the history of the Hebrew people from their first original, through the story of their imperial greatness, down to their decline. This history, however, bears a definite character throughout. It is not directed primarily, as secular histories are, to the record of their government, their manners, arts, and civilization; but to their relation towards God, and the development of his designs of mercy towards a ruined world. What may be called the secular side of their history constitutes its secondary, not its primary feature, and is given incidentally rather than directly. Yet, incidental as this side of the narrative is, it comes, nevertheless, at a great many different points of the story, into contact with the history of other nations, and with peculiarities of place, climate, habit, and circumstances, relative to which secular sources supply us with more or less exact information. There are thousands of particulars specified in the Old Testament history in which it is conceivable that mistakes might have been detected, and in which, had not the books been infallibly inspired, we conclude that mistakes would have been detected, simply because it is in these very particulars that the imperfection of human knowledge ordinarily betrays itself. Now, not only has criticism failed to discover in these varied particulars one single contradiction to known facts, but it has brought to light an astonishing accordance with them. Exactly in proportion as our knowledge of the countries, circumstances, and nations alluded to, has become more precise and minute, in that proportion have all the statements of Scripture been more and more exactly verified.

This is the case with the geography of Scripture. The Book of Genesis alone records the names of more than one hundred distinct places, adding in many cases descriptive epithets which involve local details, as in the description of the cities of the plain. The Book of Numbers contains the names of one hundred and thirty separate places, or thereabouts, distinguishing them by characteristic details, as in the case of the Jordan, Jericho, the plains of Moab, the wilderness of Sin, the booths of Succoth, and the grapes of Eshcol. The land containing these places is well known, and has been searched from end to end with restless curiosity during the last few years. The places specified, moreover, are not mentioned at random, but with a certain relation towards each other, as in the enumeration of the journeys of the people in the wilderness. Random guesses, names used at haphazard, or fictitious references to spots having no real existence, would have exposed the narrative to immediate and positive disproof. Not only, however, is there a total absence of the slightest evidence of any mistake in these geographical details, but there is a vast accumulation of evidence in favor of their minute accuracy. Scarcely a traveller has trodden the soil of the Holy Land without furnishing some new illustrations of the sacred narrative, and bringing to light fresh corroborations of its truthfulness.

The case is the same with the details of nations and peoples, and the characteristic circumstances of manners and habits attributed to them. The narratives of the Pentateuch find the illustration of their details in the existing manners of the descendants of Ishmael at the present day. The fortunes of the Hebrew people brought them into contact with all the most eminent nations of antiquity—Egyptians, Phœnicians, Assyrians, Babylonians, Persians, Greeks, and Romans; yet in every case, without one solitary exception, the circumstances of date, place, persons, and events, are true to the reality, as far as modern research has been able to trace and identify them. It constitutes an argument of singular strength that not one solitary case of historical inaccuracy has ever been made out.

A specific instance will best illustrate the minute accuracy of the sacred history and its singular multiplicity of detail. Let Egypt be taken as an example. The whole references to Egyptian manners and customs are incidental rather than direct. Yet many minute details are contained in them, exactly corresponding with all we know of ancient Egypt, alike from the pages of history, and from those silent and impartial witnesses of the past, the monumental records. The separation of the native Egyptians from foreigners, and yet their allowance of them in their lands, their special hatred of shepherds, the character of the government, the power of the king, the influence of the priests, the tenure of land, the existence of the military class, their use of horses and chariots in war, their great buildings, and the employment of foreigners in their construction, the use of bricks, and of bricks with straw in them, the taskmasters, the embalming of the dead, the importation of spices for this purpose, the violent mournings, the dissolute morals, are all more or less fully specified. Our knowledge of their gross idolatry throws peculiar light upon the history of the plagues. The use of Egyptian names, such as Pharaoh, Potiphar, Asenath, Zaphnath-paaneah, and

Moses, together with some ordinary words, complete the striking chain of evidence. The proof of historical evidences thus afforded is so much the stronger because of their incidental occurrence. They do not enter into the formal purpose of the history, and yet are so intimately connected with the narrative, that the events could not have existed separate from the local and national peculiarities. For instance, the events of the settlement in Egypt, and the Exodus, could not have taken place in the same way in Nineveh, or Babylon, or Susa, or Macedon, or Rome. Another striking instance of this accurate delineation of national manners is afforded by the Book of Esther, and the picture drawn of the Persian manners and habits. The character of Artaxerxes, himself the hero of profane history, the prolonged feast at court, the relation of the queen towards the monarch, and the court.etiquette with reference to her, the public records, the wholesale massacre, the methods of reward, the posts hasted by the king's command, the diversity and number of the provinces, are all true to the very life.

A little consideration will show what an immense field of inquiry is opened in this direction, when we glance hastily down the line of history alike throughout the Old and New Testaments. Or if any one fails in this mode to form an adequate appreciation of the prodigious number of details contained, directly or by inference, in the scriptural books, let him take up a modern Bible dictionary, and let him remember that the whole voluminous work is directed solely to the elucidation of these details.

Yet from this vast area, searched as it has been, with increasing diligence, alike by the foes and the friends of the Bible, not one solitary case of proved inaccuracy has yet been gathered. This very fact is itself a wonder, and witnesses trumpet-tongued to the more than human Authorship, which alone can explain this more than human accuracy over so vast a lapse of time and variety of topics.

But the truth must be stated in greater detail. Enough having been said to indicate the extent of the accuracy of Scripture, it is now necessary to indicate its degree. Cases of minute accuracy in little things and single words occur very extensively; and it is by them that the extent of scriptural inspiration can best be ascertained. This purpose, moreover, can only be served by instances where an exact confirmation of the accuracy can be derived from independent sources. For this reason the New Testament supplies them most abundantly, and especially the Acts of the Apostles, because a larger number of geographical and other details occur in it than elsewhere. In the New Testament we find ourselves within the period of recognized history. We have abundant sources of information, and the evidences of the minute veracity of Scripture are proportionably multiplied. But while the New Testament is, for these natural reasons, most peculiarly rich in instances, they are to be found likewise in the Old Testament; and the constant enlargement of our information is as constantly enlarging their number. Over the whole extent of inquiry open to us it will be impossible even to glance in a work like the present. The instances now to be adduced are offered only as special illustrations of a general truth.

1. In Genesis 10:10, the ancient empire of Nimrod is described: "And the beginning of his kingdom was Babel, and Erech, and Accad, and Calneh, in the land of Shinar. Out of that land went forth Asshur, and builded Nineveh, and the city Rehoboth, (or the streets of the city, *margin*,) and Calah, and Resen between Nineveh and Calah." As the names stand in the record, they might be mere names, incapable either of identification or of disproof, and so the case stood till a very recent date in our own epoch. But modern investigation has examined the mounds of Mesopotamia, and has deciphered inscriptions of three thousand years ago. These inscriptions not only prove the existence and importance of these cities, but have enabled explorers to identify the very sites on which they once stood. Babylon, and Erech, and Accad, and Calneh, and Nineveh, and Calah, and Resen, now stand upon our maps as precisely noted by the geographer of the nineteenth century after Christ as they were chronicled by the inspired historian fifteen centuries before Christ.

2. In the same passage, Genesis 10:8, 9, Nimrod is spoken of as a prince so great and celebrated that his name had become a proverb: "Wherefore it is said, 'Even as Nimrod the mighty hunter before the Lord.'" The inscriptions confirm this celebrity of Nimrod, and local tradition still consecrates his name. We are told that all the great

ruins in the Mesopotamian valley are still popularly associated with his name, and "are made in this way monuments of his glory."

3. In Numbers 34, Moses describes the borders of the territory to be occupied by the people, and in the eighth verse draws the line of their northern boundary: "From Mount Hor unto the entrance (or gate) of Hamath." Mr. Porter describes the scene as follows: "On its southern side the ridge of Lebanon rises abruptly to a height of ten thousand feet; and on its northern the lower ridge of Bargylus terminates in a bluff promontory. Between the two lies the only opening from the land of Hamath to the coast of the Mediterranean." This is "the entrance" from that great sea. "There is but one, and it cannot be mistaken. That pass between Lebanon and Bargylus is the only opening from the west into the land of Hamath. I have been told that to this day it is called by the people of Tripoli Bar-Hamath, 'the door of Hamath.'"* "Freshwater Gate" is an instance of the same kind of descriptive epithet in our own country.

4. In Judges 3:8, Chushan-rishathaim is spoken of as "king of Mesopotamia." Now this country was included in the great Assyrian empire, and the existence of an independent monarch over this special region would therefore appear like an inaccuracy in the historian. But the cuneiform records of two centuries later than the date of Othniel show that the Assyrian empire did not even at that time extend over this land. It was not till the middle of

* Porter's "Giant Cities," p. 310.

the twelfth century before Christ that the country between the Rhabour and the Euphrates was included in the Assyrian empire. The inspired historian is consequently perfectly accurate.

5. In the account of the slaughter of the kings given in Joshua, it is recorded: "It came to pass, as they fled from before Israel, and were in the going down to Bethhoron, that the Lord cast down great stones from heaven upon them, and they died," Josh. 10:12. The phrase, "going down to Bethhoron," might appear to our modern habits to express only the direction of the flight; but an examination of the locality shows its exact accuracy and the meaning of the whole passage: "The Israelites chased them along the way that goeth up to Bethhoron. A quarter of a mile west of Gibeon is a sharp ascent to a low ridge. Up this the Ammonites fled, hard pressed by their pursuers. From the top of the ridge a long and rugged descent leads to Bethhoron, which now appears in front, crowning a projecting shoulder of the mountain. The nature of the ground favored the fugitives; but 'as they fled before Israel, and were in the going down to Bethhoron, the Lord cast down great stones from heaven upon them.' Joshua led the van of his troops. He saw that the victory was complete, but yet that night must eventually save the Ammonite army from total destruction, and enable a large body of them to escape to their cities through the valley of Ajalon, at the foot of the pass down which they were rushing. Then, standing on some commanding rock in the sight of the whole people, in

the fulness of faith and enthusiasm, Joshua gave utterance to that wondrous prayer-prophecy; glancing back towards Gibeon and forward upon Ajalon, 'Sun, stand thou still upon Gibeon; and thou, moon, in the valley of Ajalon.'"*

6. Tyre and Sidon occur early and frequently in the scriptural narrative. But there is this peculiarity in the occurrence of the names, that Sidon only is mentioned by Moses, and that twice over in the Book of Joshua it is described as "great Sidon," while in the same book Tyre is only described as a "strong city." It is implied, therefore, that at this period Sidon has the preëminence in opulence and power. But at a later period of the history this is changed; Tyre is specified, while Sidon appears to have sunk into comparative insignificance. In 2 Sam. 24:6 it is simply "Sidon and the stronghold of Tyre." The whole intercourse between David and Hiram implies this reversed order of preëminence between the two Phœnician cities. Profane records exactly confirm this order of superiority. Homer, Strabo, and Justin, record the ancient superiority of Sidon, and this is confirmed by the ancient Egyptian lists, in which Sidon takes the precedence; but Dius (Josephus c. Apion, i. 17) and Menander affirm the superiority of Tyre at the time of David. If, therefore, Moses and Joshua had used the language of the writer of the Book of Samuel, or the writer of the Book of Samuel had used the language of Moses and Joshua, they would have been guilty of historical inaccuracy. But each wri-

* Porter's "Giant Cities," p. 174.

ter preserves the exact order of the facts at his own day, and all three are right.

7. The prophet Isaiah, in chapter xx., mentions an Assyrian monarch, not specified in the historical books of Kings and Chronicles, as attacking and taking Ashdod. In the sixth verse of that chapter the prophet predicts that he should take the Egyptians captive. For a long time criticism identified Sargon with some other of the Assyrian kings, as with Shalmaneser, Sennacherib, and Esarhaddon; but the native records are now found to contain the name of Sargon as an independent monarch reigning at Khorsabad, and relate the fact that he captured Ashdod, to which they add the further statement of his conquest of Egypt, in exact accordance with the declaration of Isaiah.

8. The tribute paid by Hezekiah to Sennacherib is stated to have been three hundred talents of silver and thirty talents of gold. The annals of Sennacherib record the same campaign, and state the payment, so far as the gold is concerned, at exactly the same sum, " thirty talents of gold." The amount of silver stated is larger—eight hundred talents instead of three; but it is natural to suppose that the Assyrian account is exaggerated, and includes portions of the spoil.

9. Both the writer of the Book of Kings and the prophet Isaiah record that Adrammelech and Sharezer, after the murder of their father, fled into the land of Armenia. In the history of Moses of Chorene the fact is recorded, with additional information as to the parts of the country in

which they were settled by the then reigning monarch.

10. Sennacherib was succeeded by Esarhaddon, 2 Kings 19:37. Isaiah records the same fact, and the monuments confirm it. No further mention of Esarhaddon's name occurs, however, in Scripture. But as Sennacherib was contemporary with Hezekiah, Esarhaddon must have been contemporary with his son Manasseh, and is therefore identified by a natural inference with the king of Assyria who "took Manasseh among the thorns, and bound him with fetters, and carried him to Babylon," 2 Chron. 33:11. But why should an Assyrian king carry his prisoner to Babylon, and not to Nineveh? Had the fact been recorded of any other Assyrian monarch but this one, it must have been reckoned to be a misstatement. But Esarhaddon, and *he alone* of all the Assyrian kings, reigned at Babylon, and held court there. The minute accuracy of the history on a point wholly incidental is thus singularly confirmed.

The foregoing list of specific and minute instances of exact accuracy in the inspired narratives might be very greatly enlarged, even in the present imperfect state of our information, and therefore imperfect means of verification. Nor are the instances already known confined to historical details. Thus, an instance of scientific truth is contained in the first chapter of Genesis. The order in which the tribes of the vegetable kingdom are specified in verse 11, and the orderly creation of animal life in verses 21 and 27, have been shown to "fit into the most scientific system of classification." An instance of another kind, touching a matter of personal observation, is found in the account of the prospect of the promised land afforded to Moses from the top of Pisgah. "And the Lord showed him all the land of Gilead, unto Dan, and all Naphtali and the land of Ephraim and Manasseh, and all the land of Judah unto the utmost sea." The Rev. H. B. Tristram, one of the latest as well as one of the most trustworthy explorers of Palestine, describes the view as he saw it with his own eyes, in language singularly illustrative of the scriptural accuracy: "Looking over it (the Jordan) the eye rested on Gerizim's rounded top; and farther still opened the plain of Esdraelon, the shoulder of Carmel, or some other intervening height, just showing to the right of Gerizim; while *the faint and distant bluish haze beyond it told us that there was the sea, the utmost sea.*"

The instances already given have been taken from the Old Testament. It is, however, from the New that the proofs of scriptural veracity can be most abundantly and conclusively drawn. The Acts of the Apostles, as already stated, is peculiarly rich in them. The evidences are supplied from those portions of the Bible where, from the closer proximity of the period to our own, and our greater familiarity with the places and persons mentioned, they might most reasonably be expected. To endeavor to give any thing approaching a list of these correspondences would extend this chapter far beyond its necessary limits. I shall, therefore, both for the sake of brevity and clearness, group a few instances together, under the two heads of the persons and places mentioned in the New Testament.

I. The remarkable and discriminating accuracy exhibited in the scriptural references of the New Testament to conspicuous persons known to profane history is worthy of all attention. The political circumstances of Palestine during the period covered by the New Testament history were to the highest degree intricate and peculiar. I cannot do better than quote the description of Mr. Rawlinson, to whose research I have been greatly indebted in the selection of the illustrative instances already adduced in this chapter. "The political condition of Palestine . . . was curiously complicated and anomalous. It underwent frequent changes, but retained through all of them certain peculiarities which made the position of the country unique among the dependencies of Rome. Not having been conquered in the ordinary way, but having passed under the Roman dominion with the consent and by the assistance of a large party among the inhabitants, it was allowed to maintain for a while a species of semi-independence not unlike that of various native states in India, which are really British dependencies. A mixture, and to some extent an alternation, of Roman with native power, resulted from this arrangement, and a consequent complication in the political status, which must have made it very difficult to be thorougly understood by any one who was not a native and a contemporary. The chief representative of the Roman power in the East, the president of Syria, the local governor,

10*

whether a Herod or a Roman procurator, and the high priest, had each and all certain rights and a certain authority in the country. A double system of taxation, a double administration of justice, and even, in some degree, a double military command, were the natural consequence; while Jewish and Roman customs, Jewish and Roman words, were simultaneously in use, and a condition of things existed full of harsh contrasts, strange mixtures, and abrupt transitions. Within the space of fifty years Palestine was a single united kingdom under a native ruler; a set of principalities under native ethnarchs and tetrarchs; a country in part containing such principalities, in part reduced to the condition of a Roman province; a kingdom re-united once more under a native sovereign, and a country reduced wholly under Rome, and governed by procurators dependent on the president of Syria, but still subject, in certain respects, to the Jewish monarch of a neighboring territory."*

During this period the notable persons mentioned more or less fully by the sacred writers are six members of the family of Herod, and four Roman governors of Judea. Five of the Herodian family exercised the authority of government; but neither were their dominions and authority in any one case identical, nor did they succeed each other in order of time. Herod the Great reigned by the favor of Augustus over the whole of Palestine. On his death his dominions were divided into three parts. Archelaus received Judea, Samaria, and Idumea, with the

* Rawlinson's "Bampton Lectures." p. 237.

title of tetrarch. Antipas was made tetrarch of Galilee and Peræa; and Philip tetrarch of Trachonitis and the adjoining regions. But these three governments did not continue for an equal period. The power of Archelaus came speedily to an end, and Judea was reduced to the condition of a Roman province under the government of procurators. Four of these preceded Pontius Pilate; then for a time the dominions of Herod the Great were reunited under his grandson Agrippa. But on the death of Agrippa they became again a Roman province; and yet immediately afterwards there was another king Agrippa, but without authority in Judea. Yet through this tangled maze the scriptural narrative finds its way without fault and without stumbling. Not a single inaccuracy is to be found, either as regards person, place, or time. This veracity is the more remarkable because the narrative does not proceed from the pen of the same author, but from four authors. These authors, moreover, were not men of the higher rank, conversant with political changes and the balancing of concurrent authorities; yet the narrative steps firmly and unerringly along its course.

Moreover, to the maintenance of the historical order of events it adds the precise discrimination of individual character. Each person appears in connection with exactly those events and that conduct which our independent information shows to be as consistent with that particular person as it would be inconsistent with the person preceding or succeeding in the order of the narrative.

First comes Herod the Great, so jealous and suspicious, so treacherous and cruel, that one of his own Roman patrons declared that it was better to be Herod's dog than his son. Then step upon the scene Archelaus, with a character so much dreaded that Joseph "was afraid to go" (Matt. 2:22) into Judea; Antipas, crafty and sensual, and yet weak and impressible, and Philip, undistinguished by any special decision of character. Then suddenly we find ourselves in the presence of the Roman procurator Pontius Pilate. If we are perplexed to understand the motives of his conduct towards Jesus Christ, we have but to turn to the illustrative statements of profane history, and there in his inconstant and cruel character, and in the relation of mutual distrust and reciprocal dislike existing between himself and the Jews, we find the explanation of it all. Then all at once, as it were, without any previous hint in the sacred pages of political changes, which did not touch the great purpose of the inspired narrative, we find ourselves confronted with another Jewish monarch excessively popular, but through that very cause engaged in a bitter persecution of the church. His luxurious tastes, love of popularity, delight in state and show, with the particulars of his dreadful death, are all touched with a graphic brevity equally remarkable and impressive. Then two successive governors of Judea are presented to us; not as mere names, but as living persons with their living peculiarities of character upon them. First appears Felix with his Jewish wife, himself vigorous indeed in his administration,

but personally so unprincipled, that he is said by
Tacitus "in all kinds of lust and cruelty" to have
exercised "the power of a king with the temper of
a slave." How natural it was that such a man,
crouching before the complaints against him presented by his enemies at Rome, should seek to gain
popularity with a party by an act of injustice towards an apostle. "Felix, willing to show the Jews
a pleasure, left Paul bound." Acts 24:27. How
natural that, with a conscience laden with many
crimes, such a man should have trembled beneath
the preaching of righteousness, temperance, and
judgment to come, and yet should have trembled
without repenting. Felix was succeeded by Porcius
Festus, a man of very different character—just, and
firm, and equitable. It is a natural part of the same
argument, to remark that the character of Gallio,
the Roman governor at Corinth, is also drawn in
exact accordance with the high character borne
by him by the historians of his own country. Thus
the scriptural narrative is precisely true throughout, as tested by the most accurate information of
our own day.

II. But the case is still stronger with the references to places occurring in the Acts of the Apostles. Here again the complicated political condition
of the Roman empire and the minute variations
arising from it in the political status of different
cities, or even of the same city at different times,
must be kept clearly in mind. The relation of the
various cities of the empire towards Rome herself
differed very widely. Conquest, or settlement, or

peculiar amity, or special services rendered at some crisis of the imperial fortunes, led to the gift of very different degrees of independence. Thus some were municipal, or foreign cities adopted into a close political connection. Some were settlements (απoικιαι), offshoots from the parent empire, legally independent, but retaining a filial obedience to the mother state. Some were free cities, and in virtue of freedom were self-governed in all internal affairs within the territory assigned to them. Some were colonies, being military settlements designed to protect the frontier, or to keep a disaffected province in subjection. In addition to this it was possible for individuals to possess the right of Roman citizenship, either by purchase, as in the case of Claudius Lysias, or by reward for some signal service, as in the case of Paul's father, or by inheritance, as in the case of St. Paul. Privileges accorded to citizenship by the Roman law were many and great. In addition to these intricate relations, arising from the wide extension and varied circumstances of the Roman law, other local peculiarities of title, name, and office prevailed, in the apostolic times, from the admixture of Greek and Roman habits in the same civilization.

Now, we should recall how difficult it is for a stranger passing from city to city to enter into these exact distinctions, how much more difficult to maintain them where no personal acquaintance exists to suggest by the mere force of familiar association the particular title. It would be very difficult for a foreigner, for instance, and it is not always easy for an Englishman, to understand the diversities of local government, and the specific titles of local offices in his own country. In regard to the sacred writings the difficulty was increased in proportion to the vast diversities of race, circumstance, and constitution, welded together by the administrative genius of Rome into the one imperial unity. The accurate knowledge exhibited by the scriptural narrative on all these questions, and the accurate use in each case of the especially appropriate name is the more significant, because there is evidence that it did not arise from personal acquaintance with the places and persons described, on the part of the writer. There is an evident reason for concluding that St. Luke was with St. Paul at Troas and Philippi, for he uses the first person "we." But there is nothing whatever to indicate his attendance on the apostle at Thessalonica, Athens, Corinth, or Ephesus. If, therefore, unfailing accuracy of language is maintained, it must be attributed to the overruling inspiration of God, and not to the special information of man.

This accuracy is illustrated in the following instances. Cyprus is described as governed by a pro-consul, the title ascribed to Sergius Paulus by St. Luke being exclusively applied to that dignity. Philippi is expressly stated to have been a colony, and the coins of that city bear the title. Thessalonica was a free city, and this is expressed by St. Luke, by the distinctive title he gives to the magistrates of that place. The authorized version simply uses the word "rulers of the city." They brought "Jason and certain brethren unto the rulers of the city." Acts 17:6. But these rulers were native magistrates, as is expressed in the term πολιταρκαι. The remains of a marble arch still remain in Thessalonica, and on this arch is an inscription beginning with this very name. It records the existence of seven politarchs at Thessalonica. At Athens the evangelist records the existence of an altar inscribed "To the unknown God." Two secular writers, Pausanias and Philostratus, confirm the statement that altars with this inscription existed at Athens. Corinth is designated a pro-consular province by the application to Gallio of the official title of the pro-consul applied to Sergius Paulus. Yet, in fact, Corinth underwent three changes, having been a pro-consular province under Augustus, then in the time of Tiberius being governed by imperial procurators, and again becoming a pro-consular province under Claudius, only ten years before the date of St. Paul's visit, and his use of the official title "anthupatos." In the account of the visit of St. Paul to Ephesus, in the nineteenth chapter of the Acts, four distinctive names are used. The first instance is the peculiar word translated in the authorized version as "town clerk." The word occurs with unusual frequency on the Ephesian coins. The second is furnished by the still more peculiar word translated "worshipper." "The city of the Ephesians is a worshipper of the great goddess Diana." Acts 19:35. The word is expressive in the strongest degree of extreme reverence and humility, its literal meaning being "a témple sweeper." The expression is found in an inscription at Ephesus. The third instance is the application of the distinctive pro-consular title to the governors of Asia, both the coins and the inscriptions confirming the fact that Asia was a pro-consular province. The fourth is furnished in the one compound word translated "the chiefs of Asia." The original word is "Asiarchs." The title belonged to the presidents of the public games, for which Asia in general and Ephesus in particular were famous. They were persons of great wealth, dignity, and influence, and are represented by St. Luke as the friendly counsellors of the great apostles.

I cannot close this reference to the verbal accuracy of the New Testament Scriptures without briefly referring to two other topics. Foremost of these is the account given by St. Luke of St. Paul's voyage towards Rome. This account has been laboriously examined and carefully compared with known facts of the present day, by persons professionally conversant with nautical matters. The result has been, not only to establish the veritable and trustworthy character of the narrative, but to enable the whole voyage to be traced as accurately as if a log-book of the particulars had been handed down from that day to this. The very spot has been determined on which the necessary action of the wind and current would cast a ship situated as was the Alexandrian corn-ship of the narrative; and this particular spot is found exactly to correspond with all the circumstances of St. Luke's narrative.

The second point is the wonderful particularity with which the simple incidental notices of the inspired narrative depict the peculiar features of Roman habits and civilization. I again quote the language of Mr. Rawlinson: "If we turn to Rome and the Roman system, how truly do we find depicted the great and terrible emperor whom all feared to provoke; the provincial administration by pro-consuls and others, chiefly anxious that tumults should be prevented; the contemptuous religious tolerance; the noble principles of Roman law, professed if not always acted upon, whereby accusers and accused were brought face to face, and the latter had 'free license to answer for themselves concerning the crimes laid against them,' (Acts 25:16;) the privileges of Roman citizenship, sometimes acquired by birth, sometimes by purchase; the right of appeal possessed and exercised by the provincials; the treatment of prisoners; the peculiar manner of chaining them; the employment of soldiers as their guards; the examination by torture; the punishment of condemned persons not being Roman citizens by scourging and crucifixion; the manner of this punishment, the practice of bearing the cross, of affixing a title or superscription, of placing soldiers under a centurion to watch the carrying into effect of the sentence, of giving the garments of the sufferers to these persons, of allowing the bodies after death to be buried by the friends; and the like. The sacred historians are as familiar, not only with the general character, but even with some of the obscurer customs of Greece and Rome, as with those of their own country. Fairly observant and always faithful in their accounts, they continually bring before us little points which accord minutely with notices in profane writers nearly contemporary with them; while occasionally they increase our knowledge of classic antiquity by touches harmonious with the spirit, but additional to the information which we derive from the native authorities."   (Rawlinson's "Bampton Lectures," p. 245.)

CHAPTER XIV.

THE EVIDENCE OF EXPERIENCE.

Supposed Difficulties proved to be Real Confirmations of the Truth of Scripture—Their Origin in Human Ignorance—Defective or Erroneous Information—Light thrown by these Instances on Difficulties still unsolved—Instances in Detail—The Truthfulness of Scripture a Common Characteristic of all its Writers—Exhibited in Incidental Particulars—Cannot be referred to the Personal Information of the Authors—Illustrated in Matters of Detail—No other Mode of showing it Possible.

THE preceding chapter was occupied with instances of minute accuracy on the part of the sacred Scriptures. Before I proceed to point out the characteristics of these cases, and the conclusion they justify us in forming, the argument must be further strengthened by another class of instances. The foregoing have not been made the subject of skeptical objection; but a considerable number of cases exist where passages ostentatiously paraded as evidences of mistakes in Scripture, and as, therefore, conclusive against its plenary inspiration, have been found on fuller information to bear the most positive evidence in the other direction. The importance of these instances is great, not simply because the weapons of the skeptic have become the weapons of the believer, but because of the truth illustrated by this very transference of the argument from one side to the other; for it is now proved that the difficulty experienced in reconciling them with known facts was exclusively the product of human ignorance. The information on which the objection was based was either erroneous or defective.

It was in some cases erroneous, and this in spite of apparent ground for believing in its accuracy. The prejudice entertained by many critics against Scripture, and the disposition to prefer any other authority to the authority of the sacred records has, however, been illustrated in instances where this plea of apparent credibility can scarcely be advanced. I may adduce in proof the case of a book entitled "A Million of Facts," and which, probably, from the multiplicity of its subjects, has acquired a circulation even among Christian people engaged in instructing others greatly disproportioned to its real merit. In this publication, among other strange things of the same character, is an article on Jewish history, in which the entire narrative of Moses is quietly rejected on the authority of statements imputed to Sanchoniatho, Diodorus Siculus, Tacitus, Celsus, and others. (P. 986.) On another page it is explained that the use made of the first writer's authority depends wholly on the supposition that "the allies of Ilus or Chronus, whom he called Elohim after Ilus, were Jews." (P. 620.) A more instructive instance of the tendency of many writers to give more authority to the slightest hint of a profane author, than to the most explicit and circumstantial statements of a sacred author, cannot well be conceived. For let it be supposed that Diodorus Siculus, Tacitus, Celsus, and Julian, do contradict Moses in regard to the early history of the Hebrew race, yet on no conceivable principle can it be pronounced that they are certainly right, and Moses certainly wrong. Every fair canon of historical criticism leans decisively to the other side. This case, therefore, illustrates the general tendency to treat the scriptural books with foregone prejudice. Instances where the case has been fairly tried, and the veracity of Scripture finally established beyond the possibility of a doubt, constitute its strongest rebuke. Let it be allowed that there was apparent reason on the other side, yet the stronger these reasons were for doubting the veracity of the Bible, the more triumphant is the testimony borne to its inspiration when this veracity has been finally established.

Or the skeptical objection may have rested on information, accurate as far as it went, but defective; and the supply on this one deficient point may have cleared up all the difficulty. That the omission of one fact out of a series will make the rest unintelligible, and perhaps apparently contradictory, is a matter within familiar experience. The experiment may be tried by a little exercise of the imagination. As it is important that this truth should be clearly seen, it may be worth while to adduce an illustration. The following instance is quoted by Dr. Lee from "Ebrard:" "On the evening of Sept. 5, 1839, a rumor prevailed in Zurich that an attack was to be apprehended from an armed force. The greatest commotion was excited, and a body of men were drawn together in the district of Pfäffikon to repel the attack. The rumor was soon found to be without any foundation, and means were taken by the government to allay the popular tumult. On subsequently inquiring as to these events, Ebrard was informed by one person that the government despatched N., one of their number, at a late hour, with a letter to Pfäffikon. On another occasion Ebrard was told by a second informant that N., after going a short distance, returned with the intelligence that the tocsin was already ringing in Pfäffikon. A third related that two persons on horseback had been despatched; while a fourth averred that N. had sent his messengers on horseback to the disturbed district. If ever four accounts appeared irreconcilable, these do so. And if a harmonist were to conjecture that N. had been sent to Pfäffikon, that he had been met on the Zurichberg by two peasants coming from that place, with the intelligence that the people were already on the march; that he had returned with them to Zurich, and entering the neighboring house of a magistrate, had caused two horses to be at once saddled, and commanded the peasants to ride back in haste to proclaim peace; all this would, no doubt, be set down as a highly improbable and artificial conjecture. And yet it is no conjecture, but the simple, true account which N. himself gave me when I asked him about that event."

Now, in records so condensed as are the scriptural narratives, and dealing as many of them do with great periods of time, omission more or less is inevitable. Yet its effect may be to lay the whole narrative open to speculative objections by some ingenious mind employed in analyzing the details in order to impugn their accuracy. In such a case nothing but the discovery of the missing fact can with absolute certainty make the narrative complete. Without it we might be able to show that the narrative was not improbable, because such and such suppositions would render it congruous with itself and consistent with the probability. In this way it is that we are left to argue in many instances. The case may be illustrated by a dissected map. Suppose one piece of the map to be absent, it would be evidently impossible to compose the whole map. It is argued that these pieces remaining cannot really be the parts of one complete map, because they cannot be put together into a finished whole. Another person might fairly reply that a piece is probably absent, and might suggest the kind and shape of the piece which would render the whole map consistent. But if the missing piece were actually discovered, the proof that the skeptical objection was inconclusive would not only be sound argument, but would become veritable and indisputable fact. This is exactly the evidence furnished by instances where passages urged as the grounds of skeptical objection have proved to be conclusive arguments on the other side. The following illustrations are presented:

I. Much objection has been made to the Mosaic account of the Creation on the ground that the production of light on the first day was contradictory to the creation of the sun and moon upon the fourth day. It was commonly supposed that the sun was the source of light to our globe, and it appeared, therefore, a manifest contradiction to describe light as existing three days before its source. The authorized version gave apparent force to the argument: "God called the light Day, and the darkness he called Night," was the record of the creative work of the first day. On the fourth day, we are subsequently told, "God made two great lights, the greater light to rule the day, and the lesser light to rule the night." Gen. 1:5, 16. The objection appeared to be conclusive, and constituted one of the stock arguments of the earlier forms of infidelity. "How did God make light before the sun?" asked Voltaire with apparent triumph, repeating the objection urged by Celsus in the early ages of Christianity. "Modern astronomy found it contrary to order that the earth should not only have been created before the sun, but should also, besides day and night, have distinction of the elements and vegetation before the sun," were the words of Strauss. Recent investigation has not only succeeded in removing the difficulty, but in the removal has confirmed the inspired account, by virtue of the latent scientific truth assumed in it. A more accurate scholarship has on one side corrected the translation of Gen. 1:14–16. The word translated light is really light-bearers or luminaries, instruments for the diffusion of light, but not the sources of light in themselves. On the other side, natural science advanced to the same solution by successive stages. First, it showed that the transmission of light to our globe was dependent on the luminous atmosphere surrounding the sun, and that, upon what is called the nebular hypothesis, the earth and the other planets of our system must necessarily have been constituted before the sun received the luminous atmosphere. Then it began to accumulate evidence confirmatory of the fact that light existed independently of the sun, and consisted of the undulations of a luminous ether. The latest theory maintains that the body of the sun is simply an irritant, having the property of setting the undulations of this ether into motion, but wholly devoid of light in itself. Light is, therefore, no longer an emanation from the sun, but exists independently of it. Thus, the inspired narration is not only consistent with science, but actually embodies its latest discoveries, and therefore must be held to have anticipated them by more than three thousand years.

II. In Genesis 10:8 we are told that the earliest inhabitants of the great alluvial plain at the mouth of the Tigris and the Euphrates were of Ethiopian origin. "Cush begat Nimrod ... and the beginning of his kingdom was Babel, and Erech, and Accad, and Calneh in the land of Shinar." The great majority of modern ethnologists have held an opinion directly contradictory to the scriptural statement. They believed them to be Aramæans, sprung from Shem, and not from Ham, the father of Cush. A whole array of great names supported this conclusion with the utmost confidence. The contradiction thus given to Scripture was supported by affinities of language between the Babylonians of the time of Nebuchadnezzar and the Hebrews, and by the close international connection existing between the Babylonians and Assyrians. So irrefragable were these arguments held to be, that the attempt to maintain the accuracy of the Biblical account was scouted almost with contempt. And yet it is now certain that the Bible is right, and the ethnologists wrong. The mounds of Chaldæa have been recently explored, and inscriptions have been discovered proving that the language of ancient Babylonia was not the language of the times of Nebuchadnezzar, but belonged to a different family, and this family Cushite or Ethiopian. With such a remarkable instance at hand, no one need be afraid of putting the accuracy of the inspired Scripture in points of minute detail against the rash conclusions of a science which is at present imperfect in its facts, and therefore hasty and inconsequent in its conclusions.

III. In Joshua 8:33 we find an account of the reading of the law by Joshua in the hearing of the people along the sides of Ebal and Gerizim, and in the valley lying between them: "All Israel, and their elders, and officers, and their judges, stood on this side the ark and on that side before the priests the Levites, which bare the ark of the covenant of the Lord, as well the stranger, as he that was born among them; half of them over against mount Gerizim, and half of them over against mount Ebal." The space between the two hills is considerable, and it has been thought to be absurd to suppose that the assembled people could have heard, under these circumstances, the voice of Joshua, and still more that they could have carried out the instruction of Moses, given, it should be remembered, before the entrance into the land, that the people, divided into two parties, should ratify with a loud "amen" the justice of the Divine commandments. Yet it has been discovered that this particular spot, under the sides of Ebal and Gerizim, possesses such special acoustic properties as to have made a transaction wholly credible here which would have been justly incredible elsewhere. The sides of Gerizim especially are steep, and broken by caves and cells, which serve to collect and repeat the sound. The Rev. H. B. Tristram writes: "A single voice may be heard by many thousands shut in and conveyed up and down by the enclosing hills. In the early morning we could not only see from Gerizim a man driving his ass down a path in mount Ebal, but could hear every word he uttered as he urged it on; and in order to test the matter more certainly, on a subsequent occasion, two of our party stationed themselves on opposite sides of the valley, and with perfect ease recited the commandments antiphonally." A similar statement will be found in an interesting and valuable work on Scripture lands by Rev. G. S. Drew.

This instance naturally carries the thoughts forward to the astonishing harmony existing between the geography of the Pentateuch, and the events of the exodus and the wanderings. The rocky platform of Sinai, for instance, strikes every observer by its wonderful adaptation to such a purpose as the giving of the law. Thus Dean Stanley writes: "The whole impression of that long approach was even more wonderful than I had anticipated. Whatever may have been the scene of the events of the exodus, I cannot imagine that any human being could pass up that plain, and not feel that he was entering a place above all others suited for the most august of the sights of earth." Lack of space makes it impossible to enter largely upon this subject; but it should be borne in mind as the natural groundwork from which points of special and minute accuracy are thrown into notice. Where the whole broad platform of the history is found to correspond with existing things, the most minute accuracy of details is no more than may consistently be expected.

IV. Deuteronomy 3 contains an account of the conquest of the lands east of the Jordan. Among the conquests effected at that time was the overthrow of Og, the giant king of Bashan, and the capture of his cities. "We took all his cities at that time, there was not a city which we took not from them, threescore cities, all the region of Argob, the kingdom of Og in Bashan. All these cities were fenced with high walls, gates, and bars; besides unwalled towns a great many." The province of Argob, the Trachonitis of the New Testament Scriptures, measures not more than thirty miles by twenty. The existence of so large a number of cities within so narrow an area appeared to many persons to be absolutely incredible; and the feeling, on human grounds, was not altogether unnatural.

The exploration of this region is a work of extreme difficulty and danger, and it is only within the last few years that Mr. Cyril Graham, Mr. Porter, and a few others, have succeeded in partially penetrating it. Enough, however, has been discovered to confirm in a very remarkable manner the inspired narrative. The cities are still there. Unlike the ancient cities of Palestine in general, they still survive, some of them complete as when they were first built. They are cities desolate and without inhabitants, crowding the plains and hills of Bashan far and wide with their ruins, the silent witnesses to the truth of the word of God. "That one city," writes Mr. Porter, "nurtured by the commerce of a mighty empire, might grow till her people could be numbered by millions, I could well believe. That two or even three great commercial cities might spring up in favored localities, almost side by side, I could believe too. But that sixty walled cities, besides unwalled towns a great many, should exist in a small province, at such a remote age, far from the sea, with no rivers and little commerce, appeared to be inexplicable. Inexplicable, mysterious though it appeared, it was true. On the spot, with my own eyes, I had now verified it. A list of more than one hundred ruined cities and villages situated in these mountains alone I had in my hands, and on the spot I had tested it and found it accurate, though not complete."

V. In 2 Kings 20:12 we read, "At that time Berodach-baladan, the son of Baladan, king of Babylonia, sent letters and a present unto Hezekiah." The statement is repeated less circumstantially in Isaiah 39:1, with the sole difference that the Babylonian king's name is written Merodach-baladan. To this statement it was objected that there was no such king, and that Babylonia did not constitute a separate monarchy in the days of Hezekiah. Further inquiry, however, brought to light a statement of the Ephesian historian, Polyhistor, to the effect that Merodach-baladan was a usurper, who reigned at Babylon for six months, and was overthrown by Sennacherib. The answer was thus complete. But the Babylonian inscriptions have now carried our information much farther. The annals of Tiglath-pileser record that on the invasion of Mesopotamia by that prince, the country on the seacoast was under the dominion of Merodach-baladan, who made his submission to the Assyrian monarch, and retained his own authority as a vassal king on payment of a tribute. During the reign of Shalmaneser, the successor of Tiglath-pileser, the monuments afford no information of the relations between Babylon and Assyria; but on the successful usurpation of Sargon, Babylonia revolted and placed itself under the independent government of Merodach-baladan. After a reign of twelve years, this king was conquered by Sargon; but on the death of Sargon, again revolted, and was finally overthrown by Sennacherib. Thus the veracity of the Bible in this one isolated mention of a Babylonian monarch, of whom nothing was known till the buried monuments of the past again found voice, is literally and indisputably established.

VI. Daniel 4 records the capture of Babylon by the Persians, and the death of Belshazzar, the king of the Chaldeans. On two other occasions he marks the date of visions by "the years of the reign of king Belshazzar," in which they occurred. It is objected that these references are in direct opposition to the statements of the Babylonian historian Berosus, who records that the last Babylonian monarch, Nabonadius, shut himself up in Borsippa, and was there taken after the capture of Babylon. But the inscriptions on the Babylonian cylinders again confirm the absolute truth of Scripture. At two different places have cylinders been found in which the name occurs of Belsarussar or Belshareser. He is stated to have been the eldest son of Nabonadius, to have been associated with him in the kingdom, and to have been slain at the capture of Babylon. The facts are stated by Sir H. Rawlinson to receive further and independent corroboration from "the inscription of Bisutan, in that the impostor who caused the Babylonians to revolt against Darius Hystaspes, and who personated the heir to the throne, did not take the name of the eldest son of Nabonadius Belsharezer, but of the second son, Nabukudurusur."

VII. The preceding instances have been taken from the Old Testament Scriptures, and their number has only been limited by the rule already explained, that such instances only should be given (1) as consist of minute points of details; (2) as admit of positive evidence from profane sources. In passing from the Old into the New Testament, it is worth our notice that the instances under the present head are fewer just in proportion as our information relative to this period is more full and precise. This comparative paucity of instances arises from no want of exact correspondence between the scriptural narrative and the known facts of history; for it has been shown in the preceding chapter that the New Testament writings are peculiarly rich in evidence of this kind. It arises from this very abundance of corroborative evidence, which has so narrowed the circle of possible objection, that the cases are very few indeed where the slightest positive evidence has been produced against the minute veracity of Scripture. Instances where apparent objections against the truth of Scripture have been converted into positive evidences in favor of it are few, simply and solely because the instances even of apparent inaccuracy are few. This tacit evidence is itself well worthy of being remembered.

VIII. Among the few instances where historical inaccuracy has been alleged against the New Testament writings, the case of Quirinus or Cyrenius, governor of Syria, stands prominent. St. Luke, referring to the decree issued by Cæsar Augustus that all the Roman empire should be taxed, adds that "this taxing was first made when Cyrenius was governor of Syria," Luke 2:2. Now Josephus states that he was made governor after the banishment of Archelaus, A. D. 6; consequently the taxing which took Joseph and Mary to the city of David before the birth of Mary's "first-born Son," could not have been made under a governor who did not accede to power till six years afterwards. A large variety of suppositions have been offered to remove this apparent contradiction between Josephus and St. Luke. But a discovery has recently been made by A. W. Zumpt, of Berlin, which removes the very ground of the apparent discrepancy. By a process of argument alike marked by its singular ingenuity, and by the forcible array of facts on which it is based, he has proved that Cyrenius was twice governor of Syria. He has even been able, by an exhaustive process, to prove that his first period of office was from the year B. C. 4 to B. C. 1, when he was succeeded by M. Lolius. Consequently, not only is the objection removed, since the statement of St. Luke and the statement of Josephus may both be true, but a positive evidence is afforded for the minute accuracy of St. Luke; for if Cyrenius was governor during the years B. C. 4 to B. C. 1, the taxing which brought Joseph and Mary to Bethlehem must have been "first made when Cyrenius was governor of Syria."

IX. Another notable instance has already been alluded to among the indisputable proofs of scriptural accuracy, and must therefore be but briefly touched in the character now presented, of an objection converted into an evidence. I refer to the pro-consular title given by St. Luke in the thirteenth chapter of the Acts to Sergius Paulus, the governor of Cyprus. It was objected that the title was improperly applied to him. This allegation was based on the statement of Dio Cassius that the emperor Augustus retained Cyprus as an imperial province, and that it would consequently be governed by a pro-prætor, and not by a pro-consul. But the historian goes on to explain that an exchange of provinces took place between the emperor and the senate, in which Cyprus was transferred from the emperor to the senate. It would, therefore, be governed by a pro-consul; and the fact is confirmed by the discovery of Cyprian coins bearing the very title used by the sacred historian.

A review of the instances given in the present and in the preceding chapter will exhibit in them the following characteristics:

1. The minute veracity illustrated by them is not confined to a single book, or to a single writer, or to a single section of the scriptural writings. Instances have been given from the Old Testament and from the New. The instances from the Old comprise passages from the Pentateuch, from Joshua and Judges, from the books of Kings and Chronicles, from the prophets Isaiah and Daniel. The New Testament instances are gathered alike from the gospels and from the Acts of the Apostles. The veracity of Scripture is not confined to these instances. They are but particular illustrations— cases where sufficient information has been given from independent sources to enable us to prove to moral demonstration the accuracy of the sacred narrative. These cases are found wherever the books themselves are of such a nature as to deal with facts in detail. They show, therefore, that the accurate truthfulness of Scripture is not a quality

of one or two individual writers, but the quality of the Scriptures in general. It is not, therefore, the result of any thing personal to the individual man, but of some general influence, of which they partake in common.

2. This accuracy has been traced in particulars which are more or less incidental to the main object of the narrative. They refer to details which a human writer, diffident of the extent of his own knowledge, might have omitted altogether, or in regard to which an indefinite expression might have been selected, or where a bold or careless writer might have added particulars at haphazard. For, on the supposition of the skeptic, that the scriptural books are human compositions, it is impossible that their authors could ever have anticipated for their productions that prodigious circulation and world-wide importance which they have actually attained. They could not, therefore, have supposed that their works would ever have been submitted to such a sifting and reiterated criticism as skepticism on one side and faith on the other have brought to bear upon them. Comparative carelessness as to details would have been perfectly natural to them. For instance, whether the path of the discomfited Canaanites was an ascent towards Bethhoron as far as Azekah, and a descent beyond—whether the sons of Sennacherib fled into Armenia or any other neighboring country—whether the Jewish captives of Sargon were carried to Babylon or elsewhere—are points incidental to the main purpose of the narrative. They are, therefore, ex-

actly the points by which, for this very reason, the veracity of a narrative and the extent of knowledge displayed in it are most conclusively shown.

3. Many of these details are such as could not possibly have fallen within the personal knowledge of the writer, and for which no effort of memory nor extent of information can account. For instance, Moses could not possibly have known out of his own knowledge the line of descent of the ancient Babylonians, nor have selected Ebal and Gerizim for the public recitation of the law from any individual acquaintance with the acoustic properties of the spot. The flight of Adrammelech and Sharezer into Armenia could not have fallen within the knowledge of the author of the Book of Kings. Nor is it conceivable that the political arrangements of the Roman empire should have been so minutely known to St. Luke as to enable him to exhibit from his own individual human information the minute accuracy distinguishing his history. No doubt there were sources of information open to them of which they may have availed themselves, but there is no source of historical error so common as reliance upon hearsay information. How is it that they selected just that information, and that only, on points equally numerous and varied, which was true to the utmost limits of accuracy? Whether we regard them as recording facts lying beyond the range of their own knowledge, or as supplementing their own information by the information of others, in either case there must have been some help common to the whole series of writers,

and over and above human prudence and discrimination.

4. The instances given are all, without exception, drawn from matters of detail. The passages furnishing them do not deal with the sublime doctrines of the faith, but with their human setting in the history of the Hebrew race and of the world at large. They are taken from that class of subjects which some men are disposed to exclude from the proper topics of Divine inspiration. The doctrines of the Bible they acknowledge to have been communicated by God, but not the historical facts; yet it is not in the doctrines, but in the historical facts alone, that these proofs of the truth of the sacred Scriptures are furnished to us.

Further, it should be noted that this limitation is just what might have been expected, and arises from the nature of the case. We believe the truth of Scripture everywhere, and the belief is justified by solid reasons; but it is not everywhere that we can prove it in detail. This, I repeat, is natural; for as the sublime doctrines of the faith lie beyond the reach of human discovery, so they lie beyond the reach of human proof. Let it be supposed that the Divine Author of the Bible was mercifully pleased to confirm the faith of mankind in the truth of his revealed word by proofs drawn from independent sources within human knowledge and discovery. It is only in the minute historical facts that verification could, in the nature of things, be possible. It must be in history, because this alone admits of undeniable moral evidence. It must be in definite and therefore minute particulars, because otherwise chance, and not intelligent design, might be alleged to be its cause. The proof must be afforded in exactly the manner we find to be the case, and could be given in no other way.

I submit that we have in this fact a new explanation of the reason why the same revelation should contain the sublimest doctrines and yet the smallest details. The dependence of the doctrines for their verification upon the little historical details with which, as I have shown, they are inseparably interwoven, only confirms the arguments already adduced for unity of authorship, and therefore for identity of authority for the whole Scriptures.

But one other conclusion must be asserted before we pass on to the next stage of the inquiry. It has been shown that Scripture is wonderfully accurate in details, and that where ground has apparently existed for impugning its accuracy, further information has confirmed the Scripture, and proved the objections urged against it to be only the product of human ignorance. Mistaken or defective information on our own part, not on the part of the Bible, has been the source of all the difficulty. It is therefore natural to conclude that what further information has done for some difficulties, it would do, should it be vouchsafed to us, for all. That some things in Scripture should appear obscure to us is natural, if we judge the Scripture simply as we judge any other old book. We can, moreover, understand that if Scripture be a revelation from God, at once intended to communicate saving knowledge, and to be the instrument of moral probation, God might in perfect consistency intentionally leave some difficulties to exercise faith and discipline submission. To accept the authority of Scripture as a Divine revelation, although it contains some things we cannot understand, is so far from being unreasonable, that reason herself compels us to this conclusion. Multiplied proofs are afforded us of the truth of the Bible. As a matter of indisputable fact, objections against its accuracy, in some cases apparently well founded, have been found to arise solely from ignorance in ourselves. Hence we are justified in judging of the future by the experience of the past. Not only do we assert that no mistake has ever been proved to exist in Scripture, but we proclaim likewise our conviction that no mistake ever will be found in it. We lift up our hearts to God, and exclaim with the psalmist, "Thy word is true from the beginning: and every one of thy righteous judgments endureth for ever." Psalm 119:160.

CHAPTER XV.

ALLEGED INSTANCES OF INACCURACY IN SCRIPTURE EXAMINED AND EXPLAINED.

The Proofs alleged for and against the Accuracy of the Sacred Books compared with Reference to their Character and Relative Value—The Supposed Inaccuracies resolved into Mistakes respecting the Human Element and its Operation—Rules for testing Them—Interpolations and Errors in Transcription—Figures of Speech—Variations of Statement—Omission of Facts—Differences of Style—Analogous Transactions and Discourses—*A-priori* Probabilities.

THE facts specified in the last two chapters, and the conclusion founded upon them, must be borne in mind in passing from the positive to the negative side of the controversy. Hitherto attention has been directed to the evidences confirmatory of the minute accuracy of the sacred writings. Attention must now be directed to the evidences adduced in disproof of it, in order that both sides of the argument may be taken into account and fairly balanced against each other, before the final conclusion is reached. To examine into the character and value of these asserted disproofs will be the object of the present chapter. In entering upon the examination there is manifest reason why both the facts and the conclusion already considered should be kept constantly in mind.

Without bearing the facts in mind, no fair estimate can be formed of the comparative weight due to the two opposite classes of evidences. It is not enough to count objections, and to decide the question by the numerical balance of one side over the other: their worth must be taken into account. One conclusive proof will outweigh a thousand inconclusive objections. It may be that the two classes of evidence differ **widely** in their character, and that the one may be as rich in claims for credibility as the other may be devoid of them.

This is actually the case. The instances of scriptural veracity already adduced rest upon proofs wholly independent of themselves, and absolutely above suspicion. The inspired statement has been placed on one side, and the proof of its accuracy over against it on the other. This proof has been very largely drawn from material monuments of the past. Ruined cities—the very sites of which had been forgotten for ages—have been called, as it were, out of their grave. Their remains are found to be so rich in written history as to enable us to reconstruct the past as it was never known to us before. The restless spirit of modern investigation has deciphered them, and gathered from them, over and over again, the exact corroboration of the literal truth of Scripture. These are witnesses that cannot be charged with prejudice: the vain-glorious records of a past ambition are beyond all possible suspicion of partiality. Here, as in other sources of information less wonderful but equally trustworthy, not only do we find the general references of Scripture to profane history confirmed without one single failure, but we find minute particulars of person, place, and date, and little details of personal adventure and natural history, all corroborated even to a marvel. So complete is the proof, that the Christian is filled with adoring gratitude to the providence which not only so moulded national character and habit as to cause these inscriptions to be made, but which has also preserved them intact through intervening ages, and now laid the marvellous pages open to the instruction of an age peculiarly critical and inquisitive. Such evidence as this removes the instances enumerated out of the category of probable arguments into that of demonstrative facts. The case is not, therefore, that the believer in Divine revelation asserts the sacred Scriptures to be true, but it is, that in many specified instances their truth is proved, not only beyond the possibility of disproof, but even beyond the possibility of doubt.

We have, therefore, a right to require evidence equally conclusive in its character on the other side. The resources of an age rich in antiquarian discovery and historic information could not fail to supply the material for this evidence, if any inaccuracy of Scripture had rendered its existence possible. We ask for some record of authentic history—for some monument of the ancient past—for some inscription of the days that are gone, which contradicts in any one clear point any one clear statement of the sacred Scriptures—those Scriptures which are so contemptuously declared to be a mere patchwork of old myths and traditions, unhistorical and incredible! We say, If it be so, show us the proof of it. Where is the false fact, the historical anachronism, the contradiction of known events? And where, among the multitudinous witnesses of the past, is the evidence to make conviction complete and denial impossible?

We ask in vain for any such proof. It is a memorable fact that not one such instance has been found. There is not a solitary fact disproved by the silent evidence of the monuments of Egypt, Assyria, Babylon, or Persia. The positive proof stands alone, and not a single witness is found to raise a voice on the other side. Doubts, cavils, suspicions, conjectures, we have in abundance; but positive evidence we have actually none.

In its room we are confronted with a host of shadowy objections, resting largely on arbitrary assumption and personal opinion. One part of Scripture is laboriously forced into opposition to another part. Speculative judgments are advanced as to what the sacred writers, and the Spirit who inspired them, knew or did not know, expressed or meant to express. Individual variations of manner, style, and narration, are treated as irreconcilable contradictions. Facts are summarily denied, and doctrines contemptuously discarded, on the sole authority of an alleged critical instinct. But in all these cases a course of speculative reasoning is substituted for the evidence of facts, and this reasoning, however honest, is tainted with human ignorance, fallibility, and prejudice. Alleged proofs of such a kind cannot be placed side by side, even for a moment, with the demonstrable facts which confirm, on the positive side of the argument, the singular and, under the circumstances, superhuman accuracy of the sacred writings.

But here comes in the conclusion already drawn from these undeniable facts. The familiar instances where apparent difficulties have been converted on fuller information into real harmonies show that, in these cases at all events, the difficulty arose solely from human ignorance. We are therefore not only justified, but compelled to form the conclusion that what is true in these cases is, in all probability, true in other cases likewise. Supposing it to be admitted that a certain number of insoluble difficulties still present themselves in Scripture, we must believe that defect of information is their producing cause, and that, could the defect be supplied, these cases, like others, would turn out to be convincing proofs of the veracity they are now alleged to impugn. I fully grant that the force of this conclusion depends upon the number of the difficulties alleged, because evidences very small in themselves may yet become strong by accumulation, and by the consilience of proof, as it is called, may conceivably amount even to moral demonstration. To ascertain what their number and force may be is now, therefore, my object. But it must be admitted at the beginning, that the presumption established in favor of the truth of Scripture weakens them, whatever they may be, and detracts an appreciable percentage from any value they might otherwise possess.

The number of these objections is very large, and, if numerical preponderance had weight, would apparently be very formidable. The unwearied in-

dustry exhibited in searching throughout the length
and breadth of Scripture for the grounds of adverse
evidence, proves that, if the veracity of the Bible
remains unimpugned, it will be neither from want
of will nor want of ingenuity in its assailants.
They cover so wide an area that it is impossible, in
such a work as this, to notice or even to enumerate
them. It is necessary to draw some line between
what are appropriate to my immediate subject and
what are not. I purpose, therefore, to omit all
alleged evidences which are directed to overthrow
the whole authority of Scripture, and confine myself to those which have recently been put forward
in disproof of its Divine inspiration and consequent
inerrability.

Even so the number is very large, amounting to
nearly four hundred distinct passages of more or
less length. The number might receive apparent
increase, if passages were broken up into their individual parts, and single objections separately enumerated. Nevertheless, it will appear that the very
largeness of the number only serves to attest the
more absolutely the authority of Scriptures capable
of passing unscathed through so strict and searching an ordeal.

Definite rules can alone guide the inquiry
through such a tangled mass of objections. All
arguments, moreover, incapable of being reduced
to rule, must lie under just suspicion of arbitrary
caprice. The rules will follow necessarily from a
principle already asserted, and to which, as to a
point settled, I claim the right to appeal as the

groundwork of further argument. This principle is that a revelation implies, indeed requires, two parties, and therefore two elements, and that the two elements are to be maintained everywhere, always distinct, but never separate. The part which God had in producing the Bible must not be so pushed as to absorb the part which man had in producing it. The part which man had in producing the Bible must not be so pushed as to derogate from the part which God had in producing it. Consequently, if the human element be admitted as indispensable, whatever is essential to the human element must be admitted likewise; and yet the admission will not take away any quality essential to the Divine element. The principle is very simple; yet the great mass of skeptical objection has arisen from denying it, and from falsely assuming that whatever is characteristically human cannot be at the same time characteristically Divine. I have already shown that no conceivable reason can be given why the human and Divine should not be as closely and invariably united in the written word as, by the admission of all orthodox believers, they are united in the personal Word—in Him who, born of the Virgin Mary, was yet God of God, Light of Light, very God of very God.

The rules to be borne in mind as a soldier may grasp his weapons when he descends into the conflict, are as follows:

RULE 1.—*Passages interpolated into the original autographs, or errors made in transcription, are no parts of Scripture, and furnish, therefore, no argument against its truth.* The liability to causes of error of this kind arises from the human language of Scripture, and the human instruments employed to convey the revelation. We are not at liberty, however, to fall back on this explanation as a mere means of escape from a difficulty, unless some reason can be alleged to justify it. There is no difficulty in laying down canons for guidance in such a case. We are justified in adopting this explanation (*a*) whenever the evidence of the MSS. suggested it; (*b*) wherever Scripture itself furnishes the data for discovering or correcting the mistake; (*c*) where the nature of the passage or the characters of the words render an error in transcription easy, and therefore probable. Where none of these reasons exist we have no right to adopt this mode of evading a difficulty. Mere arbitrary and capricious exercise of individual opinion constitutes no justification for it. For instance, the majority of the MSS. attest that 1 John 5 : 7 is an interpolation, and the fact that it only interrupts the argument of the apostle is an internal evidence to the same effect. Again, the number of men who drew the sword in Israel and Judah, as taken in the census made by Joab at David's command, differs very widely in 2 Sam. 24 : 9, and 1 Chron. 21 : 5. We are therefore at liberty, on the authority of either statement of the two, to suppose an error of transcription in the other, if other explanations fail to satisfy us. On the other hand, a similar error on the part of the copyist has been suggested relative to the number of the Hebrew people at the Exodus;

and it has been supposed that, by a very easy and natural error, six hundred thousand has been written for sixty thousand. But in this case, so far is Scripture itself from affording any authority for the alteration, that it positively forbids it; for the correction would bring this particular passage into contradiction with other passages, such as Exod. 30:11–16, 28:25; Numb. 11:21; Deut. 11:22; 26; 1 Cor. 10:8, etc. We are, therefore, bound to reject it. The reconstruction of the book of Genesis into the two supposed documents, the Elohistic and the Jehovistic, by the disciples of the "higher criticism," affords an instance of the arbitrary, and therefore unjustifiable, suggestion of interpolations on the part of the transcriber. Certain passages are found not to yield themselves to this theoretical treatment, and are therefore arbitrarily declared to be interpolations. Thus Eichhorn conjecturally alters Gen. 4:25; 9:27; 17:1; 22:12; 27:28, etc., solely on this ground.

The limitation expressed in this rule is applicable to some cases not at present claiming consideration. Of the instances taken into calculation in this chapter, it is applicable to four: 2 Sam. 24:9; 1 Chron. 21:5; Matt. 27:9; and 1 John 5:7. It may also be fairly applied to another instance, to which a further examination will be given hereafter, viz., Acts 7:16.

Rule 2. *The employment of figures of speech and of artificial or conventional forms of statement constitutes no violation of literal truth.* Both these peculiarities belong inseparably to the human element.

Figures of speech are employed for the very purpose of conveying the idea of facts with a greater intensity than would otherwise be possible. They must therefore be resolved into their meaning, before the accuracy or inaccuracy of the description can be tested. For instance, when St. Luke records that at the crucifixion of Christ " there was darkness over all the earth,"* he employs a figure (synecdoche) of familiar and undisputed use in all secular writers, by which sometimes a part is placed for the whole, and sometimes a whole for a part. In this instance, " all the earth " is used to express the wide and unbroken prevalence of the darkness. When a great quantity or number is expressed by such phrases as the sand of the sea, the dust of the earth, and the stars of heaven—as in Gen. 13 :16; 41 :49; Judges 7 :12 ; 1 Sam. 13 :5 ; 1 Kings 4 :29 ; 2 Chron. 1 :9 ; Jer. 15 :8 ; Heb. 11 :12—a graphic hyperbole is employed to impress upon the mind the more vivid conception of the idea. Of artificial modes of statement we have a striking instance in the genealogy of St. Matthew. Of conventional forms, an illustration is afforded by the round numbers of Scripture, as in Numb. 1 :21–46; 2 Sam. 24 :9; 1 Chron. 21 :5. In the same manner, secular historians familiarly speak of armies as consisting of so many thousand men ; but nobody accuses them of inaccuracy because of the improbability that an army should actually consist of the round numbers, without a single man either more or less.

* Luke 23:44. The word rendered earth, however, probably means land, *i. e.*, the land of Judea.

Alleged objections falling to the ground under this rule are based upon the following passages: Gen. 13 : 16; 46 : 12; Exod. 6 : 14–27; Judg. 7 : 12; Numb. 1 : 21, 46; 1 Sam. 24 : 9; 2 Chron. 21 : 5; Matt. 1 : 1, 17; 27 : 6, compared with Acts 1 : 18, Luke 23 : 44, Acts 24 : 5. But a list of similar passages might be prolonged almost indefinitely.

RULE 3. *Variations of statement are not contradictions, when they arise either from recording different parts of some common event, or from assigning a different emphasis and importance to the same parts.* If the mental peculiarities of the sacred writers were to be maintained, as I have shown that they must be maintained—or the human element would be destroyed—these variations are inevitable. The same common facts will strike different minds differently; or rather, different minds will take hold, so to speak, of different aspects of them. This variation is a matter of familiar experience. Let the accounts of the same battle by three or four different historians be compared, or the reports of some current event as given in half a dozen different newspapers; an absolute similarity will be found to exist in no two of them. Yet on the very points of variation all the accounts may be equally true. So it is with the scriptural narratives. It has already been pointed out that no history intended for human readers can possibly be a mere transcript of the Divine mind. The object is not to give a complete account of every event as the omniscient mind of God sees it, but to record such parts as God has seen to be necessary for human instruction. It has pleased God that the evangelical writers, in recording the same event, should record different parts of it; and in this very variation we find the evidence for the independent truthfulness of the narrative. We must apply to the sacred writings the standard applied to other writings. If variations of narrative were contradictions, secular history would be a mass of inexplicable confusion. It is admitted that variations may exist in writings purely human without any diminution of truth; and the same principle must be admitted with the sacred writings, inasmuch as they are the production of human authors, none the less for being inspired authors, and must therefore be expected to present human peculiarities.

Under this rule fall, as might be expected, the great mass of skeptical objections against the truthfulness of Scripture. An illustrative instance or two must be specified. Thus, the accounts of the infancy of our Lord given by St. Matthew and St. Luke have been represented as irreconcilably contradictory to each other; and the reasons alleged are the following: (a) Matthew simply records the birth of Christ at Bethlehem, and does not give the explanatory circumstances supplied by St. Luke. (b) St. Luke does not record the adoration of the Magi or the flight into Egypt, narrated by Matthew; but, after recording the presentation of the infant Jesus in the temple, fixes the next scene of his narrative at Nazareth. I believe that to most minds the mode in which the two accounts fit into one consecutive story will appear a signal instance of harmonious truth, instead of an illustration of irreconcilable contradiction.

Another instance is alleged in the cure of the centurion's servant, recorded in Matt. 8 : 5–13, Luke 7 : 1–10.   Here the point of alleged discrepancy is, that St. Matthew states, "There came unto him a centurion," while Luke states, "He sent unto him [Jesus] the elders of the Jews;" again, "The centurion sent friends unto him."   The two statements are perfectly consistent, and may both be true.   It is but a touch of nature that the centurion, in deep anxiety about his servant, should in his humility send friends, and yet, in his earnestness, himself follow, and repeat in person the message previously entrusted to others.

Where instances are so numerous, a detailed explanation of individual cases is impossible.   I can only indicate the source of the difficulty, and the key by which it is to be removed.   Passages in the Old Testament alleged to be discrepant, but which are reconcileable under this rule, are as follows :

Gen. 1 : 24–28, compared with Gen. 2 : 7–23 ;
Gen. 6 : 19 with 7 : 2 ;
Gen. 28 : 10–19 with Gen. 35 : 6–9 ;
Exod. 12 : 40 with Acts 7 : 6 ;
Exod. 16 : 35 with Josh. 5 : 10–12 ;
Exod. 20 : 1–11 with Deut. 5 : 4–22 ;
Exod. 3 : 1–20 with Exod. 4 : 10–31, 5 : 1–23, 6 : 2–30, 7 : 1–7 ;
Exodus 16 : 1–35 with Numbers 9 : 1, 2, 10 : 11–33, 11 : 1–35, 33 : 10–17 ;
Lev. 17 : 1–9 with Deut. 12 : 13–22 ;
Numb. 21 : 33–35 with Deut. 3 : 11 ;
Numb. 1 : 1–49 with Numb. 2 : 32, 33, 3 : 10–47 ;
Numb. 4 : 1–48 with Numb. 8 : 23–26 ;

Numb. 18:8-19 with Deut. 12:5-9, 15:19-22, 18:1-5, and Lev. 27:26, 27;
Numb. 18:20-26 with Deut. 14:22-29, and Neh. 10:35-38;
Deut. 3:13, 14 with Judges 10:1-4.

Passages of the same character in the New Testament are as follows:

Matt. 1:1-17 with Luke 3:23-38;
Matt. 1:18 with Luke 1:26;
Matt. 2:1, 5-23 with Luke 2:4-42;
Matt. 3:1 with Mark 1:1, Luke 3:2-22, and John 1:6-15;
Matt. 4:18-22 with Mark 1:16-20, Luke 6, 1-11, John 1:28-44;
Matt. 4:25 with Luke 6:12-20;
Matt. 6:9-15 with Mark 11:24-26, and Luke 11:1-4;
Matt. 6:19-21 with Luke 12:33, 34;
Matt. 6:22, 23 with Luke 11:32-36;
Matt. 6:24 with Luke 16:11-14;
Matt. 6:25-34 with Luke 12:21-35;
Matt. 7:1-5 with Luke 6:37-42;
Matt. 7:7-11 with Luke 11:5-13;
Matt. 7:12 with Luke 6:30-32;
Matt. 7:13, 14 with Luke 13:22-25;
Matt. 7:15 with Luke 6:43;
Matt. 7:12-23, 8:10-13, and 19:30, with Luke 13:22-30;
Matt. 8:5-13 with Luke 7:1-10;
Matt. 11:10-14 with Luke 16:14-18;
Matt. 14:3-11 with Mark 6:17-28;
Matt. 20:29-34 with Mark 10:46-52, and Luke 18:35-43, 19:1;
Matt. 19:6-19 with Mark 10:7-19, and Luke 18:18-20;
Matt. 22:34-42 with Mark 11:28-35;
Matt. 21:11-18 with Mark 11:11-15, and Luke 19:45;
Matt. 21:19 with Mark 11:2;
Matt. 26:33-75 with Mark 14:29-72, Luke 22:31-62, John 13:36-38, and 18:16-27;
Matt. 26:17-20 with Mark 14:12-17, Luke 22:7-15, John 13:1-30, and 18:28,29;
Matt. 27:45, 46 with Mark 15:24-34, Luk 23:44-46, and John 19:13-15;
Matt. 27:54 with Mark 15:39, Luke 23:47;
Matt. 26:30-32, and 28:1-20, with Mark 14:26-28, 16:1-20, Luke 24:1-53, Acts 1:3-9, John 20:1-28, and 21:1-22;

Matt. 18 : 6–15 with Luke 15 : 1–10 ;
Matt. 22 : 1–14 with Luke 14 : 15–24 ;
Matt. 25 : 14–30 with Luke 19 : 11–29 ;
Matt. 24 : 3–36 with Mark 13 : 4–32, Luke 21 : 33 ;
Acts 19 : 3–17 with Acts 22 : 6–15, and 26 : 12–19.

RULE 4. *Omissions of parts of a series of facts, or of particulars making up facts, are entirely consistent with the truth of the narrative in which they occur.* The reasons for this rule are similar to those alleged for the rule preceding, and will not require, therefore, to be repeated. It will suffice to repeat part of a quotation from an impartial source already made in a previous chapter (chap. 12) : " Since the facts out of which we must construct our histories in idea are but a small proportion, a mere remaining shred, of that enormous intertwined infinity of facts which actually went into the histories while the web was being woven, are there any kinds or orders of facts which more than others it is desirable, for the purposes of history, to secure and keep hold of?" The relative importance of facts, it must also be remembered, is strictly and solely related to the objects proposed by the writer. A variety of points of view and of modes of viewing things are inseparable from the human element. A varying proportion given to facts, even up to their omission altogether, is therefore inseparable from the human element likewise, since the effect must be coextensive with the cause. Variations of narrative, arising from the omission of some facts out of a series, might consistently have fallen under the previous rule ; but as they constitute a variation of one specific kind, I have thought it best, for the sake of clearness, to classify them by themselves.

An omission of this kind occurs in Matt. 14:5, compared with Mark 6:18. For Mark records a foregone purpose on the part of Herodias to kill John the Baptist; but Matthew records no such design. Again, John records a visit of Jesus to Jerusalem at the feast of the dedication, John 10:22, in regard to which the other three evangelists are silent. St. John describes the raising of Lazarus from the dead, John 11:7–17; but no account of such a miracle is given by Matthew, Mark, and Luke.

Or to take instances of a more detailed kind: Matthew records the curing the two blind men at Jericho, Matt. 20:29, while Mark and Luke (Mark 10:46; Luke 18:35) record the curing only of one. St. Matthew narrates the words of our Lord to Peter to be, "This night, before the cock crow, thou shalt deny me thrice," Matt. 26:34, without specifying any definite number of times when the cock should crow, Matt. 26:75; whereas St. Mark specifies that the cock should crow twice, Mark 14:72. St. Matthew and St. Mark, in the account of our Lord's crucifixion, record that the thieves who were crucified with him reviled him. Matt. 27:44; Mark 15:32. But they make no mention of the further circumstance narrated by St. Luke, of the repentance and confession of one of the two. Luke 23:42.

Other instances of omitted facts alleged to constitute cases of contradiction are as follows:

Matt. 19 : 1, 20 : 17, 21 : 1–23, 24 : 1–3, 26 : 1–12, compared with
   Mark 9 : 33, 10 : 1–46, 11 : 1–27, 12 : 35, 13 : 1, 14 : 1–9, Luke
   9 : 51–53, 10 : 38, 39, 17 : 11, 12, 18 : 35. 19 : 1–47, 20 : 1,
   22 : 1–7, John 10 : 22–39, 11 : 7–53, 12 : 1–19 ;
Matt. 23 : 8–22 with Luke 11 : 37–54 ;
Matt. 27 : 41–45 with Mark 14 : 32–42 ;
Matt. 22 : 1–14 with Luke 14 : 15–24, 22 : 40–46 ;
Matt. 25 : 14–30 with Luke 19 : 11–29.

The same objection is brought against the following passages in the book of Genesis :

Gen. 4 : 1–26 compared with Gen. 5 : 1–6 ;
Gen. 26 : 34, 35, with Gen. 28 : 6–9, and 36 : 1–6.

Many other objections have been taken similar in kind, which yet do not fall within the class here dealt with.

RULE 5. *Differences of style in the composition, of personal character in the mode of thinking, and of standpoint in looking at common truths, are neither inconsistent with truth, nor with the action of a Divine inspiration.* These differences are inseparable from the free use of human messengers as the instrument of communicating truth to mankind. The only conceivable mode of avoiding them would be for God in employing human instruments, to merge their separate peculiarities, mental, moral, local, circumstantial, in one common and indistinguishable type. Such a mode of acting would have been contrary to all the ordinary principles of God's moral government, and would have destroyed the foothold of the revelation on the historical realities of the world. But if God did not see fit to do this, then the personal peculiarities of the sacred writers must have been retained. God in selecting one man rather than another to be his messenger must have had regard to the special gifts, character, position, period, and preparatory education of the messenger. It has been shown in chapter 9 that the peculiarities of the men were a necessary condition of the human element in Scripture. But these peculiarities have necessarily left their stamp on their productions. The style is different in different men, or even with the same man under different circumstances and on different topics. Their modes of thinking affect their modes of speaking. Each man regards the common subject from the standpoint of his own particular theme, particular purpose, or particular mode of thought. If, therefore, the existence of a human element in Scripture is so essential to the very idea of a revelation as to constitute no argument against its Divine inspiration, all the peculiarities arising from the human element must be consistent with it likewise.

Forgetfulness of this simple truth has been the originating source of many adverse criticisms upon Scripture. The discriminations of the difference in style has been as accurate as the conclusion founded upon it is unjustifiable and absurd. Thus the Mosaic authority of the book of Deuteronomy has been called into question because the earnest and elevated style of the book stands in such strong contrast with the formal language of Leviticus. In the same way it has been argued that the teaching of the Pauline epistles and the teaching of the Pentateuch cannot have proceeded from the inspiration of one and the same God, because one starts from the point of view supplied by a completed salvation, the other from the point of view of a preparatory and imperfect dispensation. One instance of the same difficulty in detail is afforded by the well-known passages of Romans 4:1–5, where the apostle is arguing against the hope of salvation by the deeds of the law; and James 2:14–26, where the apostle speaks against the reality of faith that is not evidenced by its effects on the life and conduct.

Thus the standpoint of a Divine prescience in the speaker is wholly overlooked in the objections brought against such passages as Exod. 36:31, Gen. 12:6, Numb. 15:32–36, Deut. 3:12, Lev. 18:24–28. The peculiar position of the Hebrew people, and the necessity of pressing, over and over again, upon a half-civilized people respect towards others, are forgotten in the objection raised against the reiterated injunctions of Exod. 22:21; 23:9, 17–19; 34:23–26. The relation in which the times of the gospel are declared to stand towards the second coming of Christ, as being themselves the sole intervening period before the accomplishment of that great event, is overlooked in the skeptical comment made in reference to the second coming in the epistles: *e. g.*,

> Rom. 13:11, 12; 1 Cor. 1:7, 8, 7:19–31, 11:26, 15:51, 52; Phil. 1:6–10, 3:20, 21, 4:5; Col. 3:4; 1 Thess. 1:9, 10, 2:19, 3:13, 4:13–18, 5:1–23; 2 Thess. 2:1–12; 1 Tim. 6:13–15; 2 Tim. 4:1–8; Titus 2:12, 13; Heb. 9:28, 10:24–37; James 5:3–9; 1 Peter 1:4–20, 4:4–7, 5:1–4; 2 Peter 3:3–12; 1 John 2:17–28, 3:2, 4:3; Rev. 1:3–7, 2:25, 22:10–26.

The nature of predictive prophecy and the characteristic difference distinguishing the prediction of the future from the narration of the past are likewise overlooked in commenting upon the variations perceptible in such passages as Matt. 24:3-36, Mark 13:4-32, and Luke 21:20-33.

The wantonness of such conjectural criticism is illustrated by another class of instances. In some cases it has been remarked that skeptical objection is based on the diversity of style. But a further class of objection is based on the similarity of style. Doubt has been attempted to be thrown upon the accuracy of St. John's gospel, from the similarity of expression traced between it and some passages in the first epistle of the same apostle. The plea is that the peculiar style of expression belonging to the apostle St. John has colored the language imputed, and as it is hinted, falsely imputed to our blessed Master. The argument is urged in characteristic forgetfulness that the reverse alternative is at least equally probable, in that the language of our Lord may naturally have colored the mode of thinking and speaking belonging to the apostle whom Jesus loved, and who, in the familiarity of intimate friendship, lay upon his breast. The passages adduced are as follows:

John 1 : 1-14, 21 : 24, compared with 1 John 1 : 1, 2 ;
John 1 : 5, 13 : 34, with 1 John 1 : 5, 2 : 8 ;
John 1 : 12. 15 : 19, with 1 John 3 : 1 ;
John 1 : 18, with 1 John 4 : 12 ;
John 3 : 3, with 1 John 3 : 9 ;
John 3 : 16, with 1 John 4 : 9 ;
John 3 : 21, with 1 John 1 : 6 ;
John 3 : 31, 8 : 23, 15 : 19, with 1 John 4 : 5 ;
John 3 : 36, with 1 John 5 : 12 ;
John 5 : 23, 15 : 23, with 1 John 2 : 23 ;

John 5 : 24, with 1 John 3 : 14 ;
John 5 : 36, 37, with 1 John 5 : 9 ;
John 8 : 12, 12 : 35, with 1 John 1 : 7 ;
John 8 : 32, with 1 John 2 : 24 ;
John 8 : 44, with 1 John 3 : 8 ;
John 8 : 46, with 1 John 3 : 5 ;
John 8 : 47, with 1 John 4 : 6 ;
John 9 : 31, with 1 John 3 : 2 ;
John 11 : 51, 52, with 1 John 2 : 2 ;
John 12 : 35, with 1 John 2 : 11 ;
John 13 : 15, with 1 John 2 : 6 ;
John 14 : 13, with 1 John 5 : 14 ;
John 14 : 15, with 1 John 5 : 3 ;
John 14 : 16, 17, with 1 John 2 : 1 ;
John 14 : 21, with 1 John 2 : 5 ;
John 14 : 26, with 1 John 2 : 20–27 ;
John 15 : 10, with 1 John 2 : 3 ;
John 15 : 11, 16 : 24, with 1 John 1 : 4 ;
John 15 : 13, with 1 John 3 : 16 ;
John 15 : 18, with 1 John 3 : 13 ;
John 16 : 33, with 1 John 5 : 4 ;
John 20 : 31, with 1 John 5 : 13.

RULE 6. *Separate transactions are not to be identified with each other because of a parallelism between some circumstances of an event, or some portions of a discourse.* It is a true and profound remark, that human history has a tendency to repeat itself; under analogous circumstances men are likely to adopt an analogous course of action. A partial similarity is therefore no proof of identity. This caution is practically needed in regard to the transactions of our Lord's life and his recorded discourses. The resources of his own wisdom, knowledge, and power, were indeed infinite; but the sphere of his ministry was narrow, being confined to the Jews. The circumstances were rigidly peculiar.

The general characteristics of the persons with whom he came into contact were, from the strong and peculiar type of the Jewish character and the religious condition of the Jewish church of his day, marked by a strongly defined similarity. In his teaching under such circumstances there could be but little comparative variety. The same truths, the same warnings, the same expostulations, the same promises, must have recurred over and over again; for why should a perfectly wise teacher vary the form of his words, when the circumstances to which they were addressed were not varied? A certain monotone and repetition was inevitable. But if this existed in our Lord's teaching, it must equally be expected to exist in the records of his teaching. To argue from a similarity of circumstances or of truth for the absolute identity of two transactions or two discourses, is to put a forced and unnatural construction upon the inspired record.

It is not necessary for me to enter elaborately in each case upon the consideration of these asserted cases of identity. It is enough for me to assert that the conclusion is, in such cases, precarious in the extreme, to say the very best of it; and that any further argument, based on this precarious supposition, cannot have higher certainty than belongs to its foundation, and can be esteemed little better than a superstructure of shadow built upon a foundation of sand.

Yet this argument has been freely used. It has been deemed necessary to establish the existence of contradictions in the scriptural narrative. What more easy than to assume that two varying accounts refer to one and the same transaction, and therefore must be contradictory to each other? Of the extreme uncertainty of such identification at the best we have an illustration in what is the strongest of all the alleged cases, the sermon on the mount, as recorded in Matt. 5 to 8, and the discourse recorded by St. Luke in 6:20–49. A quotation from a posthumous publication by the Rev. Josiah Forshall, the merit of which suggests how great a loss the church of Christ has suffered by his removal, will serve to show the bearing of the question. After pointing out the antecedent probability that no indefinite variation would be found in our Lord's teaching, Mr. Forshall continues:

"Do the gospel narratives enable us to say positively whether our Lord did or did not repeat his lessons in the same manner and in like words? Our Lord taught his disciples to pray on two different occasions widely apart: did he think fit to command the use of the same or of different forms? They are nearly the same. Our Lord taught, on three different occasions, the true doctrine of marriage and the unlawfulness of divorce: did he do it in different or in the same terms? Nearly in the same. Our Lord twice wept over Jerusalem with touching lamentations: were they expressed in different or in the same words? They were in the same. Our Lord, when he was approaching Jerusalem, on his last journey from Galilee, delivered a parable, Luke 19:12. Within a few days, when he quitted Jerusalem, he again delivered a parable, Matt. 25:14. How far do these parables differ. They agree literally in the greater part of each."

He then illustrates the same fact from the sermon on the mount itself, in passages all of which have perversely been made the subject of skeptical objections. We conclude this topic by asking, "Why, then, should he not have repeated a part of what he had said in the sermon upon the mount on another occasion recorded by St. Luke?" He then proceeds to show that, so far are the two discourses from being identical, that of the whole matter contained in the two accounts, *less than one fifth is common, and more than four fifths peculiar, to one or the other*. But if this strongest of all the instances be weak, what shall be said of the rest, or what weight be placed upon arguments which contradict in some cases the express declarations of the narrative itself?

Yet the following passages have been called into question, solely on the authority of this speculative identity:

Gen. 12 : 10, 20 : 1–18, 21 : 22–31, 26:6–11. 17–33 ; Matt. 20 : 20–34 ; Mark 10 : 46–52 ; Luke 18 : 35–43 ; Matt. 18 : 15 ; Mark 9 : 33–37 ; Luke 9 : 46–48 ; Matt. 20:20. 29 ; Mark 10 : 35–46 ; Luke 22 : 21–30 ; Matt. 21 : 15, 16 ; Luke 19 : 38–40 ; Matt. 21 : 11 ; John 2 : 13 ; Matt. 23 : 1–39, 24 : 1; Luke 11 : 37–54 ; Matt. 4 : 18–22 with John 1 : 28–44.

RULE 7.—*No private estimates of probability or improbability, either as to facts or doctrines, can be of force to neutralize the testimony of a positive record.*

As far as this proposition relates to historical facts
the common proverb that "fact is stranger than fiction" expresses the ordinary experience and convictions of mankind. The course of human events is
not represented by the even current of some smooth
river, flowing upon its uninterrupted course through
smiling plains into the sea. But it is represented
by a river interrupted by rocks, and broken into
rapids and cataracts. Sudden changes, startling
vicissitudes, and strange calamities, form the common features of history. Those who have lived but
for a few years can recall repeated instances of
events which excited common wonder and astonish-
ment, from having taken place in a manner previously deemed to be impossible. Who could have
foreseen the past history of the world—who can
predict its future history? But if we are wholly
incapable of judging from antecedent considerations
of the probability and improbability of events, still
less are we capable of anticipating the fluctuating
course of human action; still less of judging of
Divine action. Doctrines, still more than facts,
because they have their origin in the mind of God,
lie wholly beyond and above the reach of the human
mind. All objections, therefore, founded on personal opinion on the part of the critic, and which
find expression in such phrases as "I do not think
it probable," "It does not appear to me likely," are
devoid of all argumentative force, and, as evidences,
are literally valueless.

Yet no inconsiderable number of objections
against the veracity of Scripture have no other

foundation than this, as will be seen in the following instances :

Gen. 12 : 6, 13 : 7, 18, 14 : 14, 17 : 17, 18 : 11, 19, 23 : 2, 36 : 31 ;
  Exod. 30 : 11–16, 35 : 27, 38 : 25–28, with Numb. 1 : 1–46 ;
Exod. 6 : 21, 22, 11 : 3, 12 : 3, 37, 13 : 18 ; Lev. 8 : 3, 13 : 43 ; Numb.
  2, 3 : 16, 26, with 26 : 43 ; 9 : 1–13, 10 : 11–14, 11 : 1–35, 12 : 3–16,
  13 : 3–26, 14 : 13, 15, 25–34, 15 : 22, 18 : 20–26, 20 : 1–29, 21 : 4–
  13 : 16, 26 : 62, 32 : 1, 33 : 15–39, 34 : 5–12 ; Deut. 1 : 2–46,
  2 : 1–14, 3 : 43, 5 : 1, 10 : 6, 7, 12 : 2–18, compared with Josh.
  18 : 1, 24 : 1–26 ; Judges 2 : 4, 5 ; Deut. 17 : 14–20, 28 : 36, 37 ;
  Josh 8 : 34, 35, 19 : 47 ; Judges 8 : 22, 23, 18 : 27, 28 ; 1 Sam.
  8 : 4–22, 10 : 24, 25.

Under this rule falls another class of objections, where the judgment of the critic is set up as the standard of conclusive argument, or the test of conclusive evidence. The very form of these objections involves the denial of that Divine inspiration, and consequent authority of Scripture, which are the questions for proof or disproof. The objection quietly ignores that Divine element whence Scripture derives its authority as the rule of faith. What is taught in the inspired Word as an express revelation from God is brought down to the measurement of human opinion, and accepted or rejected on the sole verdict of the critic. As example is afforded by the quotations made by St. Paul in Romans 3 : 9–19 ; from Psalms 14 : 1–7, 5 : 1–12, 140 : 1–13, 10 : 1–12, 59 : 12, 109 : 17, 18. The object of the critic is to show that the reasoning of the apostle is illogical and inconclusive. He first determines in his own judgment that the language of the psalmist could not bear that universal application which the inspired commentator gives to the inspired declaration. Having thus settled beforehand that St. Paul must be wrong, his course is easy. Let him speak in his own words: "*It is quite evident* that the whole of a nation, and still more so the whole of mankind, could not *justly be described* by all the epithets which have been quoted by St. Paul in the passage under consideration. But if this be so, if the writers of these Psalms, when they denounced the wicked in the language to which the apostle has appealed, had in view only a limited class of persons, the enemies, oppressors, and persecutors of the 'righteous,' or of the 'people' of God, it results that these texts cannot be received as evidence of what St. Paul adduces them to demonstrate, viz., the universal depravity and guilt of the entire Jewish nation, or even of the whole human race."

This mode of quietly begging the question, and then using this foregone conclusion as an evidence, has been freely applied to the writings of St. Paul. The following passages have been specially called into question, and are vindicated by the rule now under consideration:

Rom. 3 : 9–19, 4 : 1–5 ; Gal. 3 : 1–10, 8–15, 29, 4 : 21–31, 5 : 1–9 ; Heb. 1 : 1–13, 2 : 5, 3 : 7–19 ; 4 : 1–11, 10 : 14–18, 36–39, 11 : 8–16 ; 1 Cor. 11 : 5–11, 15 : 12–20 ; also to 1 Pet. 1 : 23–25, and James 2 : 14–26.

I have now enumerated three hundred and twenty-six passages of Scripture which have been called into question. I have taken them without any selection from recent works directed against the inspiration of the Bible, and have knowingly

omitted none. They constitute the entire weapons
of the skeptical armory; and if they fail, there are
none others. Yet the seven simple rules enumerated above overthrow their very foundation. Rule 1
is fatal to 4 of them, rule 2 to 12, rule 3 to 144, rule
4 to 47, rule 5 to 116, rule 6 to 23, rule 7 to 80. The
whole area of skeptical objection is now swept, and
what cases remain must be solved by the exercise
of faith, and by the reasonable presumption established in the last chapter, that difficulties arise from
erroneous and defective information, and would disappear in these cases as in others, could the information be corrected or supplied. Of the present list
none remain. The whole army of difficulties arise
from misapprehensions relative to the Divine and
human elements. They are consequently removed,
when we clearly see that all the characteristics of a
human composition may exist in the Scripture to
the full, and yet not detract in the least from its
plenary inspiration and authority.

It will be impossible, I think, to examine the
instances enumerated without perceiving another
fact. The difficulties suggested are so subtle that
in many cases it requires an effort to understand
them. Passages alleged to be contradictory may
be put side by side without an ordinary reader
being conscious even of discrepancy between them,
much less of contradiction. It needs a commentary
to elucidate the nature of the supposed difficulty,
so trivial is it for the most part in itself, and so
dependent for its force upon suppositions without
proof, and suspicions without evidence. Such ob-

jections stand in singular contrast to the broad facts, the strong, clear lines of proof, and the independent sources of evidence by which the minute accuracy of the scriptural books is signally illustrated.

There is, however, one solitary instance where a contradiction does stand on the face of the narrative, and to this case our attention must briefly be directed. I allude to Acts 7:14–16. Supposing this instance to lie wholly beyond explanation, we should fall back on the belief that some ignorance or misconception of our own was really the cause of the difficulty. But the solution is to be found in the very simplicity and absoluteness of the contradiction involved, and the palpable manner in which it stands out upon the very surface of the narrative.

The avowed inaccuracies are principally three: 1. That the household of Jacob, who went down into Egypt, consisted of seventy-five persons, whereas seventy only are specified in Gen. 46:27. 2. That Jacob is stated to have been buried at Sychem, whereas we are told in Gen. 49:30 that he was buried in the cave of Machpelah at Hebron. 3. That Abraham bought the sepulchre of the sons of Hamor; whereas, according to Gen. 23:19, the purchase was really made by Jacob. But of these three difficulties the latter only admits at present of no positive explanation. For Stephen's enumeration of Jacob's kindred as seventy-five persons may be explained in several ways, especially considering that the Septuagint version reads the number as seventy-five, not seventy, in Gen. 46:27, Exod. 1:5, and in some very ancient copies of Deut. 10:22; whereas the Hebrew has the round number seventy in all these cases. 1. Joseph may have "called for" seventy-five in ignorance of the death of three wives of Jacob and two sons of Judah, although seventy only survived to avail themselves of the invitation. 2. In addition to the sixty-six mentioned in Gen. 46:26, Stephen reckoned the twelve wives of Jacob's sons, omitting Judah's, who was dead, and Joseph's, who was in Egypt, as well as Joseph himself, for the same reason. 3. The Septuagint, quoted by Stephen, may have added the sons of Ephraim and Manasseh from 1 Chron. 7:14–21, while the Hebrew text omits them as not born till afterwards.

As regards the second objection, it is not specifically stated that Jacob was buried in Sychem. The words used are "were carried over and were laid," not "was carried over and was laid." Hence it is not Jacob who is intended, but "our fathers." Jewish tradition asserts that their bodies were carried over and buried in Sychem. Certainly there is not a word in Scripture to contradict the fact.

Thus the only real difficulty is in the alleged fact of Abraham's purchase of the sepulchre. But if the principle asserted in rule 1 of this chapter be admitted to be correct, we are at liberty to suppose that the mistake has arisen in the transcription, the word Abraham being written for Jacob. To suppose that Stephen, speaking to an assembly familiar with every word of their ancient Scriptures, even counting the letters and cherishing every link of their genealogy with almost superstitious reverence, should make a palpable blunder, is incredible. Equally incredible is it that St. Luke, familiar, like Stephen, with Jewish habits and information, should put into Stephen's mouth by any mistake of his own such a gross and patent blunder as this would be. The very greatness of the mistake takes from it any argumentative weight; for either it is a mistake of the copyist, or else the expression of St. Stephen was founded on some familiar mode of speech recognized among the Jews, and only embarrassing to us from want of the key to explain it; or lastly, there is some unknown fact involved in the statement which it has not pleased God as yet to make known to us. It can scarcely be called a trial of faith to find in the whole range of Scripture one solitary contradiction which we cannot solve.

It follows from all the foregoing that the evidence adduced in disproof of the truth of Scripture is both weak in its character and altogether devoid of proof; the alleged difficulties turn out to be no difficulties at all to those who are willing to accept man's part in the composition of the Bible on the one side, and God's part upon the other. The positive evidences previously adduced in support of the absolute truth of Scripture stand therefore in all their strength, wholly unshaken by any evidence on the other side. We maintain not only that Scripture clearly asserts by implication its own infallibility, but also that the claim is supported by the plain facts of the case. With what might have been we have nothing to do; we are only concerned with facts as they are. The case stands thus: that we have the most unanswerable evidence for the truth of Scripture, and not a tittle of evidence against it.

CHAPTER XVI.

THE WORD OF GOD IS VERBALLY INSPIRED.

Inspiration Coextensive with the Truth of Scripture—What is meant by Verbal Inspiration, and what is not meant by It—Other Theories shown to be Inconsistent with the Facts of the Case—*Post-hoc* Testimony of Scripture Itself—The Inspiration of the Old Testament as asserted by the Writers of the New—The Separate Words Authoritative, and therefore God-inspired—Old Testament Quotations, and the Principles involved in Them—The Verbal Inspiration of the New Testament.

THE course of argument followed in this work has been to prove the inspiration of Scripture from its truth, and not its truth from its inspiration. (See chapter 8.) Having proved its truth by an accumulation of those minute instances by which alone it is possible that it should be proved, I am now entitled to deduce from it not alone the fact of an inspiration, but likewise its extent. In every one of the instances adduced the accuracy or inaccuracy of the scriptural account has turned upon single words. Had any other word been used than the one particular word actually employed, the sacred narrative would have been inaccurate. It has been already pointed out that the variety of these points of detail, the vast scope of history they cover, alike as regards periods of time and geographical extent, and the minute acquaintance they involve with the particulars of place, person, order, and event, are only explicable on the supposition of a Divine and coöperating superintendence exercised over and upon the minds of the writers. Whatever force attaches to this argument to prove the Divine authority of Scripture as a revelation from God is available equally to prove that it must be verbally inspired, since it is by the accurate use of words alone that its marvellous truth and consequent inspiration can be proved.

The state of the case must be considered. It is not that now and then, and here and there, men have existed claiming to speak in God's name, and attesting their claim by a more than human knowledge of events, past, present, and future; but it is that this claim with its accompanying evidence has been advanced by one definite succession of sacred writers, and by them alone. The claim, indeed, has been very frequently made by others. This is natural, for when has the counterfeit ever failed to follow the true coin? But the evidence has not accompanied the claim. In this one succession of writers the evidence has not only been afforded to the generations contemporary with them, but it has survived in their writings to the present day. I call them a succession of writers, not alone because they have sprung from one race, as if it were a race rich in God-inspired men, but because they themselves and their writings have formed the successive links of an unbroken chain. Each one has not only taught the same doctrinal truth as his predecessor, but each one has taken up the line of teaching just where his predecessor laid it down. All the books of this series of writers taken together constitute a complete history and a complete system of truth, to which nothing can be added, from which nothing can be taken away. But they have grown into this completeness by the successive contributions of men identified by unity of race and similarity of faith, but separated from each other by long periods of time—sometimes by hundreds of years—as between Malachi and Matthew, and by every imaginable diversity of personal circumstance, position, education, fortune, and character.

No other connected series of sacred writings, constituting one whole system, exists in the world except this one. No such continuous descent of office is to be found in the history of the world but here. No other line of men authenticating a Divine commission by prophecy and miracle can be found. No literature survives comparable in the antiquity of its date to some portion of these books; while its later portions reach down into the epoch of authentic history, like a great mountain whose solid base lies within reach of sight and touch, while its cloud-capped peaks are above the clouds, inaccessible to human foot. The writers and the writings are therefore an orderly series, without a parallel. This literature is marked throughout by the most marvellous accuracy of historical detail; and this accuracy is expressed, as it could only be expressed, in words, and simple words. Surely, whatever is the authorship of the accuracy must be the authorship of the words which express it.

By ascribing the words of Scripture to a Divine inspiration, I only carry to its inevitable conclusion the principle stated in another chapter, (chapter 8,) namely, that every part of Scripture is equally human, and every part equally Divine. Thus the words were human. Verbal inspiration does not imply that a supernatural influence made the words, or communicated the knowledge of them, for the first time, to the writers. Nor does it involve that the peculiar habits and familiar mode of language of the writer did not mould the sentences and the place of the individual words, perhaps their very form. Nor does it exclude the possibility that the fact affirmed by the use of some particular word— as, for instance, that the sons of Esarhaddon found refuge in Armenia—might have been known to the writer, where such knowledge was possible, by the ordinary channels of human information. In short, it does not involve any denial that the man wrote it to whose authorship the particular book is imputed. Verbal inspiration admits all this, but goes on to assert that there was a concurrence of the act of God with the act of man. First He endowed the man with those particular gifts, and chose him to be his instrument. Secondly, He guided his mind in the selection of what he should say, and of the revelation of the material of his writing, where such revelation was made necessary, through the defect of human knowledge. Thirdly, He acted in and on the intellect and heart of the writer in the act of committing the words to writing, not only bestowing a more than human elevation, but securing the truthfulness of the thing written, and moulding the language into the form accordant to his own will.

To sum up the whole, verbal inspiration simply amounts to this, that while the words of Scripture are truly and characteristically the words of men, they are at the same time fully and concurrently the words of God.

Many excellent persons are unable to accept this doctrine of a verbal inspiration. Two explanations have accordingly been suggested to avoid the necessity of adopting it. The first is, that God communicated the matter of the revelation to the minds of the writers, but having done so, left it to the action of their own human faculties to put it into words. The other is, that the sacred writers were inspired in all matters lying beyond the range of human discovery, such as doctrinal teaching relative to the nature of God himself and the mode of man's salvation; but that on all matters falling within the natural range of human knowledge, such as historical and biographical details, they were left to the unassisted use of their own faculties. Both of these explanations will be found to be insufficient, and to involve insuperable difficulties which are avoided by the simple belief that, in the production of the Scripture, the superior mind of God concurred with the mind of man throughout.

It has already been noted (chapter 10) that, on the supposition that the Divine action ceased with the communication of the matter of the revelation to the minds of the writers, we do not possess a revelation from God at all, but only the human account of it. The sacred writers possessed it, but we have only the impression produced by it on the minds of men no longer inspired. For the suggestion is, that inspiration ceased with the communication of the matter; and as soon as that was accomplished, the men became uninspired men. As writers, and in the act of writing what had been communicated, they were, therefore, ordinary men, with no special advantage above others. All that we have, therefore, on this theory, is the uninspired account of an inspired revelation.

Now, when this theory is placed in contrast with the marvellous accuracy of Scripture on minute points such as are illustrated in the preceding chapters, it is found to be full of difficulties. For such an inspiration must have acted in one of two ways. It must have acted once for all, revealing the substance of a given message or given book all at once, and then ceasing; or it must have acted continuously, supplying the matter as the author wrote it down, verse by verse and line by line.

Let us suppose that the action was complete at one time, and not revealed during the process of the writing. Then the retentiveness and accuracy of memory involved in the faithful transcription of the matter becomes itself a miracle of no ordinary kind. The separate communications made by God at one time were of considerable length, and this in cases where no use of some old long-existing document can have been possible. For instance, five chapters and rather more in the Book of Exodus—viz., 25, 26, 27, 28, 29, and part of 30—stand as one consecutive and undivided communication. The twenty-fifth chapter begins with the words, "The Lord spake unto Moses, saying," expressions clearly denoting that what followed were God's actual words. These chapters contain a great variety of minute details relative to the construction of the tabernacle, comprising numbers, and measurements, and varieties of material, which must have been retained by Moses, on the present theory of inspiration, as a mere act of human memory. Isa. 8, 9, 10, 11, 12, contain a continuous message of the same kind. Hosea 4, 5, 6, 7, 8, 9, 10, 11, is another instance.

Or let the case of the historical books be considered—the storehouse of evidences to the marvellous accuracy of the sacred Scriptures; the Book of Numbers, of Deuteronomy, or the Acts of the Apostles. It would be itself a wonder that any human memory could retain so great a variety of facts with such minute truthfulness. Yet if the inspiration which communicated the knowledge operated at wide intervals and in completed acts, the accurate transcription of these details must be imputed altogether to the human faculties of the writers. Great efforts of memory have, indeed, been accomplished in the world, and men have been known to repeat what they have once heard without a mistake. But in this case not one man, but a succession of men, must have been thus extraordinarily endowed. If this be so, then the credit due to the veracity of Scripture must be divided between the God who communicated the knowledge and the men who so wonderfully remembered and so accurately transcribed it. Half the honor must belong to God, and half to man. If, to avoid this conclusion, it be said that God gave extraordinary help to the memories of the sacred writers, this is the same as saying that he inspired them, not alone by communicating truth to them, but in assisting them to communicate it to others. If inspiration be admitted to have acted in both directions of receiving and conveying, then the theory under discussion is confessed to be untenable.

But let us suppose that the action of the Divine mind, in communicating to the sacred writers the matter of their books, did not consist of perfect acts done and then ended, but of a continuous influence acting on the memory all through, then another kind of difficulty arises. It involves the idea that God was acting on the mind of man throughout, and yet only on one part of his mind; strengthening the memory, but leaving all the other faculties untouched. Such a thing would be as wonderful as it was that the dew fell upon Gideon's fleece and not on the floor around it, and again fell on the floor and left the fleece dry. It would be as if a breath from heaven could touch one note of a harp, and set it thrilling with music, and yet not draw from the other strings a single harmonious note. If we are driven by the facts of the case to admit that there must have been a continuous action of the mind of God on the mind of the writer during the act of the writing, surely it is better to admit still more, and believe that it concurred with the writer's whole mind, and strengthened every faculty that was called into exercise by the act of conveying in writing the revealed will of God to man.

But difficulties not less will be seen to exist in the second of the two explanations now under consideration, when placed side by side with the detailed proofs of the characteristic truthfulness of Scripture. This explanation is to the effect that the scriptural writers were inspired in delivering the great doctrines of revelation relative to the nature of God and the salvation of man, but were not inspired in recording historical and biographical facts; that the jewel of Divine truth, in short, is of God, but that its historical setting is of man. But the effect of this theory is, to deprive of their heaven-given authority those very portions of Scripture which constitute the evidence for the veracity of the whole, and in which alone such evidence could conceivably be afforded.

That God, in giving a revelation, should supply at the same time some internal means of verifying it, will be admitted to be congruous not only with the gracious character of God, but with the mode of action he has actually adopted. It would be strange if God had provided in miracles and prophecy an attestation to the authority of Scripture, and yet had afforded no means of ascertaining its truth. No Christian will doubt that the whole fabric of evidence possessed by us to prove the Bible to be a revelation from God has been intelligently provided. It has not grown by chance, but has been schemed by the mind of God, ordered by his goodness, and framed by his wisdom. But of this scheme, the confirmation of its truth by the testimony of secular history and archæological discovery constitutes an important portion. But this proof lies altogether in the historical details of Scripture, not in its doctrines. We have no possible means of putting to any practical tests its doctrines, such as the trinity of persons in the Godhead, the union of two natures in Christ, the justification of the sinner by faith, or the person and operation of the Holy Ghost. We cannot climb up into heaven, and see the eternal realities to which the revealed doctrines correspond. We accept them, because we find them contained in a revelation we believe to have come from God. But we have no possible means of proving them. We have means of testing the accuracy of historical facts; and in these facts, therefore, it is natural that God should supply the means of verifying his own words.

This reference to things intelligible to man in proof of things lying beyond the reach of his knowledge, is illustrated by an incident in the life of our Lord. When he had declared to the paralytic man at Capernaum, as he was let down on his couch in the assembled throng, the forgiveness of his sins, "Son, be of good cheer, thy sins be forgiven thee," the scribes and Pharisees murmured at him, "Who can forgive sins but God alone?" The thought in their minds was probably some such thing as this: "It is very well for this man to say, 'Thy sins be forgiven thee,' for who can tell whether they are forgiven or not? But if he had cured the man's bodily illness, we could have judged of the reality of that, and so known whether his words are true." To this thought our Lord replied alike by his words and by his act: "Whether is easier, to say, Thy sins be forgiven thee; or to say, Arise and walk?" that is, they were both equally easy to his Divine power. But as they doubted what they could not prove, he would give them an evidence they could prove: "that ye may know that the Son of man hath power to forgive sins;" then he turned round to the sufferer with the words, "Arise, take up thy bed, and walk." Mark 2:1-11. The lower exercise of power which lay within the human sphere was the evidence of the higher exercise of power which lay within the Divine.

It is on the same principle that He supplies in historical facts, lying within human proof or disproof, the verification of a revelation whose highest object is to reveal doctrines altogether belonging to another sphere. The simple and self-evident fact, that in this way alone could a verification be possibly afforded, is enough to prove what has already been insisted upon from several points of view in the preceding chapters; viz., that the historical portions of Scripture are inseparably identified with the doctrinal, and form component parts of one and the same revelation, invested with one and the same authority.

But if the explanation be accepted that the doctrinal portions of the Bible are inspired, but not the historical, the whole of this falls to the ground. The argument for the Divine authenticity of Scripture derived from historical evidences can no longer be sustained, because, according to the theory, the historical portions are human, while the doctrinal are acknowledged to be Divine. If the one are to be accepted as evidences for the other, they must both proceed from the same origin and authority. The accuracy of uninspired writers in narrating history can be no proof that they are inspired when they teach doctrine. It may be argued, indeed, that if these writers are worthy of credit in that which proceeds from themselves, they must be much more worthy of credit in that which they profess to have received from God. But the argument, however apparently plausible, does not hold good; for history supplies many instances of writers, sensible and trustworthy on secular subjects, but fanatical to the extreme and utterly untrustworthy on religious. I may mention the instance of Baron Swedenborg, an able and learned man on matters of science, but on matters of religion, the author of one of the wildest systems known to modern times. Because the sacred writers wrote sensibly and accurately upon secular matters, it would not follow that they are to be accepted as authoritative teachers in religion. The credibility of the historical portions of Scripture can only be a proof of the credibility of the doctrinal portions, so long as both have proceeded from one authority, and have been written under one and the same influence.

A twofold answer is supplied by these considerations in disproof of the theory which would limit inspiration to the doctrinal portions of the Word only. (1.) The wonderful accuracy of Scripture in these minute details can only be explained by the exercise of a Divine omniscience. (2.) If inspiration be confined to subjects beyond the scope of human knowledge, we neither have nor can we possibly have any means whatever of verifying the whole revelation.

Hence the natural conclusion arising from the proofs already adduced is confirmed, not weakened, by the explanations advanced with the view of getting rid of it. The proofs are verbal, and turn upon single words. Therefore inspiration must be verbal, and deal with single words likewise.

It must be remembered that this conclusion rests on scriptural evidence. This will be made clear by a recapitulation of the argument. I have shown that Scripture advances the highest conceivable claims relative to its own source and authority. These claims necessarily involve the truth of Scripture. This truth has been tested by an appeal to the facts, both to the facts existing in support of the claim, and the facts alleged in disproof of it. The result of the appeal has confirmed by independent evidence the character of perfect truthfulness ascribed by Scripture to itself. The conclusion that inspiration must be verbal because the truthfulness is verbal, is but the sequel of this line of argument, and partakes of the scriptural character of the premises on which it is founded.

I now desire to carry this scriptural evidence a step farther. I have shown that the inspiration of the words of Scripture necessarily follows from its own general teaching relative to itself; I now add that this conclusion is asserted by the immediate and direct testimonies of the inspired writers.

Now, the contents of Scripture are of two kinds.
1. We have direct messages from God. These portions I venture to call "ministerial," in reference to the writers. And 2. We have historical and biographical narratives, and the description of visions presented to the eyes of the prophet. These portions I venture to call "personal." The direct messages from God constitute a very considerable proportion of the whole. It includes the latter portion of the Book of Exodus, the entire Book of Leviticus, many chapters in Deuteronomy and Numbers, the greater part of the prophecy of Isaiah—the later chapters, from chapter 41 to chapter 63, expressly and in form bearing this character; thirty chapters out of the fifty-two comprising the prophecy of Jeremiah, thirty-five chapters out of the forty-eight of the prophet Ezekiel, with some slight occasional exceptions, where the words of the prophet are professedly intermingled with the immediate words of God; twelve out of the fourteen chapters of Hosea, almost the whole of the prophecy of Joel, six chapters of Amos out of nine, six chapters of Micah, the whole of the prophecies of Zephaniah and of Haggai, nine chapters of Zechariah, and the entire Book of Habakkuk.

In all these cases we find direct communications ascribed immediately to God himself. They are introduced with the words "said" or "saying," "Thus saith the Lord." What God said must have been said in words. It could not have been that a certain impression of truth was made by the Spirit upon the mind of the prophet, and that he was then left to convey it in his own language. The word is expressed and reiterated over and over again, as if on purpose to shut out the possibility of mistake. God "said." Throughout all these passages God is presented as the speaker. The message is couched in the first person, so that the messenger almost disappears, and God is all in all. "I" will save, defend, or punish. So far as concerns these passages of Scripture, no assertion of the existence of inspired words, that is, of words which carry with them a Divine authority, can be stronger than this. The positive expression, "Thus saith the Lord," must imply a verbal message if it implies any thing.

To the same class belongs the personal teaching of our blessed Master. Surely his words were inspired. Not only did he speak as one to whom was given without measure the Spirit of wisdom and understanding, the Spirit of counsel and might, but as one who was himself Divine, and within whom dwelt the fulness of the Godhead bodily. In his teaching, the supposition that a Divine mind only provided the matter, and that a human mind framed it into words, can have no place. The speaker was himself Divine, one with the Father and the Holy Spirit, God blessed for evermore.

The existence of a verbal inspiration throughout these portions of Scripture does not prove the extension of the same character to all its other portions. I have already said that in addition to those parts where God is himself ostensibly the speaker, there exists a further portion where the writer is ostensibly the speaker; parts which are either the record of what other people did, or of what the writer himself saw or did. The relation between these two parts is analogous to the relation between the recorded words of some great personage of ancient times and the words of the historian who records them. We can no more argue that because the Scriptures contain the express words of God they are therefore the express words of God throughout, than we can argue that the historian of Plato possesses the genius of Plato because the words of that philosopher are contained in his pages.

This is true. Yet these acknowledged instances of a verbal inspiration are none the less instructive; for they serve to illustrate how human words can be the words of God, and they thus clear our way of imaginary difficulties in advancing to the evidence of verbal inspiration in the other parts of Scripture likewise.

That these specified portions contain the very words of God is expressly asserted in the word "said," and no consistent believer in the authority of Scripture can call it into question. Yet even these very words are the words of man while they are the words of God. The language is human language, and is employed according to human usage and custom. There is the same kind of difference between the language of God in the Pentateuch and the language of God in the Book of Isaiah, as there is in our own English language at two different periods of our history. This is perfectly natural. It arises out of the human element in Scripture, on that side of it where the human element itself arises from the two parties involved in the very idea of a revelation, the party receiving it as well as the party giving it. God spoke in order that his words might be clearly understood and faithfully conveyed, and he therefore employed such words and such a usage of them as were intelligible to the generation to whom he spoke.

But this variation in the language is not all. The distinctive style of the several prophets exists in these portions as in other portions of their prophecies. The words of God recorded by Isaiah are not identical in style with his words by Jeremiah and Ezekiel; for in each case the prophet had to speak the words as well as write them. God used the human instrument; and as he used him not as a dead mechanism, but as the living being he was, so he permitted his words to be colored by the personal peculiarities of the instrument. To use the familiar but much-perverted illustration of the ancient fathers, the prophets were like instruments of music, and God's was the hand that touched them. A master's hand may display the same consummate skill and exhibit the same peculiarities of style, whatever be the instrument he uses, whether harp, or flute, or violin. But the several instruments will not, therefore, lose their own peculiarities, or cease to be distinguishable from each other. So it was with the prophets. The same God spoke through Moses and Isaiah, Jeremiah and Ezekiel, and the words were his. The style impressed on them by the prophet was much the same as the difference of accent and emphasis, of tone and manner, with which four separate speakers might deliver one and the same message.

It is as if God had left his Word in this form in order, among other gracious purposes, to illustrate in these acknowledged instances the concurrence of the human and the Divine elements in one result. As on the one side in these portions of Scripture the words are immediately God's, and yet the trace of the human instrument remains, so in other portions of the Bible the words are immediately man's; and yet the Divine power and authority survive in them all the same. An inspiration of the Word is as consistent in the one case as it is undeniable in the other. In the words already employed in a former chapter, all the parts of Scripture are equally human, and all the parts are equally Divine.

It is, therefore, certain that a verbal inspiration is as possible in the historical, biographical, and narrative portions of Scripture as in the rest. But the possibility is not enough. What is the evidence for the fact?

Here we must deal with the Old and New Testaments separately. The writers of each Testament constitute a class of themselves, identified by unity of subject and fellowship of the Spirit, but separated by a lapse of four hundred years in time, and also by the circumstances that the one belonged to the period of the preparatory, the other to the period of a completed and perfect dispensation. The writers of the Old Testament consequently had inspired successors; but the writers of the New had none, since with the completion of the New Testament canon the Book of Revelation was finally sealed up.

It is natural, therefore, that in the books of the New Testament we should find reiterated testimonies to the verbal inspiration of the Old Testament Scriptures such as we do not equally possess to the verbal inspiration of the New. Some evidence there is, but it is necessarily supplied by the New Testament itself. Such testimony is, however, the less necessary, because if the verbal inspiration of the Old Testament be once proved, there can be neither motive nor interest to withhold the same amount of inspiration from the New.

Now the question to be decided is this: Did the office of the inspiring Spirit cease with communicating to the minds of the writers of Scripture the truths they were chosen to convey, and were they then left to their own unassisted human faculties to express them in words? or, did the Holy Ghost concur with the minds of the writers throughout, not only making truth known to them, but preserving them likewise from all error in communicating truth to others?

If inspiration be in the matter only, not in the words, then we might expect that whenever the New Testament writers appealed to the Divine authority of the Old, they would do so by quoting the matter only, and not the words. If inspiration extends to the words, then we might expect that they would quote the words as well as the matter. Reference to the authority of the words will, therefore, constitute in every case evidence to the inspiration of the words. This evidence will be proportionably strengthened by the use of single sentences or single words, and by the amount of weight and authority ascribed to these single sentences and single words.

That it is possible to quote the sense without quoting the words is proved by the occasional adoption of this method by the writers of the New Testament. Forgetfulness of this, and the mistake of supposing that they profess to quote the words when they really do no more than refer to the sense of the more ancient writers, has been one among others of prolific causes of misapprehension relative to the New Testament quotations of the Old Testament Scriptures. Some instances will make this clearer. Thus St. Matthew wrote of our Lord: "He came and dwelt in a city called Nazareth, that it might be fulfilled which was spoken by the prophets, He shall be called a Nazarene." Matt. 2 : 23. The attempt to find some definite passage where this title is applied to the Messiah is rebuked by the use of the plural number by the evangelist, "the prophets:" and the word translated "by" is "through" or "throughout" the prophets ($\delta\iota\alpha$ with the genitive); where the phrase makes it certain that the evangelist referred to the general scope of the prophetic teaching, and not to any specific passages. Thus St. John records the words of our Lord: "It is written in the prophets, They shall all be taught of God." John 6 : 45. Again, "He that believeth in me, as the Scripture hath said, out of his belly shall flow rivers of living water." John 7 : 38.

Our Lord gives his own authoritative explanation of the language of the prophets, but does not quote any particular words. In the narrative of our Lord's trial and crucifixion the same general phrase occurs repeatedly, "that the Scriptures might be fulfilled," John 19 : 28. Yet neither is any definite passage quoted, nor is the particular point of the fulfilment explained. Further instances of general reference to the sense, and not the words of the Old Testament, will be found in John 8 : 17; Acts 10 : 43; Romans 1 : 2, 7 : 1, 9 : 4, 10 : 11, 12 : 9; 1 Cor. 1 : 31; 2 Cor. 7 : 18; and in many other passages.

If, therefore, another method is adopted in the vast majority of instances; if the quotations are verbal quotations; if elaborate arguments are founded on single phrases, or even on single words—this method was not followed because no other was practicable. It might not be easy for us to separate the sense from the words; indeed I believe it is not possible for us to do so. But it was possible to inspired apostles whose minds were guided to interpret by the same Holy Ghost by whom the ancient writers were guided to write. With this teaching they could pass infallibly through the words to the the sense. If, on the contrary, it was their ordinary method to use the words, there must have been reason and intention in it. What could the reason be, but that the words had God's authority upon them, and were themselves sacred? What could the intention be, but to witness to the church of all ages the verbal inspiration and therefore verbal authority of the Scriptures?

Thus our Lord himself quotes the words of Moses in Deut. 8:3, that "Man doth not live by bread alone;" where the stress is laid on the last word, "alone." Yet more strikingly, in the narrative of the same temptation, he refuted the tempter by words taken from 1 Samuel 7:3, "Him only shalt thou serve;" where the force of the answer depends upon the emphatic word "only," "him only." Satan would have been content if our Lord had rendered him worship, even though it had been divided with Jehovah. His offer was not, "If thou wilt fall down and worship me alone," but, "If thou wilt fall down and worship me." He would have been ready to go halves in the Divine honor due to God. But God will have none of such divided allegiance: "Him only shalt thou serve." It was by a phrase consisting of two words, "my Lord," that our Saviour retorted upon the Jews with the question how Christ could be the Son of David, and yet be addressed by the psalmist with the title, "The Lord said unto my Lord." Psalm 110:1; Matt. 22:44. To the memorable quotation from Psalm 82, recorded in John 10:34, our Lord adds the further and most emphatic declaration, "The Scripture cannot be broken." In the personal teaching of our Master, further instances of the same character occur, in Matthew 3:3; 19:5; 21:13, 16; and Luke 4:21.

The narrative of our Lord's trial and crucifixion supplies several notable cases of similar verbal references on the part of the evangelist. Thus he marks the fulfilment of Zechariah's prophecy of the "thirty pieces of silver," and "the potter's field;" of the "parting" of the outward garment by the soldiers, and the "casting lots" for the inner woven vesture, as exactly predicted in Psalm 22:18; of the piercing of our Lord's side, foretold in the same psalm; and the not breaking a bone of his blessed body, as expressed in Psalm 34. In all these cases, the correspondence between the prophecy and the fulfilment is wholly dependent upon single words and upon their mutual combinations.

In the Acts of the Apostles the same method of verbal quotation is continued. St. Peter, in his sermon on the day of Pentecost, declares the resurrection of our Lord to be the accomplishment of David's language in Psalm 16:10 and Psalm 111. At the first persecution, the assembled apostles not only quote the words of the second psalm, but they expressly state them to be the words of God: "Lord, thou art God, who by the mouth of thy servant David hast said." Acts 4:25. A more striking declaration of verbal inspiration—and what I have ventured to call the concurrence of the human and Divine elements—than these words can scarcely be conceived. God spoke them, but he spoke them by the mouth of David. Two other references of the same general character will be found in Acts 2:34; 13:46.

It is, however, in the argumentative portions of the epistles that we find these illustrations most abundantly; and the more frequent the quotations, the more prominently we find them. Thus St. Paul rests his proof that the Jews as well as the Gentiles

were concluded under sin on two little words occurring in the fourteenth psalm—on the word "none,"
in the first verse, and on the word "all," in the third.
Let these two little words be changed, and the apostle's argument fails at once. Rom. 3 : 10–20. In
the fourth chapter of the same epistle, he declares
justification by faith only to be the immutable counsel of God, on the sole strength of two phrases—the
phrase "counted for righteousness," in Gen. 15 : 6,
and the phrase "not impute sin," in Psa. 32:2. He
teaches the equality of all men before God, and the
freedom of this Divine mode of saving, on the authority of a single emphatic word used by the prophet
Joel—"whosoever." On this word he elaborately
argues, Rom. 10 : 12, "There is no difference between the Jew and the Greek; for the same Lord
over all is rich unto all that call upon him." Then
comes the authority for the assertion : "For *whosoever* shall call upon the name of the Lord shall be
saved." In Rom. 14 : 11 he rests the solemn assertion, "We shall *all* stand before the judgment-
seat of Christ," on the word "every :" "As I live,
saith the Lord, *every* knee shall bow to me." The
doctrine of faith is illustrated in 2 Cor. 4 : 13 by the
single expression of David, "I believed." In arguing, in Gal. 3 : 16, that the promise of eternal life is
annexed to faith, and not to human merit, he argues,
not alone from a single word, but from a single letter, from the fact that a word is used in the singular,
not in the plural : "He saith not, And to seeds, as
of many, but as of one, and to thy *seed*, which is
Christ." The word "all," in Psa. 8 : 6, is the apos-

tle's proof of the universal triumph of Christ, in Heb. 2 : 8. In Heb. 3 : 7–15, he enlarges, during nine consecutive verses, on the force of the word "To-day," as quoted from Psa. 95 : 7.

The fourth chapter of this epistle contains an elaborate and profound argument relative to the "sabbath-keeping" remaining "for the people of God." In verses 4 and 5 he argues from the use of a tense of the future in Psa. 95 : 11, as contrasted with a tense of the past in Gen. 2 : 2. "He (God) spake in a certain place of the seventh day in this wise, And God *did rest* the seventh day from all his works;" and in this place again, "If they *shall* enter into my rest." In his exposition of the great high-priesthood of our Master, he points out its superiority over the Levitical priesthood, in virtue of its perpetuity : "They truly were many priests, because they were not suffered to continue by reason of death ; but this man, because he continueth ever, hath an unchangeable priesthood." Hebrews 7 : 23, 24. But how is it proved that he continueth ever? By the use of the two words "for ever," in Psa. 110 : 4 : "Thou art a Priest for ever." He deduces the purpose of God, that the Mosaic covenant should pass away, from the word "*new*," employed by Jeremiah (31 : 31): "In that he saith, A *new* covenant, he hath made the first old." Heb. 8 : 13. He supports his explanation of the same truth by the relative order of two sentences in Psa. 40 : 6, 7. "Above *when* he said, Sacrifice and offering. . . . . *Then* saith he, Lo, I come to do thy will, O God." Heb. 10 : 8, 9. He illustrates the superiority of the good things of the latter covenant, over the promises of the first covenant, by the full remission of sin contrasted with the constant repetition of the Mosaic sacrifices. This final remission of sin is proved by the two words, "no more," in Jer. 31:34: "Their sins and their iniquities will I remember no. more." Heb. 10:17. And lastly, he teaches the immutability of the gospel kingdom, the "kingdom that cannot be moved," in comparison with the transitory nature of all earthly glory, from the single word, "once," employed by Haggai: "And this word, Yet once more, signifieth the removing of those things that are shaken." Heb. 12:27.

The great majority of the preceding instances are taken from the personal rather than the ministerial portions of the word, four only belonging to the latter class. Additional illustrations will be found in the following passages:

Matt. 3:3 compared with Isa. 40:3;
Matt. 4:4 with Deut. 8:3;
Matt. 19:5 with Gen. 2:24;
Matt. 21:13 with Isa. 56:7;
Matt. 21:16 with Psa. 8:2;
Luke 4:21 with Isa. 61:1, 2;
Luke 12:40 with Isa. 6:1;
Rom. 9:7 with Gen. 20:12;
Rom. 9:12 with Gen. 25:23;
Rom. 9:15 with Exod. 23:19;
Rom. 9:17 with Exod. 9:16;
Rom. 9:17 with Hos. 2:23:
Rom. 9:21 with Isa. 10:22;
Rom. 10:15 with Isa. 52:7, and 53:1;
Rom. 10:19-21 with Deut. 32:21, and Isa. 65:1;
Rom. 10:5, 6 with Deut. 30:11;
Rom. 11:4 with 1 Kings 19:18;

Rom. 11 : 8-10 with Psa. 69 : 22, and Isa. 29 : 10 ;
Rom. 15 : 9-12 with Psa. 118 : 1, and Isa. 24 : 15, 16 ;
1 Cor. 2 : 9 with Isa. 44 : 4 ;
1 Cor. 15 : 54 with Isa. 25 : 8 ;
Gal. 3 : 11 with Hab. 2 : 4 ;
Gal. 4 : 27 with Isa. 54 : 1-5;
Gal. 4 : 9 with Psa. 68 : 18 ;
Gal. 5 : 14 with Isa. 60 : 1 ;
Gal. 6 : 2 with Exod. 20 : 12 ;
Heb. 1 : 5-13 with Psa. 2 : 7, 2 Sam. 7 : 14, Psa. 97 : 7, 65 : 6,
    7, and 33 : 6 ;
Heb. 2 : 12-14 with Psa. 22 : 22, 18 : 2, and Isa. 8 : 18 ;
Heb. 4 : 14 with Gen. 22 : 16;
Heb. 12 : 5 with Prov. 3 : 11.

In all these cases it will be found, on a careful comparison of the two passages, that the inspired writers of the New Testament rest positive doctrines and frame elaborate arguments on the authority of single sentences and single words of the Old Testament Scriptures.

If any person will take the trouble of examining these evidences he will find them marked by two peculiarities.

I. He will find the quotations, when the whole sentence is taken together, frequently incomplete, and not exactly corresponding with the original. The explanation of this circumstance corroborates in the strongest manner the fact of a verbal inspiration. For, although the quotation of the whole sentence be inaccurate, the quotation of the particular phrase or particular word on which the stress of authority is laid is invariably accurate. The comparative indifference displayed as to the rest of the quotation only serves to fix attention the more, and to lay the more emphatic weight on the special phrase or word. The remainder of the sentence did not enter into the purpose and argument of the writer, and is therefore quoted generally to show that it is unimportant. Thus in Heb. 10:17, "Their sins and iniquities will I remember *no more*." The last two words are the emphatic and authoritative words, and the rest of the sentence differs from the words of Jeremiah by the addition from other passages of the same prophet of the words " and iniquities." It has been shown in a previous chapter (chapter 12) that an evidence must be as extensive as the thing to be evidenced, but need be no wider. In all these quotations accordingly the phrase or word alleged in proof of the doctrine is there, and there accurately; and the context is added generally in order to identify the passage, but for no further reason. The exclusive attention thus fixed on particular words can only have arisen from the belief that these single words are God's words, selected by his intention, and therefore clothed with his authority.

II. It will be observed that passages and parts of passages from different writers are grouped together as the harmonious evidence of some common truth. For instance, the Divine nature and glory of the Son of God are proved in the first chapter of the Hebrews, by parts of sentences selected for the sake of their emphatic words from three different Psalms, and from the first Book of Samuel. The Divine fitness of the incarnation of the Son of God is proved in the second chapter by passages from two different Psalms, and from the prophecy of Isaiah. Justification by faith is proved by passages from Moses and David, writers separated from each other by a period of between four and five hundred years, and whose productions belong to different classes altogether. In the argument of St. Paul, in illustration of the eternal sovereignty of the Divine will, in Rom. 9:7, 21, a yet stronger instance is given; for here two passages from different chapters in the book of Genesis, two from different chapters of Exodus, one from Isaiah, and one from Hosea, are all brought side by side in attestation of the common truth. A reference to the passages already enumerated will furnish additional illustrations of the same thing.

Now, on the supposition that inspiration belongs only to the truths the prophets were commissioned to convey, and that their words are simply human words and no more, this mode of quotation is utterly inexplicable. Not only is there no appeal to the general sense of the passages in which the quotations are found, but the words are, as it might appear to some, violently separated from the context, and are employed as authoritative without the slightest reference to the general object of the whole passage. Thus, for instance, there is no apparent allusion to any such mysterious doctrine as the electing sovereignty of God in the simple and unadorned narration by Moses of the fact that Isaac was preferred over Ishmael, and Jacob over Esau. Still less would any one not possessed of a Divine key trace any bearing on the doctrine of the incarnation in the sentiments of David in Psa. 18:2, and 22:22. In repeated instances it will be found that no appeal whatever is made to the general sense of quoted passages; but that single expressions and single words are sharply separated from the context, and used in a sense which the sentiment of the context would not of itself have suggested.

If there be a verbal inspiration, this mode of quotation is as consistent and reasonable as it is utterly inexplicable without it. For if the words were selected under the guidance of the perfect wisdom of the Omniscient Being to whose infinite grasp all times, all persons, all events, are present at one and the same time in the eternal "now" of his own existence, then they are full of God, and must have a depth and reach of meaning, a profound force and significance, a faultless and unerring appropriateness investing each single word with the full authority of the Deity. The question to be asked in such a case is not what the human writers meant to say, but what "the Spirit which was in them did signify." Who shall interpret the words but He who first inspired them?

I do not forget that these facts are treated by many persons in a widely different manner. The mode of quotation adopted by the New Testament writers appears to them loose, wild, and inaccurate. These passages are therefore adduced as affording, in the balances of a human criticism, undeniable proof of the human infirmities and ignorance of the writers. And I believe these critics are right so far that they present the only possible alternative to the conclusion of the preceding paragraph. If the words of the Old Testament are solely the words of men, it is impossible to justify the New Testament use of them. I use the word "justify" with the deepest reverence, remembering that our blessed Master himself quoted them in the same verbal manner as his apostles. But if our Lord and his apostles were right in so .quoting them, and I cannot conceive how any believer in revelation can doubt it, then the words must have been divinely inspired words. In this proof of a verbal inspiration we find the authority for our own employment of them in the same way, interpreting them ever with reference to their context, but with a devout confidence that they are the very words of God, faultless as his absolute wisdom, unalterable as his own eternal will.

When we pass to the New Testament, the existence of the same positive and independent evidence is in the nature of things impossible, as has been already shown. But our Lord promised such a plenary assistance to his apostles in their time of special difficulty that it would "not be ye that speak, but the Holy Ghost," Matt. 10 : 20. This inspiration must have been verbal, and we can scarcely conceive that a lower amount of Divine help would be afforded them in the composition of the books through whose pages they were to speak even to the end of the world. St. Paul positively asserts this verbal inspiration : "Which things also we speak, not in the words which man's wisdom teacheth, but which the Holy Ghost teacheth." 1 Cor. 2 : 13. No less than this can be the meaning of St. Peter when he first traces the life of the soul in the believing people of God to an "incorruptible seed;" then identifies this word with the actual preaching of himself and his co-apostles : "This is the word which by the gospel is preached unto you." 1 Pet. 1 : 25.

This evidence appears to be incomplete compared to the accumulated proof furnished to the verbal inspiration of the Old Testament Scriptures. But, in truth, the inspiration of the one Testament includes equally the inspiration of the other. The case of the earlier books is, in the scales of criticism, weaker than that of the later. The objections urged are not against the verbal inspiration of this particular book or that, but against verbal inspiration at all, and especially in those historical details which constitute so prominent a feature of the Old Testament. Yet here we have a redundancy of proof that the words of the human writers are at the same time the words of God, as truly his as if from amid the parted clouds of his glory our outward ears could catch his own awful voice proclaiming in the ears of mankind his infallible and unalterable will.

CHAPTER XVII.

OBJECTIONS AGAINST VERBAL INSPIRATION CONSIDERED.

General Character of the Objections—Special Difficulties: 1. The Minor Details of Scripture alleged to be Incongruous with the Inspiration of God; the Relation in which They stand to the Other Parts of the Word; Their Connection with Doctrine; Their Evidential Value; What is Knowable is not Always Known; Practically Inseparable from the Doctrinal Teaching; 2. Variations of the Text; Their Supposed Talent, and What It would prove; Their Real Talent examined and stated.

THE argument for the verbal inspiration of Holy Scripture proffered in the preceding chapters has been founded throughout upon an induction from facts. The position and influence of Christianity, its identity with definite Christian doctrine, the dependence of this doctrine upon the Christian Scriptures, the grounds on which we receive the Scriptures as a revelation from God, the internal evidence for their unity of authorship and authority, the claims they advance relative to their own authority, the character of truth involved in these claims, and the proof of veracity gained by an examination of individual passages on both sides of the controversy, have formed the successive stages of the argument. In each stage the appeal has been made to the facts of the case, and reasoning has only been employed to follow out the meaning of the facts, and to clear them from misapprehension. The entire range of known facts relative to the Scriptures, when fairly combined and collated with each other, bears consentient testimony in one direction—a chorus of many voices swelling into one song of praise. An act of the Divine mind concurring, as a superior may concur with an inferior, with the minds of the human writers, throughout every step of the composition of the sacred works, from the communication or verification of the truth to be conveyed down to the form of its verbal expression, explains, and is alone adequate to explain, the case as it is.

Against such an argument no merely speculative reasoning can have any force. Arbitrary human conjectures of what might have been, or should have been, God's mode of making known his will, are out of place altogether. This is generally admitted, either directly or by implication. The effort has therefore been made to marshal an opposing array of facts on the other side, and to prove a plenary or verbal inspiration to be inconsistent with them. It has been shown (chapter 15) that these alleged proofs rest on a misapprehension relative to the two sides of Scripture, the human and the Divine. By some, the mistake is made of supposing the human element to be altogether irreconcilable with the Divine. I venture boldly to call it a mistake, because, if the union of the two be in its own nature impossible, then the great mystery of the incarnation, God manifest in the flesh, must be denied on the same ground. Others admit the possibility of the two being united, but are afraid to give fair scope to the action of the human element on the one side and the action of the Divine on the other. They timidly limit the variety of form impressed on the human revelation by the agency of man, and the absolute infallibility bestowed upon it by the agency of God. In short, they find it difficult to understand that what is characteristically human and what is characteristically Divine may exist side by side without either limitation or confusion. Let both be maintained, and the very groundwork of objection will be found to have been swept away.

There remain, however, two classes of objection against a verbal inspiration of Holy Scripture, of which a brief examination appears to be desirable.

I. The first class depends upon the distinction of the subject-matter of Scripture, and arises from the theory that the doctrines of Scripture are Divinely inspired, but not its historical or biographical details. The objection may take different forms. Sometimes it is said that it would be unworthy of the majesty and omniscience of God to suppose his Spirit to have inspired the details of genealogy or the particulars of ordinary earthly events. At other times it is urged that, as these events lie within the range of ordinary human knowledge, their Divine revelation would contradict the rigid economy of the Divine dealings, since God would be making known to man what man is capable of finding out for himself. It is further added, that such an inspiration would remove the stimulus and motive for human labor supplied by the intentional imperfection of human knowledge, and the search after truth latent enough to require search, and yet open enough to discovery to reward it.

The groundwork of this class of objection has already been removed in a great degree by the discussions of the preceding chapters. For the sake of clearness, I venture to recapitulate in a connected form the conclusions we have reached bearing upon this question.

a. It has been shown that the detailed facts of Scripture, alike in the Old and the New Testament, form the outward setting to the supernatural truths of the word. They constitute essential links in the historical unity of the entire revelation, and unite it inseparably with the actual development of the Divine plan of redemption in the calling, education, and history, of the ancient people of God. They bear the same relation to the whole revelation as the particles of human language do to its whole structure. They are necessary to the mutual connection, and therefore to the meaning of the whole. As in human language, if all words of conjunction and grammatical dependence were omitted, the intelligent sentences of human language would become mere strings of isolated words without a meaning, unstrung gems forming no whole; so, were all the human details of the scriptural narratives taken away, the unity of the plan now pervading the entire revelation would be absolutely lost, and the scheme of the Divine plan would be interrupted in the same degree. At present we see it to be as consecutive as the rise of a natural day, from the first dawning light in the horizon up to its meridian. But were these details removed, it would be no more than a series of abrupt and broken manifestations, without any apparent common design or mutual dependence. And further, the sacred history of God's dealings with the world would lose, by the omission of these details, its foothold upon the actual world of human experience. It would move altogether in the heavenly sphere, and not at all in the earthly. From these considerations it follows, that these human details are comprised in the structural unity of the whole revelation, and are essential to it. Hence it would be as unreasonable to allege these details to be unworthy of the majesty of a Divine Author as it would be to object to the particles employed in human composition, and allege the absurdity of ascribing to the genius of Milton the little words (and, if, but, for, etc.) which connect together the sublime diction of the " Paradise Lost." See chapters 4 and 14.

b. It has also been shown that minute detail is inseparable from all human action. It is therefore inseparable also from doctrines touching human life and action. This is especially illustrated by the grand central doctrine of the incarnation, life, and death, of the Second Person of the Deity. At the point where Godhead came in contact with manhood, there the little details of human life inevitably began, alike in the facts of the work and in the narratives recording it. If it was necessary for the grand doctrine of the atonement that the Son of God should become man, all that was involved in his becoming man was necessary also. The human mother, and the human body, and the human life, and the human experience, and the human wants and weaknesses, and the human home and human relationships, and the journeyings to and fro, and the incidents of hunger and thirst, and cold and weariness, must all have been there, or else the reality of a true human nature could not have been there. Will any one deny that these details were present to our Lord in fact? Or will any one say that it was unworthy of the Son of God to come into connection with them, which would be tantamount to saying that it was unworthy of him to become incarnate? But if these details were present in the fact and present suitably to the Divine glory, why may they not also be present in the record of the fact, and present consistently with the Divine inspiration? To deny it would be to deny the consistency of a revelation with the majesty of God.

But not only would the record of our Lord's work have failed to correspond with the facts—that is, have failed to be true, if these details had been absent from it--but it must be further observed, that the doctrine is so dependent upon the matter of fact that it could not have existed without it. Christ could not have atoned for human sin either without the details of his life or without the particulars involved in his trial, and sufferings, and death. In the close connection of human events with each other, every little circumstance of the marvellous events has its proper place and significance. But if the facts were necessary for the doctrine, our knowledge of the facts must be necessary to our knowledge of the doctrine. We could not have known the one without knowing the other.

Hence has arisen the peculiar form of the ancient creeds, such as the Apostle and Nicene creeds. The want of the full doctrinal statement has been alleged as a fault against them. They are mainly statements of facts. Take, for instance, the language of the Apostles' Creed, " Who suffereth under Pontius Pilate, was crucified, dead, and buried ; he descended into hell; the third day he rose again from the dead." In form, the creed is a bare enumeration of facts. But in substance it is much more than this, for the facts are the framework of the doctrine. As we could not have been "justified by faith only," unless the Son of God had thus suffered, died, and risen again ; so, on the other hand, it is possible to argue back from the facts to the doctrine, and because "he thus lived, suffered, and died," to conclude that we must be "justified by faith alone." Hence, if the doctrine be consistent with the majesty, wisdom, and goodness of God, the facts, and record of the facts, must be consistent with them likewise. See chapters 4 and 14.

c. It has also been shown that the only possible means afforded to man of verifying the truth of Scripture is supplied by these details. It is evident that we can only test the accuracy of a narration, where the things narrated fall in some way within our knowledge, either by personal experience or by analogy. What lies beyond this sphere can admit of no human test. If we suppose it to be the will of God to afford to mankind some means of verifying the accuracy of his inspired word, and thus enabling them to distinguish it from the false impostures of man, it is by the narration of historical facts alone, and these of a minute and special kind, that such an object could possibly be accomplished. In proportion, therefore, as such a purpose is consistent with the benevolent character of the Divine being, must the means whereby alone it can be accomplished be consistent with it likewise. Hence the addition of these little details, whether on points of topography or of history, is so far from being inconsistent with the majesty of God, and therefore with its inspiration, that they are only what an adequate conception of God's attributes and purposes would lead us to expect. As a matter of fact, the whole immense range of corroborative testimony afforded from profane sources to the truth of Scripture depends entirely upon these details, and would be entirely swept away by their absence. See chapters 14 and 16.

To these considerations, conclusive as they appear to be, I would add the following remarks:

There is a great distinction to be made between things which may be known by man—things knowable, as they are philosophically called—and things actually known. It appears that a certain knowledge of many of the historical facts of Scripture is of essential importance to us, since they form the foundations of the most momentous doctrines of the faith. We need, therefore, to possess an absolute certitude that they have really taken place. But this certitude can in no degree whatever be supplied by the fact that the events requiring to be known fall within the natural range of human information. For this may be the case, and actually is the case, with a very large number of particulars belonging to human history, and yet we who live after the time may be absolutely devoid of any means of ascertaining the truth in regard to them. For instance, a great deal of ancient Roman history has been conjecturally reconstructed by modern historical criticism, and the reconstruction has been made the subject of endless dispute. However probable the modern account may be, that probability must ever fall very far short of certainty; and to make such facts the subject of religious belief would be an outrage upon the human conscience.

Now it may be doubted whether the denial of inspired authority to the books of the New Testament, for instance, would not leave us in nearly as much difficulty in determining the real facts of our Lord's life as we are in determining the events of ancient Roman history. The periods of the two sets of events are not very far distant. There is, it is true, this immense difference, that in the case of our Lord's life we have four independent histories congruous with each other, and bearing on their front every conceivable evidence of authenticity and credibility. But this will not avail us in the present case. For if they were persons so superstitious as to believe in an inspiration which had no real existence, then they were ignorant fanatics. If they asserted what they did not themselves believe, then they were impostors. But men convicted either of fanaticism or of imposture cannot be accepted as trustworthy witnesses. If, therefore, we take away the inspired character of the scriptural narrative, we really shall possess little more certainty in regard to the facts of our Lord's life than we do to the facts of ancient Roman history. That this is not too strong a statement of the case is shown in the results of denying the inspired authority of the evangelists, as illustrated in the romances which Strauss, Renan, and Michelet, have proposed to substitute for the sacred history. A fact may be knowable by man, and yet may not be known nevertheless.

What can, therefore, be more consistent that the erection of an inspired superstructure of doctrine on an inspired foundation of facts? What more strange and incongruous than that we should have a Divine authority for the doctrine, and yet for the facts on which the doctrine is absolutely dependent should be relegated to the uncertainties and possible mistakes of a simply human evidence?

This consideration becomes the stronger when we bear in mind that the theory which represents matters of historical facts to be unworthy subjects of a revelation from God, does not simply deny a verbal inspiration to all these parts of Scripture, but it denies to them any inspiration at all. For if it be incongruous for the Divine Being to concern himself with the record of such facts, it must be equally incongruous to concern himself with their revelation. Not only did he not assist the writers in communicating them to others, but he did not convey or verify the knowledge of them to the writers themselves. Consequently, these portions of Scripture cannot be a Divine revelation at all, but must be simply, barely, nakedly human, and nothing more. Hence Scripture must consist of two parts; the one treating of doctrine, and divinely inspired; the other treating of the facts on which the doctrine rests, and having no authority whatever beyond what may arise from the honesty of the human writer.

Now let us see in what position this would place us. In bringing it to a practical test, I find a difficulty in drawing the line between the doctrinal and the historical portions of Scripture, unless the distinction be broadly and unreservedly maintained. If it be once said that some portions of the more important facts, such as those relating to our Lord's sufferings and death, may have been recorded under a Divine authority, but not the less important facts, it will be found that the whole distinction must be given up. It is practically impossible to draw the line where the facts are related to each other by so gradual a sequence as are all the facts of the Bible, without exception. See chapter 4.

The distinction must therefore be broadly maintained, if maintained at all. All the facts, without exception, accomplished on the earth, and within the knowledge of man, must be put on one side, as recorded only and exclusively by man; while the doctrines are placed on the other side, as recorded equally and authoritatively by God.

The truth is, that the two classes of passages are so inextricably blended together that any attempt to separate and distribute them to other respective sources reduces to an absurdity the theory which requires such an attempt. I do not speak now of the dependence of the sense, but of the mere collocation of the words, and the blending together of what is historical and what is doctrinal in the same passages, and even in the same sentences.

First, I select as an instance the memorable account of the raising of Lazarus, in John 11. The whole is narrative, and in one sense historical. On the theory under discussion, the facts cognizable by man are narrated in human words, but our Lord's doctrinal teaching, as it exists in this chapter in the most sublime form, and especially all references to our Lord's secret thoughts, feelings, and purposes, are narrated in inspired words. The result will stand thus: the first four verses are human: the fifth and sixth are inspired, for they record Christ's secret feelings and purposes. The six next verses are human. Then comes an inspired verse, the thirteenth, which gives the real meaning of our Lord's words. The nine next verses are human, and so is the twenty-fourth verse; but one inspired verse, the twenty-third, intervenes; then follow two more inspired verses; then seven human verses; then an inspired verse, followed by three uninspired; then another inspired verse, followed by six uninspired; then two inspired verses, and four uninspired; then again two inspired, and the rest of the chapter uninspired. Is it possible that a theory that so blends up in inextricable confusion the two elements of Scripture can be considered to be reasonable and accordant with the teaching of Scripture itself?

But in the doctrinal portions of the word there are yet more singular instances. Moreover, as they deal not with narrative, but argument, the separation of the two supposed classes of passages, the inspired and the uninspired, can be made with the greater ease and certainty. In the following eleven verses of 1 Cor. 10, I have marked in italics the passages which must be considered to be inspired, that it may be seen in what an inseparable connection they stand towards the parts asserted to be uninspired :

1. Moreover, brethren, I would not that ye should be ignorant, how that all our fathers were under the cloud, and all passed through the sea;
2. *And were all baptized unto Moses in the cloud and in the sea.*
3. *And did all eat the same spiritual meat.*
4. *And did all drink the same spiritual drink; for they drank of that spiritual rock that followed them; and that Rock was Christ.*
5. *But with many of them God was not well pleased;* for they were overthrown in the wilderness.
6. *Now these things were our ensamples, to the intent we should not lust after evil things,* as they also lusted.
7. *Neither be ye idolaters,* as were some of them ; as it is written, The people sat down to eat and drink, and rose up to play.
8. *Neither let us commit fornication,* as some of them committed, and fell in one day three and twenty thousand.
9. *Neither let us tempt Christ,* as some of them also tempted, and were destroyed of serpents.

10. *Neither murmur ye,* as some of them also murmured, and were destroyed of the destroyer.

11. *Now all these things happened unto them for ensamples; and they are written for our admonition, upon whom the ends of the world are come.*

Another remarkable instance of the same admixture of the doctrinal and the historical occurs in the eleventh chapter of the Hebrews. I extract a few verses by way of illustration, and mark them with italics the same as before:

7. *By faith* Noah, being warned of God of things not seen as yet, moved with fear, prepared an ark for the saving of his house, *by the which he condemned the world, and became heir of the righteousness which is by faith.*

8. *By faith* Abraham, when he was called to go out into a place which he should after receive for an inheritance, obeyed, and he went out, not knowing whither he went.

9. *By faith* he sojourned in the land of promise as in a strange country, dwelling in tabernacles with Isaac and Jacob, the heirs with him of the same promise.

10. *For he looked for a city which hath foundations, whose builder and maker is God.*

The next six verses may all be considered to be inspired. Then the apostle proceeds:

17. *By faith* Abraham, when he was tried, offered up Isaac, and he that had received the promises offered up his only begotten son;

18. Of whom it was said, That in Isaac shall thy seed be called;

19. *Accounting that God was able to raise him up even from the dead; from whence also he received him in a figure.*

The same peculiarity marks the whole chapter; but the illustration has probably been carried far enough. I fully admit that these are strong cases; but a theory cannot be true unless it can be applied to all cases alike.

I earnestly trust that I shall not be suspected of

any wish to turn the subject into burlesque.   I only
contend that one harmonious principle must be applied to the whole of such passages—that they cannot be broken up into heterogeneous fragments, but
must be invested with the same authority throughout.   It is perfectly consistent to contend that there
is no verbal inspiration in any part of Scripture;
although I believe such a belief to be wholly inconsistent with the facts of the case.   On such a theory, an inspiration would exist in the subject-matter everywhere, but in the words nowhere.   This, I
repeat, is consistent.   But it is not consistent with
the facts to break the unity of scriptural composition into two classes of passages, where the two
exist together so inextricably that it is absolutely
impossible to separate them.   Inspiration cannot
be at once present and absent.   Hence the objection against verbal inspiration on the ground that
it attributes to God a subject-matter unworthy of
him, and inconsistent with his ordinary modes of
dealing, falls to the ground.   For Scripture itself
being the witness, the historical and doctrinal portions of Scripture form parts of the same revelation, and must, therefore, have the same authorship.

A single remark will suffice in answer to the
objection that a verbal inspiration removes the
stimulus to human inquiry on all matters within
its sphere.   The whole form into which it has pleased
God to throw his revelation is one grand appeal to
the human reason and conscience.   And so long as
its sublime doctrines continue to exercise the loftiest faculties of the human intellect, and touch the

profoundest emotions of the human heart, as they have done from the beginning till now, there is no fear that the disciplinary purposes of God's works should be less effectually accomplished in the revelation of his word.

II. Another class of objection weighs much on some men's minds. This is founded on the variations of reading existing in our manuscript copies of the Scriptures. It is said by some, that if God had verbally inspired Scripture, he would miraculously have preserved the manuscripts without error or variation during every age of the church. The objection is purely speculative, and rests on a human conception of what God should consistently have done under certain circumstances. I have repeatedly protested against such a mode of argument. All speculations of our own on such a subject appear to me too utterly valueless to require serious refutation, even if their arbitrary and capricious nature made it possible.

So far, however, as the objection is urged by believers in the Divine authority of the Christian Scriptures, one remark may be made upon it. It is, that the objection would create quite as much difficulty on the theory of a general inspiration as on the belief of a verbal one. Those who believe that inspiration ended with communicating the substance of revelation, and did not extend to the mode of its embodiment in words, believe the Bible to be just as necessary to make men wise unto salvation, and its communications to be just as binding on the belief and on the conscience, as does the believer in verbal inspiration.   It is held to be given for the same purpose, and to be effectual to the same end, by them both.   If the variations in the text are sufficient to awaken any misgivings as to the authority of the Scriptures we possess, these misgivings would affect the one case just as much as the other.   A miraculously preserved autograph would be as necessary to quiet the scruples of a believer in the one as of a believer in the other.   If, therefore, its absence has any argumentative weight, it lies against the authority of Scripture altogether; since, if the existing text does not correspond with the original autographs, it is not God's word at all.   No appreciable difference is made to those who accept the Scriptures as a revelation from God, by believing its inspiration to be in the substance, or in the substance and in the words.   The absence of a miraculously preserved autograph causes no special difficulty whatever to a man who accepts verbal inspiration, and is only the speculative embarrassment of the man who rejects it.   If the fact had any weight, it would weigh equally against both parties; but, in fact, it has no weight whatever.

That inspiration can only have been in the original will be generally admitted.   But we have not got the original, is the bold assertion of the objector.   He means that the existing text cannot be considered to be identical with the original autographs, because of the various readings.   The original can only have been one.   Consequently, where there are several readings of the same passage, one only can possibly agree with the autograph.

Now, it has been already seen that the absence of the original autograph is no proof that this autograph was not verbally inspired. 1. Because the supposition that if it had been verbally inspired God would miraculously have preserved it, is a mere human speculation, and cannot have the slightest weight against a conclusion drawn from facts. 2. Because the objection, if valid at all, goes too far, and would destroy not only the verbal inspiration of the existing text, but its authority altogether. It must now be added, that the variations in the text are no proof against the existence of one original autograph, because variations of the same kind are found to exist in profane compositions as well as sacred. The only question affected by them is, To what extent are our existing copies identical with this autograph? Are the variations such as to shake our confidence in the authority of the text as it exists? If they are not sufficient to shake our belief in its authority, neither can they shake our belief in its verbal inspiration. Its authority depends upon its being the very revelation that God gave; and if it be that very revelation, then the words must be the same, for the revelation cannot be separated from the words that convey it. When it is objected that we have not got copies of the original, I reply by asking what it is the objector thinks we have got. If it is something else, its verbal inspiration must undoubtedly be given up, but its Divine authority in faith and conscience must be given up likewise.

What, then, is the state of the case, and what is

the extent and character of these variations; in
other words, how far do they affect the text? That
they are very numerous has been often repeated,
and it has been as often replied that they are as
trivial as they are numerous. This does not, however, convey a sufficiently accurate idea of the facts.
No one can adequately appreciate the character of
these variations who has not taken the trouble to
examine them one by one, as they are to be found
in any modern edition of the Scriptures. In the
absence of this personal examination, a general
impression only can be conveyed; but this impression will suffice to show, in some measure, what sort
of variations they are which are supposed to destroy
the integrity, and therefore the authority of the
sacred text.

I take an illustration of four chapters of the
New Testament: the first chapter of St. Matthew's
gospel, the first chapter of St. Mark, the first of St.
Luke, and the first of St. John. The variations of
reading in the text of these four chapters amount to
the apparently formidable number of five hundred
and fifteen. But directly, as we look at them closely,
they begin to lose their substance, and become, for
all practical purposes, as intangible as ghosts. I
divide them into eight classes. The first class consists of variations in the case, person, gender, or
number of words, of such a kind that either of the
readings falls into the grammatical construction of
the sentence, and is equally suitable to the sense.
For instance, in Matt. 1 : 21 the authorized version
renders the passage, "Thou shalt call his name

Jesus." The variation gives it thus: "She shall bring forth a son, and shall call his name Jesus." Here the Divine authority of the name is equally maintained in either case. In Mark 1:7 the authorized renders it "The latchet of whose shoes I am not worthy to stoop down and unloose." The variation reads it, "The latchet of whose shoe." The number of variations of this kind occurring in the four specified chapters is thirty-eight.

The second class consists of amplifications or contractions of the sense. Thus, in Matt. 1:21, the words "She brought forth her first-born son," are elsewhere written, "She brought forth her son." In Mark 1:6, the words descriptive of John the Baptist's dress, "And with a girdle of skin about his loins," are omitted in some manuscripts. In the thirty-fourth verse, "He healed many that were sick of divers diseases," the words "of divers diseases" are sometimes absent, but are plainly involved in the diversity of persons healed. Fifty-two variations of this kind occur in the four chapters.

The third class is made up of differences of spelling and the mere form of words, and arises wholly from varieties of usage and dialect. The first chapter of St. Matthew supplies eighteen; the first of St. Mark thirty; of St. Luke thirty-six; and of St. John fifteen; in all ninety-nine variations.

The fourth class consists of the change of conjunctions, sometimes differing from each other by a single letter, as in John 1:16. The difference is so delicate as to be beyond the appreciation of any but a practised Greek scholar, and to defy translation. Seven variations occur of this kind.

The fifth class consists of variations in the order of the words, in affixing single words to one branch of a common sentence rather than to another, or in reversing their mutual position in the same way in which poetry reverses the usual order of the sentence in prose. Thirty-eight variations arise from this cause.

The sixth class consists of variations of tense; as, for instance, in Matt. 1:20, "The angel of the Lord appeared to Joseph," where some manuscripts use the graphic and dramatic present instead of the past tense, "The angel of the Lord appears." Twenty variations are added to the list from this source.

The seventh class consists of the insertion or omission of secondary and implied words, such as the pronouns "he," "his," etc., or such as the repetition of the nominative case: "Jesus" did so and so, instead of the third person understood and the verb; or as the use or the absence of the article, the use or the absence of the preposition, and others of the same kind. No less than one hundred and thirty-six variations of reading are of this character.

The eighth class consists of the interchange of synonymous forms of expression, as, for instance, in the substitution of the word "Lord" for the word "God," the word "Peter" for the word "Simon," and other changes of expression so minute as to baffle description. In one case only is a matter of fact touched. This is Luke 1 : 46, where the words imputed to Mary are, in some manuscripts, imputed to Elizabeth.

I give these instances only as illustrations of what are called variations of the text. They are not only utterly unimportant, but they are inappreciable. Their existence is just sufficient to show that God has exercised no miracle for the preservation of the copies of the Scripture. They are so singularly slight and trivial as to make the substantial integrity of the text a proof of providential protection, so exact and wonderful as only not to be miraculous. It is not enough to say that in no case do they affect the sense. The truth is far beyond this. In no case do they affect a single important word, still less a single phrase. Let every word affected by these variations be put on one side, not as certainly uninspired, but as not being certainly inspired, because it is not certainly identical with the original autograph. It will be quite enough if the verbal inspiration of all the rest be admitted. For this inspired portion, on which variation of reading has not thrown the shadow of a question, contains so entirely every expressive and emphatic word, that the denial of inspiration to the remainder becomes simply nugatory, if it be not ridiculous.

CHAPTER XVIII.

RECAPITULATION AND SUMMARY.

The Argument founded throughout on Facts, not Theories—Its Progressive Character reviewed—Formal Propositions—The Character of the Scriptures—Mode of their Composition—Their Characteristics—Their Authority—The Divine Agency Uniform —Verbally inspired—Plenary and Verbal Inspiration—Their Infallibility and Sovereign Authority over Faith and Practice.

A RAPID review of the argument stated in the preceding chapters will constitute the best introduction to its definite conclusions. I will recapitulate, step by step, the ground it has traversed, in order to present its general scope and object.

CHAPTER I. The first step was to define the object of inquiry, and ascertain what Christianity is. This is rendered necessary by the peculiarities of modern controversy, which professes to handle with the utmost freedom the doctrines of Christianity without destroying Christianity itself. But Christianity has an historical existence, and its name cannot fairly be divorced from itself. We mean by it the system of religious truth preached in its completed form in the first century of our era, centred round Jesus Christ the Prophet of Galilee and the incarnate Son of God, described by the four evangelists, incorporated in the visible society specified in the Acts of the Apostles, explained in the apostolic epistle, and prophetically depicted in the great outlines of its outward fortunes in the book of the

Apocalypse. This definite system has continued by unbroken descent, both of an external society and an internal system of belief, down to our own day. It is the great civilizing and quickening force of the world, the moral spring of national progress and of individual happiness. If we inquire into the sources of its power, we find them to be twofold— distinct, and yet inseparably related. A superhuman energy, the influence of God the Holy Ghost— constitutes its efficient agency; but this agency works through a definite body of truth, in which historical facts furnish the basis of sublime doctrines. This body of truth constitutes an harmonious system of belief, and is incorporated in the creeds of the Christian church. As its superhuman agency admits of no human investigation, being inward and spiritual, this harmonious body of truth constitutes the substance of Christianity in its outward aspect. Christianity is identified with Christian doctrine.

CHAPTER II. This Christian doctrine is itself identified with the Christian Scriptures. We must discard all speculations as to what might have been, and must take the facts as we find them to be. As the case stands, we are absolutely dependent for our knowledge, alike of Christian facts and Christian doctrines, upon these records. We have no other source of information within the Church of Christ; for the Christian writings remaining to us from the first century in addition to the inspired Scriptures are exceedingly limited in extent, and of very doubtful authenticity. But being such as they are, they claim to have no authority of their own, but refer to the canonical Scriptures as the Church's rule of faith. All the other Christian writings of a later date follow the same rule, and are but the successive links of a chain, of which the beginning is in the sacred Scriptures of the Old and New Testaments. We possess, therefore, no source of information whatever within the church, relative to Christian facts and doctrines, beyond the written Word. Nor does any source of information exist outside the church. Profane history attests in the clearest way the wide extension and extraordinary influence of Christianity in the earliest ages, but supplies no facts regarding its details which are not of the most meager description. Nor could human philosophy supply from its own independent discovery any of the distinctive truths relative to God and man which constitute the sublime doctrines of the Christian faith. On every side, therefore, we are shut up into dependence on the Christian Scriptures. It is not more certain that Christianity is identified with Christian doctrine than it is that Christian doctrine is identified with the Christian Scriptures.

CHAPTER III. What is, then, the authority of these Scriptures? They have ever been received by the church as a revelation from God, and as, therefore, binding on human faith and conscience. The grounds of this acceptance are threefold. In the first place, they are the compositions, and the only compositions extant, of men claiming to have received a commission to teach mankind direct from God himself, and who exhibited the credentials of this commission in their possession of miraculous powers. The nature of the signs they wrought, the astonishing extension of their influence, and the known prevalence of their authority and teaching at the very dates and places of their occurrence, place the reality of these miracles beyond a doubt, and equally identify the workers of them with the authors of the sacred books. Secondly, the books thus composed at very different periods, and by men of widely varying character, position, and circumstances, are yet found to constitute one whole and single work, united throughout by as clear a unity of thought and purposes as the work of any one ordinary author. Hence it is concluded, that as collusion or mutual agreement among the separate writers was clearly impossible, this unity can only have been impressed on the work by Divine intelligence, and constitutes the stamp of Divine authority. Thirdly, the character thus attributed to the book is found wonderfully accordant with the grandeur and sublimity of its contents. It reveals truths lying beyond the utmost reach of human inquiry, and so profound in themselves that, when revealed, the loftiest human intellect is lost in their height and depth. Hence the book is believed to be a Divine book, and to constitute a revelation of God to man, claiming human belief, and binding upon the human conscience.

CHAPTER IV. Hence follows the natural conclusion, that a book so wonderfully constituted does not only contain the word of God, but that it is itself the word of God. If it only contained the word of God, then part of it must be accepted as a message from God to man, while the other parts might be rejected as carrying with them the ordinary authority of fallible human authors, and no more. Many persons have argued for such a division of its authority, on the ground of the historical and biographical details intermixed with its grand revelation of Divine things. But the facts of the case contradict such a mode of conceiving of the Scriptures, with a force which nothing but some practical disproof of the most urgent kind can contradict; for the inspired authorship of the Bible extends equally to all the contents of the canonical Scriptures, without any distinction whatever, and the identity of authorship necessarily carries with it an identity of authority. Moreover, the historical details of Scripture have their place in the structural unity of the whole books as evidently as have its sublimest doctrines. There is not a detail without its appropriate place and object. Whatever proof of a Divine inspiration is derived from the wonderful unity of compositions so widely separated from each other in all their human circumstances, extends to every part that goes to make up the unity, whether it be a detail of man's history or a manifestation of God's wisdom. Nor is there any incongruity between the minuteness of the facts and the sublimity of the doctrines. The little details arise from man's side of the scheme of redemption, and are inseparably associated with that scheme of redemption through the incarnation, sufferings, and death, of the incarnate Son of God. It follows, therefore, that an equal authority, whatever the exact amount of it may be, pervades the whole body of the Scriptures. They are the word of God.

CHAPTER V. The authority of the Scriptures is thus generally established; but its exact nature and its relation to the human conscience still need to be ascertained. Has it been given as a subordinate help to the intellect and conscience of man in finding out truth, or as an authoritative and infallible guide? Scripture itself can alone give the answer; and to those who accept it as the word of God, its answer must be conclusive. But does Scripture contain any positive assertions of absolute authority and infallibility? Some say that it does not. Undoubtedly, direct and reiterated affirmations of its own inspiration and truth are not appended to each particular chapter or particular book. But why should evidence be limited to direct assertion, and necessary inference be excluded? A little consideration shows that ostentatious assertions would alike be utterly devoid of all weight, and would be incongruous with the dignity and the self-consciousness of a Divine Author. We do not believe an earthly witness on the strength of his own assertions of credibility, but on the strength of his known character and of the evidence he adduces. Thus we may expect that it will be with God; and thus we find that it is. The scriptural writers are not always talking of their own credibility, but they speak freely of their commission, and of the authority attached to it. By necessary inference, they assert in the strongest manner their inspiration by God, and this inference demands and deserves the same implicit acceptance as a direct statement. It is equally God's teaching, whatever may be the exact form of the communication.

CHAPTER VI. These statements of Scripture relative to itself may be arranged under six heads: 1. They claim to be a communication from God; not only a revelation of him, but a revelation from him, in the truest and most exact sense in which the authority of a message depends not upon the messenger who brings it, but on the character of the person who sends it. 2. They declare themselves to be accredited with the authority of God as of a Creator, claiming by right the reverence and obedience of his creatures. 3. They affirm themselves to have been given for the specific purpose of making men wise unto salvation. The writers must, therefore, be believed to have received an inspiration suitable to and adequate for their special work, just as Bezaleel and Aholiab received the manufacturing skill needed for their special duty, and Samson the bodily strength requisite for his. They are also the only provision specially made by God for the communication of saving knowledge to his creatures. 4. They affirm themselves to have been given to supplement the light of nature, and to supply that knowledge of God which neither the outward creation nor the light of conscience were competent to afford to a fallen and guilty creature. 5. They affirm implicit credence to be due to their contents, alike by virtue of their Divine Author and of the evidences furnished in authentication of them. This belief they claim for matters of fact as well as for matters of doctrine; for events transpiring on the earth as for the deep mysteries of heavenly and Divine things. 6. They assert their claims upon believing acceptance to be so authoritative that the denial of them is a sin, and will be punished as a sin at the great judgment-day by the righteous Judge of all.

CHAPTER VII. These claims, viewed in relation to each other, involve the infallible truth of Scripture, since it is repugnant to all reason to believe that the righteous God would assert such claims for what was untrue. This truth involves the reality of the things recorded, the earnestness and gravity of the narration, the absence of unintentional errors, and the freedom from intentional fraud. It follows, therefore, that Scripture does assert its own absolute veracity, and asserts it in the mode most consistent with the self-consciousness of an inspiring Deity. All its contents are true according to the nature of their truth—its deep mysteries, its grand promises, its records of the past, its unveiling of the future, its majestic history, its graphic narratives, its ethnological and genealogical details. In the face of its tremendous claims, the supposition that the Bible is partly true and partly untrue, and that a process of elaborate criticism is required to separate the true from the untrue, becomes utterly incredible. For then, according to the positive statements of Scripture itself, life and death, heaven and hell, would be dependent on a process of selection impossible to the majority of mankind, and even to the most educated precarious and uncertain in the extreme. The simple conclusion that the Bible is all true supplies the only solution of the facts. The Scriptures are not only truly the word of God, but they are the true word of God.

CHAPTER VIII. This assertion is met by skeptical criticism with a direct negative. It asserts that Scripture is not true, and therefore cannot be Divine. The question must therefore be referred to the evidence of facts. But before we enter upon this inquiry, it is necessary to ascertain the exact nature of the question at issue, and the standard by which it is to be decided. When two parties advance contradictory assertions with reference to one and the same thing, there is reason to suspect a misapprehension of the point in dispute. To remove these mistakes, and lay a recognized basis for common argument, must be the first step. In the controversy relative to the authority and inspiration of Scripture, these misapprehensions refer to two points: first, the character asserted for Scripture as the word of God; and secondly, what is meant by its truth. Now the character of Scripture as the word of God is so far from excluding human agency, and therefore human characteristics, in its composition, that it necessarily includes them.   There must be two sides to a revelation, corresponding to the party who gives it and the party who receives it.   Hence Scripture must necessarily possess a human side or element and a Divine side or element.   They are neither to be confused together, nor are they to be separated from each other.   They are to be regarded as existing side by side, exactly in the same manner as the Godhead and the manhood exist together in the personal word.   The Scriptures are not less human because they are Divine, nor less Divine because they are human.   Whatever is essential to either element is to be retained in union, and only what is non-essential to be modified by the combination.   Every part of Scripture is human, and every part of Scripture is Divine, and the two characters together constitute " God's Word written."

CHAPTER IX. The application of this simple principle explains all the facts of the case.   On the one hand, the human element—that is, the part which man instrumentally had in the composition of the sacred books—is to be maintained intact.   It includes (1) the personal peculiarities of the respective writers, alike of time, place, circumstance, character, and intellectual gifts.   Hence it involves (2) the human point of view and the human mode of conceiving Divine things.   The object being the instruction of mankind, it was needful that truth should be conveyed in such a manner as to be understood.   The instruction so communicated is real, and the notions presented are true to the utmost capacity of human language to express and human ideas to comprehend them. The revelation is incomplete, solely because of the limits of human powers, but the knowledge communicated is true and real. (3) The human side of Scripture involves the use of all the peculiarities of human language as freely as they would be used in uninspired compositions. The force of words, the construction of sentences, the mode of stating an argument, the employment of imagery and illustration, and the free adoption of all the recognized figures of speech employed by secular writers, are naturally to be expected in Scripture. If these peculiarities were absent, the human element would be absent. To object against the existence of these human peculiarities in the sacred books is simply to object against the possibility of the human and the Divine existing together, as they do in the person of the God incarnate.

CHAPTER X. On the other hand, the Divine element, or the part belonging to God in the composition of sacred Scripture, is to be maintained with equal distinctness. This Divine element includes (1) the selection of the writers, with their special peculiarities of circumstance and character for their given work, and their education for it; (2) their instruction is the subject-matter of their writings, alike by the revelation of what was previously unknown to them, by the verification of knowledge possessed by them through ordinary human channels, and by the selection of the things to be written and the things to be omitted from the writings. As a general rule, the sacred writers were conscious and intelligent agents, understanding, more or less perfectly, the meaning of their own message; but cases have been specifically excepted, in order to prevent our limiting the sense of the words written by the intention of human writers. These two instances are found in John 11:15 and 1 Peter 1:11. Hence it follows that the Divine element includes (3) the guidance of the Spirit in the selection of the words employed by the sacred writers. If the Divine inspiration acted only in communicating truth to the sacred writers, and did not extend to their communication of this divinely given truth to others, it is certain that we possess only a human account of a Divine revelation, and not the very revelation itself. The veracity of the truth transmitted must be equivalent, neither more nor less, to the accuracy of the words which convey it. (4) It involves the absolute truth of all the things written. Man is always fallible, and liable to mistakes; but actually to make mistakes is as unnecessary to the completeness of the human element as not to make mistakes is absolutely essential to the Divine. The Bible may be truly the work of man, and yet be true; but if it be not certainly true, it cannot also be the work of God. The concurrence of the human part of Scripture and the Divine part of Scripture is thus perfect throughout. It is not, however, the concurrence of two equals, but of a superior and an inferior. Man is necessarily the subordinate instrument, and God necessarily the originating and controlling agent. Hence it follows that, as the existence of what is Divine in Scripture is no sound argument against its being human, so the existence of what is human in Scripture is no sound argument against its also being Divine.

CHAPTER XI. The character of the word of God being ascertained, we have yet to secure a clear understanding of what believers mean when they assert its truth, and what skeptics mean when they assert its untruth. Two classes of expression require to be explained. The one consists of adjectives of intensity and force, as in the phrases, "strictly true," "absolutely true," "literally true." The other of adjectives of quality, such as "logically true," "scientifically true," "historically true," Now we mean by truth, the correspondence of a statement with the reality of the thing stated. If they correspond, the statement is true; if they do not correspond, it is not true. There is, therefore, only one kind of truth, and it can admit of no degrees. One part of a statement may be true, and another part untrue; but the same part cannot be both true and untrue. Phrases consisting of adjectives of intensity only imply that every part of the whole is true without exception. Adjectives of quality imply different modes of stating truth, not different degrees of truth. Whether a fact is stated in popular language or in scientific language, the fact itself is just the same in either case, and the truth of its occurrence is the same. The fact stated in any modern almanac, that the sun will rise at a certain time on a certain day, is scientifically true, although it is not expressed in scientific language. In the same way an argument may be perfectly logical, although it is not stated logically. The Bible is neither a book of science nor a book of logic; nor is it exclusively a poem, or a history, or a biography, or a book of devotion. It is a revelation bestowed to make men wise unto salvation, and is therefore adapted, in all the truth it conveys, whether scientific, or logical, or historical, or biographical, or devotional, to the comprehension of those for whom it is intended. Its truth is one, its modes of statement various.

CHAPTER XII. The prominent objections urged against the historical truth rendered it necessary to examine the phrase historically true still more closely. Historical truth differs in no respect from any other truth, but only expresses that branch of human certitude which has reference to the past events of the world. These events have been so many and various that no one history can possibly embrace the whole, even of those included in any one branch of investigation. Particular histories can only deal with some one portion of human events, and can narrate those facts, and those facts alone, which are appropriate to their special purpose and particular principles. The idea of a universal history to sweep over the entire range of the past, trace every link without exception, and record every fact, is no more than a dream. Historical truth consequently does not require that no facts should be omitted, since such a condition would be impracticable; nor that in several narratives of the same events the facts recorded should be absolutely identical. It only requires that the facts should have taken place as they are recorded to have taken place, and that they should correspond with the statement they are adduced to prove. These conditions of historical truth are illustrated by the two accounts of the genealogy of our Lord, given by St. Matthew and St. Luke. These lists are recorded in proof of our Lord's descent from Abraham and David, according to the Scriptures. As no evidence exists to impugn any one link of the descent, the historical truth of the genealogies is neither affected by the artificial form adopted by St. Matthew, nor by our inability to explain the mode in which the two lines of St. Matthew and St. Luke met in the one person of Jesus of Nazareth. Varieties of expression affect the mode of conveying truth, but not the truth conveyed. Of this truth there are neither degrees nor varieties of kind. Truth is but one, and the written Word of God is its Divine impersonation.

Chapter XIII. These misapprehensions being removed, we are in a position to bring the question at issue to the test of facts. Are the contents of Scripture true, or are they not? An immense mass of evidence exists to prove the minute accuracy of the scriptural narratives on circumstantial points, where independent information is at hand to verify them. The number of facts specified in the sacred

Scripture is large beyond enumeration. On no one point has criticism discovered a single contradiction to known facts, while it has brought to light an astonishing accordance with them. Exactly in proportion as our knowledge of the countries, circumstances, and nations, alluded to in Scripture has become more precise and minute, in that proportion have all the statements of Scripture been more and more verified. This has been shown to be the case, for instance, with the geography of Scripture, and perhaps yet more wonderfully with its references to the governing nations of the ancient world, and the characteristic manners and customs attributed to them. Thus ancient Egypt has become known to us through its monuments, and the graphic details furnished by its still existing paintings and sculptures. But in every point the sacred narrative is so signally confirmed by these silent witnesses of the past as actually to fill up the sacred outlines with a vivid coloring not possessed before. Striking, however, as these and other similar instances are, more minute testimony is at hand. Ten specific instances have been adduced from the Old Testament as illustrations of other existing cases of historical accuracy, so discriminating and exact, that nothing short of Divine inspiration can account for them. In the New Testament similar instances are so numerous that only by grouping them under some common heads can a general conception be formed of their number and variety. The notable persons described in the New Testament Scriptures, and the most memorable places made illustrious by the events of the New Testament history, have been used in illustration, and been found to supply proofs of accurate truth equally astonishing and indisputable..

CHAPTER XIV. The case is, however, much strengthened by another class of instances. These are passages at one time alleged as arguments against the truth, and therefore against the inspiration of the Scriptures, but converted by fuller information into proofs of the very truth they were once alleged to contradict. Such cases prove the supposed difficulty of explanation to have wholly arisen from erroneous and defective information on the part of man, not from any thing really inexplicable on the part of the Word. The natural conclusion is, that the cause proved to operate in these cases now explained is still operating in cases yet unexplained, and that the difficulty experienced in reconciling different parts of Scripture with each other, or with known facts, is simply the product of human ignorance, and would wholly be removed by fuller or more accurate information. The strength of this conclusion is exactly proportioned to the apparent reasonableness of the objection once urged, but now removed. Nine instances of this kind have been given. A review of the facts adduced in this and the previous chapter exhibits the following characteristics: (1) the minute accuracy illustrated by them is not confined to a single book, or a single writer, or a single section of the inspired writings, but is the characteristic of them all; (2) it exists in particulars more or less obviously incidental to the main object of the narrative; (3) many of these details are such as could not possibly have fallen within the personal knowledge of the writer, and for which no effort of memory or extent of human information can account; (4) the instances are, without exception, drawn from matters of detail, and in such matters alone is it possible for human knowledge either to confirm or contradict the Word of God. We have no means of ascertaining the credibility of doctrinal truths beyond the character of the Being who proclaims them.

CHAPTER XV. From the positive evidence of the accuracy of Scripture it is necessary to pass to an examination of the passages alleged by skeptical criticism in disproof of it. Skeptical evidence is found to be evidently of a different and of a lower character; whereas the argument in proof of the truth of Scripture is based upon positive and indisputable facts proved by independent and impartial testimony. The argument against the truth of Scripture has no fact of the same kind to allege, but is founded on arbitrary assumption and speculative opinion. In proof of this assertion nearly four hundred passages quoted in recent works against the inspiration of Scripture have been passed under review. The objections founded upon them are found to be removed, without exception, by some one or more of the following rules, all of which are corollaries of the principle that the Divine and human elements of Scripture are equally to be

maintained in their integrity. 1. Passages interpolated into the original autographs, or errors made
in transcription, are no parts of Scripture, and furnish, therefore, no argument against its truth. 2. The
employment of figures of speech, and of artificial or
conventional forms of statement, constitute no violation of literal truth. 3. Varieties of statement
are not contradictions, whether they arise from
recording different parts of some common event, or
from assigning a different emphasis and importance to the same parts. 4. Omissions of parts of
a series of facts, or of particulars making up facts,
are consistent with the truth of the narrative in
which they occur. 5. Differences of style in the
composition, of personal character in the mode of
thinking, or of standpoint in looking at common
truths, are neither inconsistent with truth, nor with
the action of a Divine inspiration. 6. Separate
transactions are not to be identified with each other
because of a parallelism between some circumstances
of an event, or some portions of a discourse. 7. No
private estimates of probability or improbability,
either as to facts or doctrines, can be of force
against the testimony of a positive record. In one
passage alone a plain contradiction stands on the surface of the narrative, viz., Acts 7 :14–16; and here the
patent character of the difficulty at once removes any
argumentative value it might otherwise have possessed, and at once suggests the mode of its solution.

CHAPTER XVI. The truth of the veracity of Holy
Scripture, supplied by the instances under consider-

ation in the previous chapters, illustrates the extent as well as the fact of inspiration. For the accuracy is traced, as alone it could be conceivably traced, in words, and in single words. If God supplied the truth, God must equally have guided the words conveying it. This verbal inspiration in no degree limits the human element. It only involves that, while the words of Scripture are truly the words of man, they are at the same time fully and concurrently the words of God. The theories that God revealed to the sacred writers the subject-matter of the revelation, but left them to themselves to imbody it in written words, or that the doctrinal portions of Scripture are inspired, but the historical uninspired, have been shown not to agree with the facts of the case, but to involve insuperable difficulties. The only natural conclusion is, that the words of Scripture are inspired. When we turn to Scripture itself, we find this verbal inspiration to be clearly taught. In the case of the Old Testament especially, the writers of the New, including our Lord himself, testify to its verbal inspiration, since they quote it in a manner inexplicable on any other principle. In a vast majority of instances they quote not its sense, but its words, and rest the authority of great doctrines on single phrases and even on single words, taken from different parts of the Old Testament, and so separated from their context as to show that the words themselves are considered to be authoritative. In the case of the New Testament, no evidence of the same kind can possibly exist, because there has been no later succession of inspired writers to bear an analogous testimony. But both the language of our Lord himself and that of the apostles assert for the New Testament the same inspiration asserted by them for the Old. The inspiration is, therefore, in both cases verbal.

CHAPTER XVII. The great mass of the objections entertained against the verbal inspiration of Scripture proceed from a misapprehension of the meaning of verbal inspiration, and are removed, almost without exception, by the simple rule of maintaining the perfect human element on the one side, and the perfect Divine element upon the other. Two classes of objection alone require further consideration. I. Objections founded on the variety of subject-matter, and the supposed incongruity of imputing to an immediate revelation of God details apparently trivial and relative to matters knowable by man himself. It has, however, been previously shown (1) that the minute details of history enter necessarily into the structural unity of the entire revelation; (2) that the doctrines of Scripture are, in many unquestionable particulars, dependent upon its historical details; (3) that in these elements alone could the means of verifying the truth of Scripture possibly be opposed to us. It must be farther added, that what is knowable by man is not always and of necessity known, and, as a matter of fact, is frequently unknown, and beyond the reach of any human research and discovery. If, therefore, it be consistent that the doctrines should be revealed under Divine inspiration, it must be equally consistent that the facts inseparably connected with them should be under the same influence. Accordingly, when the attempt is made to separate the doctrinal and the historical portions of Scripture from each other, it is found to be practically impossible, since they are so blended together in the same passages, and even in the same verses, and so mutually dependent upon each other as to reduce the attempt to separate them to an absurdity. II. The other class of objections is founded on the allegation that our existing text is proved not to be identical with the original autographs, since, of the existing variations, one only can be true; whereas it is assumed that if the words of Scripture had been inspired, God would have provided, even at the cost of a miracle, for its exact preservation. But, in answer, it must be remembered that all speculative conjectures respecting what we think God would have done under certain circumstances have no weight whatever against the evidence of positive facts. Moreover, it goes too far. For if the existing text be not the text of the original autographs, the fact not only destroys the verbal inspiration of Scripture, but its authority likewise. Moreover, an examination of these variations proves that they not only occur in unimportant matters, but that their own character is so utterly unimportant as not to affect even a crucial word, much less touch a distinctive meaning; still less modify a doctrine. Not only practically, but substantively, the existing text of the Scriptures is identical with the original autographs. Not only, therefore, is the conclusion founded on the fact unsound, but the fact itself is misapprehended.

From these data I draw the following conclusions :

1. That the canonical Scriptures, as at present existing, are in the strictest sense of the terms God's Word written.

2. That in the composition of Scripture two elements or two parties necessarily concurred, and in no one part of the Scripture can they be separated—the part which man had in their composition being what is called the human element, and the part which God had being what is called the Divine element.

3. That the characteristics of each party remain intact, all that is peculiar to man on the one side, and all that is peculiar to God on the other side; so that the books resulting from the concurrence of the two are not less human because they are Divine, and not less Divine because they are human.

4. That the relation between these two concurring parties is the relation of an inferior and a superior, the part which man had in the composition of Scripture being throughout subordinate and instrumental, and the part which God had in their composition primary and authoritative.

5. That while the Divine agency in the production of Scripture was wider than the human, inasmuch as the origination of the plan and the selection of the agents preceded the action of the human

instruments, in no particular did it fall short of it, or leave the human instrumentality to itself.

6. That the action of the Holy Spirit upon the minds of the sacred writers did not cease with the revelation to them of the matters they were employed to write, but extended also to their conveyance of this divinely revealed truth to others.

7. That this action of the Holy Spirit is conveniently expressed by the word "inspiration," which expresses the part taken by God in the composition of the sacred Scriptures, and the authority with which they are invested by virtue of this Divine action.

8. That inspiration is both plenary and verbal: plenary, inasmuch as God's attributes of infinite wisdom and perfect truth have found expression through it; verbal, because the vehicle of its expression is—as it could only be in a communication to mankind—the vehicle of words.

9. That, because the Scriptures are God's Word written, they therefore contain infallible truth, and nothing but truth, and are invested with sovereign authority in all matters of belief and practice.

CHAPTER XIX.

CONCLUSION.

Testimony of Christian Experience—Value and Influence of the Words of Scripture—Christian Hymns and the Christian Bible—The Instrument of Conversion and Sanctification through the Spirit—Particular Texts—The Indefinable Power and Tone of the Word—Fanaticism or Faith—Practical Comforts of God's Word Written.

I HAVE endeavored, in the preceding pages, to rest my argument entirely upon facts. I have also selected such facts as lie within the knowledge of all men, and are generally admitted to be true; so that those who dissent from my account of inspiration must direct their opposition not against the facts, but only against my conclusions from them. I have therefore omitted all reference to the facts of Christian experience, lest some who are devoid of this experience should deny them as facts or demur to their validity as arguments. But I cannot do so much violence to my own convictions as to close the subject without a brief reference to them.

The doctrine of the verbal inspiration of Holy Scripture is singularly accordant with the results of Christian experience. There is a natural, and I believe inevitable tendency to cling to the very words of the Bible with an affectionate reverence entertained towards no other book. The feeling entertained towards some familiar hymn supplies the nearest parallel; and yet it differs alike in degree and in kind from the loving solemnity gathered round the word of God. Our fondness for hymns is a more familiar feeling, and arises from their adaptation to thoughts and emotions working within our own minds, and perhaps vainly seeking expression in our own words. But our love to the word of God arises from what it brings to the soul, not from the emotions it evokes from it, and is deeply colored by our sense of its power and majesty. With the hymn, we feel that the utterance is of man; with the Bible, we feel that the utterance is of God. The one touches the chords of a human sympathy; the other is clothed with the authority of a Divine wisdom and the infinite tenderness of a Divine love. The language of the psalmist expresses, now as ever, the utterance of Christian experience: " O how I love thy law." " The law of thy mouth is better unto me than thousands of gold and silver." Psa. 119:97, 72.

Thus, not the hymn, but the word of God, is the ordinary instrument of conversion. There may be exceptions, but in the vast majority of instances a text of the Bible constitutes the weapon of the operating Spirit of God. The Bible itself would lead us to expect this; for St. Peter describes the saints as " born again ... by the word of God, which liveth and abideth for ever." 1 Peter 1:23.

But the affectionate reverence thus formed for the word is deepened by the various experiences of life. It is from this that we have drawn comfort in time of sorrow, encouragement and strength in times of despondent weakness. At periods of perplexity, we have gone to this source for direction, and have found some guiding principle to solve the present difficulty, and point out the path of duty as with a ray of heavenly light. Our enlarging affections have drunk deeply of this spring. Here we have learned our deeper lessons both of ourselves and God—broad promises, so free and large that a child could understand them—mysteries so profound that the loftiest intellect is lost in their heights and depths.

In the course of such an experience, our inward life becomes bound up more and more with particular texts. Not that we rest exclusively on these, but, from their sweetness, are led on to drink the more deeply of the fountains whence they flow. One particular text was the means of conversion; another was brought to the mind at the moment of some peculiar temptation; a third was specially fixed upon the memory by circumstances of place, or time, or person; a fourth flashed upon the soul at some time of meditation, or it may be, in the midst of life's activities, with the vividness and intensity of a message from heaven. The lights and shadows of our inward life have been reflected in these special portions of the word; but in each case particular texts, and perhaps particular words of texts, have supplied the soul's nutriment. Not the word at large, in its grand perfection, but portions of the word, have blended themselves up intimately with the varying experiences of the Christian life and the events of the soul's history.

This association of our affections with the Bible at large through its separate words in particular is inevitable. Many precious truths lie as it were imbedded in other passages without themselves forming any inseparable portion of their general scope and sense. They may therefore be taken, so to speak, out of the material in which they are imbedded, and treated as of themselves utterances from the tongue of God. In so treating many texts, we only use them as the inspired writers used them; as, for instance, when St. Paul adopts the promise of God to Abraham as a ground of confidence to all Christians: "For he hath said, I will never leave thee nor forsake thee." Heb. 13:5. Not only do we, in all cases, gather the sense from the words, but we cannot separate the sense from the words without losing their depth of meaning and singular richness of comfort. Try to take the sense and to fling the words away, and we shall find that we have flung away in the effort their beauty and significance. We hang, as it were, over every word, and ponder it again and again; and yet find that we never exhaust its power and meaning. Let us take, for instance, such an expression as the wonderful words of St. John, "God is love." 1 John 4:8. Very few and simple are the words, but what mind can measure all their depths and blessedness?

I believe, moreover, that experience teaches us still more than this. It is possible for us to gather the sense out of the words of a text, and yet find, nevertheless, that the words have a power of their own, like the fragrance of some sweet flower that we lay next our hearts. The soul seems to imbibe, from contact with the very words, a certain indescribable tone and spirit, as if the mind, in its prayerful meditation, grew into the text, and through the text came into contact with the mind of the inspiring Deity. What Christian man has not repeated the words of a text over and over and over again, as if they were a strain of sweet music—a breath fresh from the other and the better world?

Certain it is that, whether we will or not, the very words of Scripture become consecrated to us, not as husks which we dismiss. after winnowing from them the precious seed they contained, but as jewels; or rather, we enshrine them in our hearts as a thousand times more precious than jewels. The soul lives upon them and feeds upon them, as being instinct with that living Spirit of God, who speaks and works in them with all the power of the infinite mind of a living Creator upon the receptive mind of the living creature. Thus we do not worship the word, however much our inner life is bound up with it, but the living God from whom it comes.

This experience must be a kind of fanaticism, a mere reflection of our own emotions, if the Scriptures be not verbally inspired. If they are, it is in accordance with the soundest dictates of the reason, as well as with the truest instincts of the affections. In the one case it is a thing to be ashamed of and to avoid. In the other case, it is a thing to be thankful for, and to cherish with all our hearts. This necessity of the soul, which compels it to cling to the very words of Scripture, appears to me to be an inward witness to its verbal inspiration. For thus the judgment of the head and the emotions of the heart go hand in hand, like two instruments touched by the same gracious Spirit of God, and emitting beneath his touch the same sweet song of love and praise. It would be strange if the head condemned what the heart felt to be a necessity; or if the heart failed to place its seal of experience on what the head believed; strangest of all would it be, if a doctrine thus accordant with head and heart should be visionary and superstitious. Let us believe that God is consistent in grace as he is in nature, and quickens the heart to feel what he enables the judgment to apprehend. The words of Scripture are of God, and the soul rightly clings to them.

I rejoice to believe that towards this doctrine of verbal inspiration the common mind of the Christian church is more and more decidedly tending, as affording the only consistent explanation of the plain facts of the case. Whatever may be the issue of existing controversies, he alone can stand in calm security who places his feet on this "word of God, which liveth and abideth for ever." 1 Peter 1:23. To him alone the past can be clear, the present blessed, the future hopeful, who believes that no human fraud has sullied the purity, and no human ignorance clouded the infallible truth, of "God's Word written."